WOMEN MYSTICS IN MEDIEVAL EUROPE

WOMEN MYSTICS IN MEDIEVAL EUROPE

Emilie Zum Brunn and

Georgette Epiney-Burgard

Translated from the French by Sheila Hughes

PARAGON HOUSE

New York

First American edition, 1989

Published in the United States by
Paragon House
90 Fifth Avenue
New York, NY 10011

Copyright © 1989 by Emilie Zum Brunn and Georgette Epiney-Burgard

Originally published in French under the title *Femmes Troubadours de Dieu* by Brepols Publishers (Belgium), 1988.

MANUFACTURED IN THE UNITED STATES OF AMERICA

Library of Congress Cataloging-in-Publication Data
Women mystics in Medieval Europe.
    Bibliography: p.
    1. Women mystics—Europe. 2. Mysticism—Europe— History. 3. Mysticism—History—Middle Ages, 600–1500. I. Zum Brunn, Emilie, 1922–   . II. Epiney-Burgard, Georgette.
BV5077.E85W65   1989   248.2′2′088042   88-25414
ISBN 0-913729-16-7
ISBN 1-55778-196-6 (pbk.)

Contents

Contents

Part V Marguerite Porete

List of Maps and Illustrations

Abbreviations

AASS	Acta Sanctorum, 1643 etc. Antwerp; 1734–1761, Venice.
CC	Corpus Christianorum, Brepols, Turnhout
CCCM	Corpus Christianorum continuatio mediaevalis, Brepols Turnhout.
PG	Migne, Patrologia Graeca, Paris.
PL	Migne, Patrologia Latina, Paris.
SC	Collection Sources Chrétiennes, Cerf, Paris.

Hildegard:

LDO	Liber divinorum operum.
LVM	Liber vitae meritorum.

Hadewijch I and II:

MD	Mengeldichten.
SG	Strophische Gedichten.
L (Br.)	Letters (Brieven).

Introduction

The Abbess and the Beguines

It is not an easy task to show briefly the link that exists between the Benedictine Abbess, Hildegard of Bingen, still of the early medieval period, and the Beguines of less than a century later: Hadewijch of Antwerp, Mechthild of Magdeburg, Marguerite Porete of Hainaut, as well as the Cistercian Prioress, Beatrice of Nazareth, brought up by the Beguines and partaking of their spirituality. The profound bond uniting them is well reflected in certain texts of those times, as for example this testimony of 1158 concerning Hildegard and her contemporary, Elizabeth of Schönau, also of the Benedictine order:

> In these days God made manifest His power through the frail sex, in these handmaidens whom He filled with the prophetic spirit.[1]

When, after these great nuns whose action still remains isolated, we turn our attention to the Beguine movement at the height of its fervor, halfway through the thirteenth century, we find a significant reference to these women in *Tochter von Syon*, the important poetical work of the Franciscan Lamprecht von Regensburg,[2] written about 1250:

> And so, in our days
> In Brabant and the land of Bayern,

> *Has the art arisen amongst women.*
> Lord God, what art is this
> That an old woman better[3]
> Understands than a man of wit?

Lamprecht is amazed that these women, the Beguines, possess the "art" (*kunst*) of understanding and expressing spiritual realities better than gifted men, instructed in matters of the spirit. He explains this in an effective manner by means of a penetrating analysis of woman's psychological constitution:

> It seems to me that thus it is
> A woman becomes good for God;
> In the simplicity of her understanding
> Her gentle heart, her frailer mind
> Are kindled more quickly within her,
> So that in her desire she understands better
> The wisdom flowing from Heaven
> Than does a hard man
> Who is clumsy in these things.[4]

This direct inspiration of the Spirit is the fundamental link between Hildegard and our Beguines and was the only competence recognized to women in the realm of spirituality—and this only in privileged cases. However, in spite of what Lamprecht seems to say, and notwithstanding their assertions to the contrary, we shall see that the women we are about to deal with possessed a solid theological and metaphysical culture. The originality and power of our nuns and Beguines lie in the perfect amalgamation of their doctrine with their spiritual experience. Their approach was, in fact, quite the contrary to that of the scholastic doctors, as Dom Porion noted when speaking of Beatrice and Hadewijch. They were sometimes called "mistresses," an appellation used to emphasize the inspired nature of their teaching.

This reminds us of the expression *Lebemeister*, "master of living," a title that Eckhart considered to be higher than *Lesemeister*, "master or reader of Scripture." We have a clear idea of the difference between these two "masters" in the work that was long attributed to Eckhart: *Also sprach Schwester Katrei (Thus Spoke Sr. Katherine).*[5] On one hand we have a nun who has reached the summit of spiritual union and on the other, her confessor who, not having attained these heights, makes her suffer under his incompetent direction. Finally he understands that she has "become God" and tries to follow her along the path where previously he believed he was leading her. But it must be borne in mind that this contrast is not so much between doctrine and life as between a doctrine that remains fettered to the level of intellect and one that is applied to life itself. This latter doctrine allows one to rise to a higher kind of knowledge, not merely theoretical but constitutive of being. This is what is meant by Beatrice of Nazareth and by Marguerite Porete when they speak of the seven degrees, estates, or *beings* of spiritual life.

John of Leeuwen, Ruysbroeck's beloved disciple, calls Hadewijch a "mistress" while Marguerite Porete, in certain manuscripts of her *Mirror of Simple Souls*, is referred to as a "Béguine clergeresse" (clerical Beguine).

Even more sensational was the recognition of this gift of divine inspiration in the case of Hildegard, who became known as the sibyl or prophetess of the Rhine. Here we might quote a Premonstratensian canon of Toul who, after reading Hildegard's answer to Guibert of Gembloux's queries about her visions, wrote:

The subtle French masters are incapable of such feats. . . . With a dry heart and puffed cheeks, they lose themselves in loud declamations, in analyses and disputes. . . . But this divine woman emphasizes only the essential: the honor of the Trinity. She draws from the fount of her inner plenitude and pours it forth, to quench the thirst of the parched.[6]

If the writings of these women astonished their contemporaries and continue to amaze us today, it is also because they are the fruit of sound learning. The quasi-encyclopaedic opus of Hildegard, cloistered from the age of seven or eight, could not otherwise be accounted for. Moreover, during the feudal epoch, the women of the nobility pursued advanced studies, almost of the same level as those of their brothers. And in the following century, the Beguines we are about to deal with, as well as the Prioress Beatrice, apparently all belonging to a well-to-do milieu, possessed a deep culture, both literary and spiritual.

Although, as we shall see, the literary aspect of their writings is important, the main achievement of these women lies in their efforts to reform the Church, undermined by schisms, sclerosis, simony, and intellectual aridity, and to install new forms of Christian life. The former task, that of reformation, was more specifically Hildegard's, while that of renewal and even innovation is what characterizes the Beguine movement. In fact, from the beginning of the thirteenth century, the aim of the great spiritual currents that were making headway was not only to restore but also to innovate. Such words as *novelty* and *liberty* are their chief leitmotivs, accompanied by that of *poverty*. This spirit of evangelical poverty, in various manners, was opposed to the corruption and lucrative ambitions rife particularly among the higher ranks of the clergy. Umberto Eco's recent book, *The Name of the Rose*,[7] has given the modern reader an excellent picture of the situation and of the struggles carried on within the Church itself among the various tendencies, both orthodox and heterodox. At one moment or another, these trends, originally of the same inspiration, parted ways, sometimes for reasons dogmatically justified, sometimes for motives that were purely political.

Affinities and Differences

After having sketched the spiritual relationship uniting the women we are going to deal with in these pages, we must now proceed in more detail, on one hand to examine more deeply their affinities, and on the other to stress the points of difference between the Benedictine Abbess and our Beguines, together with Beatrice. In fact, the latter belong to a later spiritual trend which has been called Rheno-Flemish Mysticism. (Let us not forget that the Cistercian Order, to which our Beguines are spiritually linked and to which Beatrice belonged, is a reform of the Order of St. Benedict, based on the ideal of poverty.) This current of mysticism follows in the wake of St. Bernard—who founded the Cistercian Order in the twelfth century—but more especially of his friend and disciple, William, Abbot of St. Thierry, of Liège origin. This spiritual trend developed during the thirteenth and fourteenth centuries, first in Flanders, and then along and beyond the Rhine. Although Hildegard had very close relations with Flemish spiritual milieux, and particularly with the Cistercian Abbey of Villiers (or Villers) in Brabant where, in the following century, the monks would observe with keen interest the Beguine movement, she herself does not represent Rheno-Flemish mysticism, while our Beguines and Beatrice are its somewhat forgotten mothers. Without them, and without their humbler sisters who have not expressed in literary form the mystical experiences they certainly lived, we can be certain that neither Meister Eckhart's mysticism nor that of Ruysbroeck the Admirable would have been what they are. These two great mystics elaborated theologically and gave literary expression to a type of experience which was not exclusively theirs but which had been previously lived by these women, in their Beguinages or their convents.

The term "mystic" must be understood in very different senses according to whether we are referring to Hildegard or to the Rheno-Flemish mystics, and this because of the changes of mentality and perspective which characterize the passage from the early Middle Ages to the thirteenth and fourteenth centuries. The Benedictine Abbess belongs to an age of undivided globality: she is at the same time naturalist, physician, poet, musician, theologian. Her visions integrate natural history and sacred history, cosmology and eschatology. Our Beguines and Beatrice, on the other hand, are marked by the distinctions that now appear in religion, between the philosophical, theological, and mystical perspectives. Mysticism, understood in the modern sense of the term, was to find its greatest exponents in the fifteenth century: Jean Gerson[8] and Henry Herp,[9] both of whom placed it in the realm of experience. Without forgetting that Hadewijch and Mechthild hold an intermediate position, we can consider our Beguines, with all due respect, as "specialists" of mystical experience. Their ultimate aim is to transcend themselves and "to be melted in God," in a union that excludes all intermediaries (*sine medio*). Hence their tendency to minimize the necessity of recourse to the ecclesiastical hierarchy and to reduce the exercise of the moral virtues to the condition of a preliminary and imperfect stage: in fact, the freed soul can take leave of them without any formality, according to a new version of the famous Augustinian precept "Love, and do what you like." At the very limit, this soul no longer needs God Himself, insofar as this need still implies exteriority and duality, since, having become identified with Him, she has become "what He is."[10] Nevertheless, the fact must be stressed that these mystics do not reject the human aspect of the Incarnation. For Hadewijch, before claiming to be "God with God," the soul, with Mary, must pass through all the stages of the divine maternity, and Marguerite Porete, who describes in very metaphysical terms the fusion of the soul with God, has written lines in which one can foresee the "Mystery of Jesus" of Blaise Pascal. In fact, the large majority of our Beguines seem to have been perfectly orthodox and—particularly in Flanders where the movement developed around Marie d'Oignies— constituted a rampart both against the interior corruption of the Church and against heresy. On this matter, let us quote

Dom Porion, one of those who has best understood and loved them:

> A spirit of fervor and renewal is blowing, breaking down conventions and looking for the immediate, the real, in several domains. Beghards and Beguines devote themselves to the poor and the sick, and to this day we find traces of their charitable initiatives. They encourage and spread the devotion to the Holy Sacrament; some of the pious women show, in their own person, by visible stigmata, the union they realize with the Humanity of Christ. Apart from their ecstasies and visions, it is not bereft of interest to observe the behavior that biographers have noted in women deprived of their control by the intensity of spiritual savor: laughter, clapping of hands, volts, and dances. All these expressions of irresistible joy appear in the lives of St. Lutgard, of Beatrice, Christine the Admirable and many others. . . . But the feature that is most worthy of attention remains the one we have already stressed in our authors: the inner orientation, the impetus which urges the soul to overpass herself in order to be lost in the simplicity of the Divine Being. This is what distinguishes those among our holy women whose picture is most clearly drawn by documents and testimonies. Marie d'Oignies, Lutgard de Tongres, Yvette d'Huy, as well as Beatrice and Hadewijch, plunge their gaze into the Divine Essence, showing that It is visible to the inner eye if it manages to recover its original nakedness. It is on account of this testimony that their names must be preserved and their voices transmitted: bold women who remind us why we were born.[11]

Certain prelates—such as Cardinal Jacques de Vitry (1170–1240) who was inspired by Marie d'Oignies and is still remembered for his historical works[12]—were able to appreciate this renewal and gave ecclesiastic protection to the Beguines. But the institutional Church was, on the whole,

xx (*Introduction*

more aware of the danger of this "novelty" than of the spiritual treasures it brought with it; consequently she tried to protect herself by means of the Inquisition and various interdictions. She felt that she was menaced in her very structure and this was so, at least as regards the feudal aspect of this structure and, in the eyes of a considerable part of the clergy, this aspect constituted her true nature. On this point, Hildegard is more prone towards the conservative attitude: she is still a figure of the early Middle Ages, a representative of the Benedictine and ecclesiastical order. Although she appears to have enjoyed considerable independence, speaking her mind to prelates and the important people of this world, preaching to the clergy and the laity, she nevertheless remains integrated in the feudal system and its socioreligious hierarchy, as is proved by her refusal to accept novices who were not of noble birth. (At the same time we must not forget that, in other matters, Hildegard is ahead of the generally accepted ideas of her age, as, for example, when she says that heretics should not be put to death because they are *forma Dei*.)[13]

On the other hand, the Beguine movement corresponds to a new age of Christianity, the age of rights wrenched from the feudal system: freedom of trade, communal franchises and, as a consequence, a certain personal religious independence. This was especially the case in the Rhine Valley where the densely populated towns and trade expansion favored the spread of ideas which in those days were, first and foremost, religious ideas.

We see another facet of this freedom when we consider the case of many women of noble or bourgeois origin, desirous of dedicating themselves to God. As they were unable to join religious orders, for lack of sufficient dowry or of noble origin, and also on account of the growing refusal of the religious orders to open new convents to satisfy the ever-increasing number of vocations, these women were obliged to adopt a semi-religious life. In other words, they devoted themselves to a life of asceticism, prayer, and work, but without pronouncing perpetual vows. And so the creation of the Beguinages helped to solve the serious problem of the fate of unmarried women (*Frauenfrage*) who, in aristocratic milieux could not take up an occupation, as could those of the lower classes. These few indications illustrate the fact that the movement of the women of the Middle Ages—as other movements of that period—is to be explained by factors that are indissociably religious, social, and economic. In his great work *Religious Movements in the Middle Ages*, Herbert Grundmann was the first to illustrate the relation between these factors, and it is to be hoped that his unfinished task will be resumed so that further light will be thrown on the forces at play in these new religious movements.

As regards importance, the Beguine movement (not exclusively feminine since there was a small minority of Beghards), which spread from Flanders to Germany and northeast France, can be compared only to the contemporary poverty movements of the Franciscans and Humiliates in northern Italy. None of them were started by "proletarians," as was asserted by the scholars who, towards the end of the last century, looked upon them as examples of class struggles; their real aim was to meet needs that were as much spiritual as economic. And so, during the whole of the thirteenth century, the majority of the Beguines were of noble or middle-class origin, but gradually the Beguinages became places of refuge for poor women. Certain Beguines begged for their living, often wandering from one place to another and asking for their bread in God's name (*Brot für Gott*)— these being the most ill-reputed. It is perhaps literally, and not merely figuratively, that we must interpret the expression "begging creature" that Marguerite Porete applies to herself. But the majority of these women, in the Beguinages then being organized, under the direction of a "mistress" (*magistra*), apart from their lives of prayer and austerity, dedicated themselves to activities both within and beyond the walls of the community house: care of the sick, the laying out of the dead, and all kinds of manual work. Thus they were able to earn their own living and ended up—involuntarily—

competing with certain guilds, especially with that of the weavers.

The Beguines were closely linked to the Cistercians and also, a little later on, to the Mendicant Orders, the friends of poverty: the Franciscans and Dominicans, founded and developed during the thirteenth century. The members of these three orders undertook pastoral duties in return for services offered by the Beguines. However, these women were often suspected by the clergy, and this for two chief reasons. Firstly, they were not so closely supervised as were the nuns, as they were neither cloistered nor bound by perpetual vows, and the Church had never given them official status. Secondly, by reason of their spiritual aspirations, they played an incontestable part in the revolution that was to allow the laity to become acquainted with the sacred texts and with theological knowledge, no longer exclusively through sermons and prayer books but, thanks to translations and writings, in the vernacular. This meant encroaching on a domain reserved to the clergy, a domain they defended by means of interdictions, autos-da-fé, and condemnations to death at the stake. Such was the fate of Marguerite and her book, and Mechthild knew that hers too was threatened. It has been rightly suggested that neither Meister Eckhart nor Marguerite would have been condemned if their works had appeared only in Latin. It is true that St. Bernard's *Sermons on the Song of Songs* had already been translated into French in the thirteenth century, though they were written primarily for monks. This shows that the laity already had a certain access to theology, but we must stress the fact that in this case it was the theology of a scholar who was above all suspicion of heresy or error.[14]

At this point we must draw attention to a very important fact: the vulgar tongues were emancipated at the same time as the communes and while these free communities of women, the Beguinages, were gradually being established. These vulgar languages—Flemish, German, and French— found, in the writings of our Beguines and of Beatrice, their first literary form in the spiritual field. This is what explains, to a great extent, the success and rapid diffusion of these works.

Among the earliest writings in the vernacular, of paramount importance are the works we are going to present in this book; the *Letters, Poems,* and *Visions* of Hadewijch of Antwerp; the *Mengeldichten* of Hadewijch II; the *Seven Degrees of Love* of Beatrice of Nazareth; *The Flowing Light of the Godhead* by Mechthild of Magdeburg; and lastly, Marguerite Porete's *Mirror of Simple Annihilated Souls.* It was these women who, together with the authors of the chansons de geste, the *Minnesänger* and the troubadours, are at the origins of our great literatures, thanks to their free manner of expressing the freshness and vigor of their experience in a living language just being created.

In the literary field also, we can note in what way these women are akin to Hildegard and what it is that separates them from her. They are her sisters insofar as they too are spiritual writers defending the faith and denouncing the corruption of the clergy and, as lay persons and women, they, like Hildegard, also had to excuse themselves for writing on subjects on which they were considered incompetent. The only exceptions were made for those who were judged to have received a special privilege: the direct inspiration of the Holy Spirit. But Hildegard still wrote, or dictated, in the language of the Church, although she herself said she was not conversant with the Latin of philosophers. Thus she belonged to the domain reserved to the clergy, since she used their language and had received approbation from the Pope and the Synod of Trier. On the contrary, our Beguines were often less fortunate, as was the case with Marguerite, who suffered a fate similar to that of Joan of Arc. In fact, one document relating to the latter declares that she was a Beguine,[15] an interesting indication, even if it still remains without proof.

It seems that for public opinion, as well as for the theologians, the asceticism of spiritual persons and above all their claim that it is possible *to find God in the*

soul without intermediary provoked suspicions and created
hostile prejudices. Apart from political hatred, what led
Joan of Arc to the stake was the *immediate character of
her mission*, received from an inner authority which
another power was tempted to doubt. We must also
take into account the extremism of medieval psychology:
an ecstatic must be either a minister of the Holy Spirit
or an instrument of Satan.[16]

If we now consider the doctrinal aspect of the works we
are about to examine, we shall find again a certain opposition
between the old and the "new." Hildegard is a great visionary
who, with her exceptional wealth of images, was able to
illustrate the data of the history of salvation, introducing
certain perspectives that were original for those times but,
on the whole, her works remain within the traditional
framework of Augustinian theology.

On the other hand, our Beguines introduced a "new"
theological element and this constitutes the greatest difference between them and Hildegard. Here we refer to the
doctrine of the return of the soul to her primal reality in
God, in a much more radical formulation than that of
Augustine, because it is inspired by the Greek Fathers. It is
this aspect we are now going to deal with. In fact, in spite
of its rich quality, Hildegard's work does not present any
special difficulties for the cultured reader. According to her,
the soul, at the summit of the vision, becomes similar to God
while, for the Beguines, the soul is annihilated to become
"what God is." Their mysticism of abandonment is expressed,
in fact, in an ontological dilemma: the creature must shed
his particular, created, separated being, in order to find once
again his true, "uncreated," "non-separated" being in God.
Thus it is that the "non-willing," which consists of willing
nothing apart from God Himself, leads to a real annihilation
of the soul considered in her particular and egotistic being.
But she loses herself thus only to find herself at an incom-
parably higher stage or "being," having become, as Hadewijch says, "God with God," or, as Meister Eckhart will say,

"God in God." Here we have one of our deepest mystical traditions, which will include not only Eckhart and Ruysbroeck the Admirable, but also Teresa of Avila, John of the Cross, and many others. However, the language of this mysticism has been somewhat forgotten and that is why we must briefly give it our attention.

Mysticism of Love and Mysticism of Being

In the writings of our Beguines the symbolism of courtly love mingles with the metaphysical expression of union with God, thanks to their profane as well as religious culture. This fusion is in great part due to Cistercian influence. In fact, the great development of nuptial mysticism in the West goes back to St. Bernard's *Sermons on the Song of Songs*, in which he applies the eroticism of the sacred text to the relation between the soul and the Divine Word. We must remember that St. Bernard belongs to the twelfth century, an age that witnessed the birth and blossoming of the doctrine of courtly love. Our Beguines, as we shall see, love and think in accordance with the tenets of this doctrine "which was truly to mould the soul of the West and definitely establish the features of its culture. . . . In the thirteenth century, the spiritual revolution of which we are speaking—a new awareness of the solitude of the soul with God, of her divine nobleness and intangible freedom—was to a great extent the work of the ecstatic virgins who, curiously enough, borrowed so many expressions from courtly literature. . . . And so we find the Beguines creating a language to express their passionate experiences, to seek a union more immediate and more total with God, to proclaim as a kind of inward gospel a new exigency of Eternal Love."[17]

Side by side with this extremely important aspect, that of the mysticism of Love, or *Minnemystik*, there is, with our Beguines, another facet that cannot be neglected if we really wish to understand their works: We refer here to the mysticism of Being, or *Wesenmystik*, also known as speculative mysticism. For our Beguines draw from a doctrinal source, that of the Augustinian tradition, which had been considerably enriched, and even partially transformed, by the addition of Cistercian spirituality. In fact, their works are strongly influenced by William of St. Thierry, the most "Greek" of the twelfth-century theologians. Not content, as his friend St. Bernard was, with borrowing from Origen, William (in his *Commentaries on the Song of Songs*) reintroduced into the Latin tradition a considerable amount of Alexandrian theology, which had been completely forgotten or neglected in the West except by John Scotus Erigena in the ninth century. We shall repeatedly find this theology in the works of our Beguines just as we do, a little later, in those of the masters who, in one manner or another, continued their tradition: Eckhart and Ruysbroeck.

At this point, mention must be made of the new Trinitarian theology that William developed, taking inspiration, of course, from the Alexandrians, but stressing far more than they did the close bond between Trinitarian life and our own spiritual life.[18] This integration of our relations with God within the Trinitarian relationship "so that God loves Himself by and in the very human heart," will also become a characteristic feature of Beguine spirituality. On the one hand William states that the Trinitarian relations are inherent in the mystery of the *Divine Being*, comparing the verse of Exodus 3:14 ("I *am* who I *am*") with the verse of John 10:18 ("Do you not believe that I *am* in the Father and the Father *is* in Me?"). On the other hand, William clearly shows that, for us too, there is no other possibility of *being* than that of *being in the Father* while the Father *is in us*. But, unlike Christ, Who *is* always this being since He is always born, we must *become this being*, that is, accede to this condition by birth.

To make this understood, William did not hesitate to use the expression: *"to become what God is,"* which is much bolder than anything found in the Augustinian tradition. In fact, although Augustine urges us to participate in God, that is, *to be in the only real Being*, nevertheless, in opposition to Manichean Pantheism, he insists on the point that, in this participation, the soul is not God nor "what God is." In other words, she is not a part of the Divine Substance. Without falling into Pantheism, and in a formulation we shall find later in some of our Beguines, William asserts that we must become, not God, certainly, but "what God is." That is to say, we must become by grace what God is by nature. Here he is merely expressing, in his own manner, and in the line of the Greek Fathers, the traditional doctrine of *deification*.[19] This assimilation in God which, more than union, is *"unity of spirit,"* is based on the will of love, just as it will be with our Beguines:

> It is when man becomes with God one single thing, one single spirit, not only by the union of a will that wills the same as He does, but by a more profoundly true virtue that is not capable of willing anything else. This virtue is called *unity of spirit* not only because the Holy Spirit produces it or deposes it in the spirit of man, but because it is *the Holy Spirit Itself, God-Love*. It is present . . . when the blessed soul finds herself taken up in the embrace of the Father and the Son; when, in an ineffable, incomprehensible manner, *the man of God deserves to become, not God, but nevertheless what God is*, man becoming by grace what God is by virtue of His nature.[20]

In this passage from his famous *Letter to the Brethren of Mont-Dieu* (also called *Golden Letter* and long attributed to St. Bernard), William uses an expression which was later considered suspect by Gerson. It is true that the phrase "to become God"—refused by William but close to the one he himself employs—will be found in schools judged heretical, such as that of Amaury de Bène in France at the end of the thirteenth century, as well as among the Brethren of the Free Spirit. We cannot know whether such expressions as "to become what God is," "to become God," "to be God in God," etc., all of which refer to the Greek notion of deification, are employed in an unorthodox manner or merely serve to convey the power of mystical union, unless we first try to discover in what context of doctrine and of life they were used.

The intimate union of doctrine and life is, in fact, what characterizes William and what opposes him to the scholastic doctors, particularly Abélard who, in William's opinion, ruins the true nature of Theology by introducing into the science of God a purely rational conception.[21] William, on the contrary, wants to know God otherwise than as an abstraction. He wants "to palpate, to touch with the hand of experience." This is why he does not hesitate to assert that the only faculty capable of leading to this knowledge is love. *Amor ipse intellectus est.* It is Love herself that becomes knowledge, for Love alone is able to reach God's depths which transcend the intellect.

In the course of the twelfth century both Hugh and Richard of St. Victor would also stress the primacy of Love over intellect. These two monks were the most famous representatives of the Convent of St. Victor in Paris, at that time a sanctuary of mysticism. After them, Thomas Gallus, who taught at St. Victor's at the beginning of the thirteenth century and then at the Monastery of Verceil, amalgamated the mysticism of Denys the Aeropagite with that of the Victorines. Together with William, these mystics all had a more or less pronounced influence on our Beguines.

It has been rightly said that the knowledge of Love that William teaches, *cognitio caritatis*, is a Christian gnosis, distinct from all purely philosophical speculation. "Reason cannot see God unless it is in what He is not, while Love is content to rest in what He is,"[22] says William in a text that will later be taken up by Hadewijch of Antwerp. In fact, we shall find once again this type of "Christian gnosis" in the Beguines, with the primacy they attach to Love anchored in the Trinity. In their works, we also constantly find the doctrine of "unity of spirit" with God.

Let us mention, even if briefly, some of the other influences upon these women, traceable to William of St. Thierry. It should be remembered that he considered the virtues not so much from the moral point of view, as a necessary acquisition, but rather as the normal consequence of our deification in Christ, as Origen did. This theme will be found again with our Beguines and with Meister Eckhart who will express it in such a striking manner as to make it become a cause of scandal for the Inquisitors![23] Let us also recall the theme of *epectasis*, or the infinite progress of spiritual life that never exhausts the depths of God. This theme was described by St. Gregory of Nyssa and reintroduced by William into the Latin world. Lastly, we must not forget the importance that eucharistic mysticism held for William: faithful to the Cistercian tradition, he emphasized the personal and subjective aspect of the encounter with Christ.

All these themes are to be met with again in the works of our Beguines, who formulate them in a new manner, for their mode of expression is different. In fact, their literary model is that of courtly love, their language, the vernacular. This is why their style, whether simple or learned, has nothing in common with the rhetoric of Latin medieval authors. They set about putting new wine into *new* bottles. Lamprecht von Regensburg was not mistaken about them when he recognized in them an art of expression that is also "the art of just love," as Hadewijch of Antwerp says in her first *Vision*. She herself is recognized as one of the greatest Flemish poets, while the works of Mechthild of Magdeburg and Marguerite Porete respectively may be numbered among the masterpieces of German and French literature.

But this new literary creation is sometimes expressed awkwardly, in a language in its first stages, from both the literary and theological standpoints, a language that now sounds somewhat alien to our ears. Therefore, in the texts we have translated, we have tried to respect as much as possible the literary style of our authors who very often proceed by repetition and make use of allegory to the point of saturation. It is our opinion that an over-modernized translation, while lessening these defects which doubtlessly make the text heavier, might very well destroy their vigor and lyricism. This is why we have attempted to remain very close to the medieval text, so that the reader can have as direct a contact as possible with the art of our authors.

"The art of just love" is an expression that Hadewijch took from courtly literature. The ideal proposed by our mystics is that of the *noble* soul, the proud soul who accepts all the trials imposed by God (under the form of *Lady Love*) just as the knight in the courtly romance accepts all trials that are imposed on him by his lady. In this transfer from the human to the divine sphere lies the originality of our Beguines who may very rightly be called "troubadours of God." But this primacy of Love is expressed by them also in terms of metaphysics of being and Trinitarian Theology: *God-Love* is indissociably Being and Trinity. They lived fully the encounter between Metaphysics of Love and Metaphysics of Being, already proposed in the works of William of St. Thierry. For them, as for him, "to love . . . *is to be*, and to be one single spirit with God."[24]

Hadewijch, in her turn, will unite indissolubly these two aspects: "In fruition you will experience who *I am*, I, *Love*."[25]

And Marguerite Porete, in an even denser theological formula, writes:

He is [*He*] *Who is.* That is why He is what He is by Himself: *Lover, Loved, Love.*[26]

The experience of union is, as we have already seen, that of the return of the soul to her primal being in God. She must find once more what she was when, not yet having become distinguished from Him through her exit into creation, she was "what God is," or "God with God," or even "God in God." That is why it can be called a union "without difference."

It is to this tradition that our Beguines belong, but they express it through their original, personal experience. At this point we might mention the admirable manner in which Hadewijch of Antwerp described, before Meister Eckhart, the exclusive reciprocity between the Divine Depths and the depths of the soul—the soul, that fathomless abyss which

God alone can fill. This theme is considered by some as the most famous point in Eckhart's mysticism.[27] Often, in fact, it is to these Beguines that we must turn to find the origin of expressions in the works of Eckhart and Ruysbroeck that had been thought to be without precedent until the writings of these spiritual mistresses were rediscovered or brought to light again. For example, it is in Beatrice's little book, *The Seven Manners of Love*, that we meet for the first time the expression *without a why*, which was taken up again by Hadewijch, Marguerite, and Catherine of Genoa, and which finally became famous with Eckhart. This expression refers to the gratuitous nature of Divine Love, but also to the total detachment of the annihilated soul.

Attention must be drawn to the theme of overpassing, (*überfahrt* or *überfall* in German; *overvaert* in Dutch; *trépas* in French) which is extremely important in the works of our Beguines. This theme of the soul always overpassing herself without ever being able to embrace the Divine Being is doubtlessly the most difficult for the noninitiated reader to understand since it is generally expressed in negative terms. This approach, according to the tradition handed down from Denys the Aeropagite, seeks to transcend our too human manner of understanding the divine names, such as Goodness, Intelligence, and Being, by denying them, only to assert finally that God *is* the Reality corresponding to these names, but in an ineffable and super-intelligible manner. This is why the language of the mysticism of Being, in its efforts to surpass the very words that it employs, constantly alternates positive and negative terms, the vocabulary of being and that of nonbeing, of the something (*iht* in German, *iet* in Flemish) and of the nothing (*niht, niet*). Therefore the abandonment of the soul to God is expressed more often than not in negative terms, in order to make understood this "overpassing" of the soul towards the Infinite. Thanks to the "non-willing"—which is at the same time desire for uncreated Love—the soul no longer wishes for anything finite. Thus it is that her individual will is annihilated; and, as a consequence, what she is in her individual, created, and separated being (the being that today would be called ego) will be annihilated. Then she can find again in God her original, non-separated being; in other words, she can "become what He is," or "be God with God," having gone beyond her own limits and abandoned the means that, for a certain time, helped her in this crossing which constitutes the sole aim and the sole meaning of our life in this world.

Although this is one of the deepest mystical traditions of the West, it is also one of those that has been the most unjustly condemned—here we have only to think of Marguerite Porete and Meister Eckhart. Later, the language of the Mysticism of Being more often than not deteriorated into scholastic metaphysics, almost exclusively speculative, separating theory from life and experience. However, the last few decades have witnessed the beginning of a return towards this lost heritage and attempts are being made to decipher its meaning, for so long misunderstood.

Such is the mysticism of Being that was wedded to the mysticism of Love by our Beguines and particularly by the most metaphysical among them, Marguerite Porete and Hadewijch II. This latter author wrote somewhat later and she was often confused with Hadewijch of Antwerp. But, in actual fact, Hadewijch II employs a much more abstract and theological language. The *Mengeldichten* of Hadewijch II, part of which have been translated into French by Dom Porion and entitled *New Poems*, are very close to Eckhart's formulations—as is also Marguerite Porete's *Mirror*. We must make special mention of *Mengeldicht XXVI* concerning "Naked Love Who spares nothing—in her wild overpassing (*overvaert*),"[28] an expression, in its thought and vocabulary, closely akin to the Eckhartian *Treatise XI* of Pfeiffer, *Von der übervart der Gotheit*, while *Mengeldicht XVII* resembles in a striking manner Pfeiffer's *Treatise XII, Von dem überschalle*, long attributed to Eckhart. In the two above mentioned *Mengeldichten*, as well as in the German *Treatises*, the theme is the Divine Transcendence: Whatever heights our knowledge may reach in contemplation, something of Him remains, and always will remain, beyond our grasp, and it is in this that our highest joy abides.

> The active silence of the Unity is hidden in silent depths, so that no creature ever reaches the ultimate depths of Its Being (*iht*). The fact that to us this Being (*iht*) *remains* unfathomable should make us rejoice and we must understand this through Him: in this lies our highest bliss. May the godly Three-Oneness allow us to attain it.[29]

In Dutch, this ever-unattainable Transcendence is called *ontbliven* and means literally *what remains* above our reach. With Marguerite Porete, this "what remains" is called the "*More,*"[30] that which God is over and above what He communicates to us of Himself: this constitutes one of the fundamental themes of the *Mirror*. Dom Porion has stressed the importance of this theme as a pre-Eckhartian testimony in Beguine mysticism. The same can be said as regards the theme of spiritual poverty, if we compare certain passages from the *Mirror* with Meister Eckhart's famous German Sermon 52, *Beati pauperes spiritu*.[31] Finally, let us draw attention to an anonymous poem of the thirteenth century, the *Dreifaltigkeitslied*, or *Trinitarian Hymn*, which Preger cited as an example of the development reached by the *Wesenmystik*, or Mysticism of Being, before Eckhart.[32] With both Hadewijch II and Marguerite, it is a question of attaining the Divine "No-thingness," that pure and naked No-thingness which is the desert of all created things, because it is the Uncreated Being, or, to use the words of Denys, the superessential Good.

As researches are deepened in this field, we become more and more convinced that these themes were present among the thirteenth-century mystics, especially among our Beguines; that means one or several generations before Meister Eckhart developed them. So we must admit that he partook of this trend and was not as original as was commonly thought. We say this without wishing in any way to deny his exceptional speculative genius, his profound religious experience, and his creative mastery of the German language. However, while it is generally considered that Eckhart was born around 1260, it is worthwhile remembering that in 1250 Lamprecht von Regensburg had already described in a few words, in the poem already mentioned, the manner in which the Beguines of Brabant and Bayern lived and conceived the mystical experience: "Free of themselves and of all things," they aspired "to see without intermediary what God is."

Map courtesy of Brepols Publishers (Belgium).

Map courtesy of Brepols Publishers (Belgium).

PART I

Hildegard of Bingen

(1098–1179)

Hildegard of Bingen receives the inspiration of the Holy Spirit in the form of a river of fire. She is writing down her Visions on wax tablets. They are being transcribed by the monk Volmar who is in an adjacent cell while Hildegard is attended by her spiritual daughter, Richardis von Stade.

(Illuminated MS of *Codex latinus* 1942 in the Biblioteca Statale di Lucca and reproduced with the kind permission of this Library.)

Introduction

Life and Personality

Hildegard offers us the finest example of what a woman could achieve in the twelfth century, as regards active life, as well as spiritual and artistic life.[1] She is outstanding for the quality of her natural gifts, her prophetic charisma, and her dynamic reforming attitude.

She lived in a troubled age, a period which witnessed the conflicts between the Priesthood and the Empire, as well as the early Crusades, the second of which was preached by St. Bernard at Vézelay in 1146.

Born in 1098 at Bermersheim, near Alzey in Rhenish Hesse, of a family of barons, she was entrusted when she was eight years old to the care of the female community attached to the Benedictine monastery of Disibodenberg. Here she was placed under the guidance of Jutta von Sponheim, and after the latter's death she became abbess of the hermitage. In 1148 she broke free of the authority of the monks in order to found a convent on the Rupertsberg, near Bingen, and fought tooth and nail to defend its independence by seeking directly the protection of the powerful Archbishop of Mainz, as well as that of the Emperor Frederick I, Barbarossa, elected in 1152.[2] In 1165 she set up a new convent at Eibingen, on the other side of the Rhine, which, in the twentieth century, became the center of the Hildegardian revival. Hildegard not only ensured the economic autonomy of the newly created sisterhoods—

thanks to her competence in legal matters—but she also showed great comprehension in the way she looked after the spiritual and physical welfare of her daughters, although there was sometimes danger of rupture.[3]

But her concerns soon went far beyond the convent walls. Ever since the age of forty-three, she had felt she had been endowed with a prophetic mission. For a long time she resisted this terrible divine calling, until, overwhelmed by illness, she felt compelled to write and dictate her visions, having previously consulted the abbot of the Disibodenberg monastery. She also sought advice from St. Bernard, who gave her encouragement.[4] The Abbot of Disibodenberg handed over to the Archbishop of Mainz the already compiled pages of *Scivias*, her first great work. In 1147, at the Synod of Trier which Pope Eugenius attended, Hildegard was authorized, partly thanks to the intervention of St. Bernard, "in the name of Christ and of St. Peter to publish all that she had learned from the Holy Spirit."[5]

Her fame then began to spread throughout the whole Christian world. Pilgrims came flocking to the Rupertsberg convent and this sometimes gave rise to picturesque scenes, as certain demons demanded to be exorcised only by "Old Wrinklegard" who, on one occasion, had to organize for the possessed patient a kind of religious psychotherapeutic rite.[6]

Hildegard held correspondence with all kinds of prominent people, with pope and emperor, with bishops and abbots, and she did not mince words when she considered their behavior unworthy of their callings. She addressed herself to the clery of Cologne,[7] to the monks of St. Martin of Mainz[8] to put them on their guard against the rising Cathar heresy. She also undertook four preaching missions—to both clergy and laity—visiting Franconia, Lorraine, Schwaben, and places along the Rhine as far as Werden. This role was quite exceptional for a woman of those days.

Moreover, she attempted to intervene in the schismatic situation created in 1160 and 1177 by Barbarossa, who nominated no less than four antipopes. Her courage did not fail her even at the age of eighty, when an interdict was unjustly placed upon her convent because in the convent cemetery she had permitted burial of a nobleman who had been excommunicated but who was nevertheless reconciled with the Church during his last hours.[9] The Abbess ended up by winning her case and died shortly afterwards, in 1179.

The events of this long and active life bear witness to Hildegard's strong personality. She was, however, of an extremely complex nature. Her reaction to illness is not devoid of ambiguity. There is no doubt that, throughout her whole life, she was a sickly creature: "From the day she was born, this woman lived confined within illnesses as if enmeshed within a net, so that her very marrow, her veins and her flesh are constantly tortured by pain."[10] What today we would call "psychosomatic troubles" she imputed to the work of the Holy Spirit, Who submits her to the influence of the elements, making her weather-sensitive.[11] When she is crushed by the weight of her visions, she is ill until she can express them.[12] It is actually this oversensitivity that opens her to a world of profound spiritual intuitions and images. But sometimes this psychosomatic fragility is used to exert pressure upon her entourage as, for example, when she wishes to obtain the permission of the Abbot of Disibodenberg to leave the mother-house in order to found a new convent.[13]

She wavers between doubts concerning her mission and its acceptance by the outside world and, on the other hand, her deep conviction that she has received a prophetic gift.[14] She often makes use of this conviction in an imperious manner when she is judging the behavior of the important people of this world, both clergy and laity. Here she is acting, not as the weak woman she professes to be, but as a conscious instrument of God. Although she judges from a lofty viewpoint and with deep fidelity to the Church the opposition of Barbarossa to the Pope,[15] nevertheless she is sometimes carried away by a purely human sentiment when, for example, she tries to prevent her beloved spiritual daughter, Richardis von Stade, from being appointed abbess of another convent. But her anger and disappointment gradually fade away as she realizes they were exaggerated, a fact which is proved by the fine letters exchanged with Richardis's brother, Bishop of Brême.[16]

Lastly, we must admit that, in spite of the universal character of her visions, Hildegard did not go beyond the feudal conceptions of her age. For she defended a hierarchical theory of conventual life, seen as a reflection of the cosmic order, as opposed to a more evangelical experience. This attitude is clearly seen in her answer to the questions (veiled reproaches) put to her by the Prioress of Echternach, Canoness Tengswich (Tengswidis). In fact, the latter asks the Abbess why she accepted exclusively the daughters of the noble and rich in her community, whereas Christ had chosen the poor as Apostles, and Peter and Paul both reminded us that God is no respecter of persons. (Acts 10:34, Rom. :2,11)

In her reply, Hildegard insists on the fact that the world is composed of hierarchical states willed by God, an order which under no circumstances should be overthrown. She takes as her first example the angelic hierarchy and then adds a more trivial image: does one put oxen, sheep, asses, and goats into the same enclosure? The moral argument she proffers is that a mingling of young noblewomen and commoners in the same convent would mean running the risk of encouraging the former to be proud and the latter to revolt. By practicing humility among their own equals, these young women have greater possibilities of accomplishing the divine will.[17]

Hildegard's Works

Authenticity

The editing of Hildegard's works poses several problems. In fact, her visions, as well as the words she heard, present themselves as "sparkling flames or clouds moving in a pure air," as she herself explains to Guibert of Gembloux. Her scanty knowledge of written Latin, the Latin of philosophers, as she says, allows her to write down these experiences only with extreme awkwardness (*non limatis verbis*).[18] That is why she worked with secretaries: first with Volmar, a monk of Disibodenberg, the "symmysta" (or co-initiated) who corrected her grammar and style.[19] After Volmar's death in 1173, when her chief works were already completed, one, among others, who aided her was Guibert of Gembloux (1124/25–1213) who stayed at the Rupertsberg until 1180, a year after Hildegard's death.[20] A literary scholar, he marked her last works with his most flourishing style, a fact, however, which she herself deplored. Two nuns, one of whom was Richardis von Stade, also assisted her in her task.

The first miniature of the famous Rupertsberg illuminated manuscript illustrates well the Abbess's manner of proceeding. Her head pierced by the flames of the Holy Spirit, she writes down her visions on a wax tablet. In an adjacent cell, communicating by means of a window with our visionary's cell, Volmar is writing down her words, while she is assisted by her spiritual daughter, Richardis.[21] (Illustration I: cover)

The study of the manuscripts of the letters both written and received by Hildegard, as well as historical and iconographical testimony, confirm the authenticity of her works, which has sometimes been questioned.[22]

Hildegard's Culture

The Abbess of Rupertsberg considered herself as "a simple creature" (*homo simplex*); she described herself as "a poor little womanly creature" (*paupercula mulier*), as "an uncultured woman" (*indocta mulier*). In those times, in principle, women did not have the right to teach in public and the ignorance they confessed, or was imputed to them, led to another type of experimental, inspired knowledge for which difference of sex was of no importance.[23] This concept was used to guarantee the authenticity and divine origin of writings and words deemed to be prophetic right up to the sixteenth century, even as regards men, as is proved by certain affirmations concerning Ruysbroeck, treated by his biographer as "ignorant and uncultured."

In actual fact, thanks to the Divine Office, Hildegard knew the Latin texts of the Vulgate and those of the Latin Fathers. Moreover, she lived during a period of intellectual ebullition, an age which was rediscovering the universe as a whole. It was the epoch of the schools of Chartres and St. Victor, the spoken and written influence of which she must surely have felt. There is no doubt that she had a knowledge of philosophic authors such as Lucan and Cicero[24] and that she kept up a learned correspondence with theologians of that period who sought her opinion on doctrinal matters.[25]

Her scientific knowledge derives, on the one hand, from a personal observation of surrounding nature—animals and plants—as well as from a study of the illnesses of those who came to her to be healed and, on the other hand, from a rich tradition based on a global explanation of the universe inherited from Greek antiquity.[26]

Hildegard the Visionary

In general, Hildegard's visions have been considered didactic rather than ecstatic; that is to say, through them, she transmitted her knowledge in allegorical form.[27] It is true that, as to her visions, she usually insists on the fact that she experiences them in the state of wakefulness.[28] But we must remember that in the *Vita* we find the following passage: "A little later, I had a marvelous and mystical vision; all my inner organs were upset and the sensations of my body were no longer felt. For my consciousness had been transformed, as if I no longer knew myself, as if raindrops were falling from the hand of God upon my soul, in the same way that the Holy Spirit had filled the Evangelist St. John."[29] The prophetess here describes a loss of individual consciousness which leads her into another dimension.

According to the description she gave to Guibert of Gembloux,[30] her visions are not hallucinations, even when received in wakefulness, but they allow her to penetrate "with the eyes and ears of the inner man" into the realm of the "spiritual senses," where what one sees and hears is perceived in a supranatural light, "shadow of the Living Light," and sometimes, very exceptionally, she penetrates that Light itself. This is what she tells us at the end of *Liber vitae meritorum*: "The creature who sees these things and transcribes them sees and yet does not see; he feels terrestrial things and at the same time does not feel them. It is not he who presents the wonders of God, but he is seized by them, as a chord by a musician's hand, to make heard a sound which does not come from him, but from the touch of another."[31]

The didactic element in her writings is, in reality, subsequent to the vision and is methodically conducted. This task may last for years, as is shown by the fact that about a decade elapses between the composition of her three greater works. In many passages of these works, as well as in her letters, the didactic factor often comes to the fore, although she always declares she is speaking *ex visione*. Every concrete situation is immediately translated into images and symbols, perceived in the light of Christ and in relation to His redemptive design.[32] Her major *opera* might very well be described as great inspired panoramas created as a synthesis of the history of the world and of salvation.

Hildegard's Major Writings

Apart from her secondary works—by no means negligible— such as her *Explanation of the Rule of St. Benedict*, her lives of the saints and theological commentaries, Hildegard wrote a book on natural history and one on medicine: her *Physica* deals with nature, the elements of botany and zoology, while *Causae et Curae*[33] studies illnesses, their causes and remedies.

Her most famous works form a vast visionary triptych: *Scivias* or *Know the Ways* (of the Lord), put into written form between 1141 and 1158; *Liber vitae meritorum* or *The Book of the Merits of Life*, composed between 1158 and 1163; *Liber divinorum operum* or *The Book of Divine Works*, begun in 1163 and completed in 1173.

We must also stress the importance of her correspondence, mentioned above: about 300 letters have been authenticated and published in various editions.

Hildegard was also poet and musician, having composed and set to music seventy-seven hymns of divine praise. Some of them are still sung in our own times and the recently recorded versions have met with great success.

Her famous "triptych," already mentioned above, embraces the whole history of the universe, from the creation to the end of time, a sacred history which includes both nature and mankind.

In *Scivias*, the first book describes the Creation of the angel and of man. Prepared by the call of Israel, the second book extols the coming of the Word Incarnate and the marriage of God to humankind in the fecundity of the Church and the sacraments. In the third book the various stages of salvation are represented by a series of symbolic buildings, and the conclusion describes the final assumption of the Church after the defeat of Satan.

The Book of the Merits of Life,[34] which could also be called the *Book of Discernment*, or *Retribution of Good and Evil*, takes up the vision once more and prolongs it in an ethical sense. At the center of the work is Man, the personification of God (*Vir Deus*), who dominates and sustains the cosmos. He takes part in the conflict between Good and Evil, a conflict which is expressed by the "yes" or "no" pronounced by each individual, by the whole of humanity, torn asunder one might say, by opposing virtues and vices, until the final victory of Good and the vision of Church and Earth reintegrated in eternal glory are reached. In this grandiose psychomachia, Hildegard enriches the allegory with her very subtle power of psychological observation, which accounts for the wealth of character portrayal.

The Book of Divine Works gathers in ten admirable visions the ensemble of the reflections contained in the two previous works. Beginning with a presentation of the Trinity as a threefold figure—Love, Mercy, and Goodness—the first five visions evoke the origin of the world, its internal structure, and the position of man around whom the celestial spheres are placed in concentric circles moving like a wheel, each human organ having its corresponding part in the cosmos. This comparison is the subject of the fourth vision, which continues these parallelisms with a great store of detail. The fifth vision offers a complete ethical topography of the World Beyond, with descriptions of the places of suffering and purification. As for the last five visions, they take up again the history of humanity as the history of salvation, at the center of which there stands the Word Incarnate Who, by the power of His love, creates a new world.

Throughout these works, Hildegard's theology is seen to be at once traditional and fundamentally optimistic. Although she never tries to conceal the consequences of initial refusal to obey God at the Fall, she nevertheless always ends up with final victory of the Deity and the reintegration of the cosmos in the divine sphere.

What particularly distinguishes her with respect to the theologians of her age, in like manner creators of vast symbolic constructions (Alain de Lille, Hugh of St. Victor),[35] is the dynamism and the concrete quality of her astoundingly rich visions. They inspired the illuminated codices of Wiesbaden and Lucca which, created at the Rupertsberg Convent, together allow us to catch a glimpse of this touching and colorful world. A faithful reflection of the visions, they are considered a particularly important contribution to medieval iconography.[36]

For Hildegard, a sound theologian, God is, primordially, "He Who is" (Ex. 3:14) and several of her visions begin with this traditional assertion of the *Being* of God. With neither beginning nor end, He is total life (*vita integra*), persisting identical,[37] unchangeable, eternal. "One in His uniqueness, to Whom nothing can be added".[38] The unity of Being is manifested in a triple energy: Father, Word, and Spirit.

The Creation had always existed in the mind of God: "When God, through his *Fiat* 'uttered' the creative act, all things at once took on their form, all things that divine prescience had contemplated before they became corporeal."[39]

The Word is thus the exemplary cause of all creatures, as the Abbess explains in her exegesis on St. John's prologue: "All creation appeared in the mind of this Creator. It was in His prescience, not eternally with Him, but envisaged by Him, foreseen and foreordained. God's is the only life which does not originate in another life having a beginning. Everything that has been created is life in Him, since it was in His 'providence.' All creation lived in God. In God, there has never been any questions of remembering, or of forgetting either: for everything was already in His prescience, although no form yet existed in time."[40] It can therefore be said that the Incarnation of the Word was foreseen throughout Eternity, in accordance with what will be called *praedestinatio Christi absoluta*, a doctrine later held by the Franciscan School.[41]

By creation in time, the virtualities contained in the mind of God are realized. In the universe, Man, the work of God, (*opus dei cum omni creatura*),[42] occupies a privileged position. Having been called upon to take the place of the fallen angel, he is created to the image of God, one and trinal: body, soul, and intelligence. He is the "shadow of God,"[43] a reflection, owing his existence, naturally, to the Object reflected, at the same time revealing Its splendor.

If, in all her descriptions, Hildegard returns to the Augustinian ternary image, she extends it to the dimensions of the universe, for Man bears within him the impress of all the other creatures. Man, a microcosm, reproduces, even to the smallest detail, in his anatomy and his physiology, the microcosm. Each human organ, every operation of the senses has a threefold correspondence: with the elements, with moral life, and with supernatural life.

To take just one example: the human chest represents the whole air space between the clouds and the earth and, by means of the winds, this space sets the terrestrial wheel in motion. The chest also harbors the soul which, like the air, unites heaven and earth. This soul, or divine spark, is called upon to lead the body along the right path towards Good.[44]

The seasons of the year and the very hours of the day sum up all the ages of the earth and of human life,[45] thus expressing the intimate bond existing between Man and his environment. He has been assigned the mission of continuing the work of God upon the earth. As God's workman, (*operarius divinitatis*)[46] he has been given the earth as his workshop. "Man was given the task of announcing the marvels of God, using as instrument his voice of reason, for man is 'the plenary work of God.' "[47]

Man and Woman

This work entrusted to humankind is performed in a sexed universe; it is carried out by man *and* by woman (*opus alterum per alterum*),[48] for without the latter there would be no humanity.

With different nuances, the patristic authors and those of the early Middle Ages recognized the equality of the divine image in man and woman, but not their parity in hierarchical status, man being directly subject to God, and woman to man. This attitude was assumed less on account of woman's nature or her frailty than by reason of original sin, considered more serious on Eve's part than on Adam's.[49]

Hildegard conserves the traditional opposition of man representing strength and woman frailty, but she gives it a much more positive interpretation. Of course, we must distinguish two tendencies in her: in her liturgical writings, Eve's trangression is always emphasized in order to magnify the role of the Virgin Mary.[50] In her scientific works, however, there is a much more naturalistic tone, as for example when she speaks in very frank terms about the physical union of man and woman or about female temperaments. On these occasions she seems to be more of a clinician than a moralist.[51]

In her great visionary works, she had a very wide view on the role of woman. At the beginning, before the Fall, woman is born of man as his love, to whom God has given form.[52]

In complete equality, man beholds woman and woman beholds man. That is why, notwithstanding the Fall, man and woman remain united by the bond of fidelity which joins them indissolubly, just as body and soul are united.[53] This leads Hildegard to stigmatize all forms of sexual perversion. Conjugal love alone is envisaged in God's plans, an exception being made for virginity, reminder of Paradise and herald of final blessedness.

At a period when misogynous descriptions prevailed (inherited from Theophrastus and St. Jerome), in Hildegard's works we notice an attempt to break free of traditional patterns. Of course woman continues to be the symbol of the maternal earth (*terra materna*) where all will germinate, just as the Virgin Mary will be matter transfigured (*terra Maria, terra aurea*), who, by the power of the Holy Spirit, will give birth to the Word Incarnate.[54]

But Hildegard dares to go further in her analogies, to the point of comparing the carnal act and its component parts: strength (*fortitudo*), desire (*concupiscentia*) and the act itself (*studium*) with the work of the Trinity,[55] an image which, to our knowledge, finds no equivalent in the literature of that time. This comparison reflects the importance she attaches to bodily union in the matter of love.

Hildegard also includes the feminine element in her theology: the love of God is a maternal love, a life-giving love which is manifested in its gentleness and mercy.[56] In fact she has a predilection for the parable of the woman seeking the lost drachma (Luke 15:8–10); the woman represents God, the drachma the lost soul, while the woman's lamp symbolizes the light of Christ.[57]

Lastly, with the Incarnation, there is created a conversion of values, or rather a conjunction of strength and frailty: "God had created man strong and woman frail, she whose frailty created the world. And the Divinity is strong while the flesh of the Son of God is frail, that flesh by which the world is restored to its original life.[58]

In the exegesis of the scriptural passage on the strong woman (Prov. 31:10–14), there results, perhaps in a less explicit manner, a kind of osmosis between strength and weakness which henceforth are no longer the exclusive lot of one or the other sex, but a heritage common to both— woman's strength being more supple, more flexible, than man's.[59] It may be said that Hildegard tries to get beyond the exclusively masculine concept of God and the values traditionally attributed to man and woman.

Man's Responsibility

As image of God, man is distinguished by intelligence, a quality considered less as a faculty of reasoning than as a capacity of discerning Good and Evil. Uninterruptedly throughout his life he is called upon to make his choice, and according to this choice, he draws closer to or farther from the divine design.[60] Naturally, Evil is considered as having no existence in itself,[61] and Lucifer, the fallen angel, lives in a dark deserted region where love is excluded.[62] Nevertheless, there is a penetration of his antagonistic forces, the cause of a merciless combat in which man is ceaselessly engaged. Hence the essential role of discernment (*discretio*). It is on this point that Hildegard shows that she is in perfect control of the situations into which she is sometimes drawn by her imagination and gives us proof of her enlightened wisdom.

This *discretio* is a "joyful knowledge" (*laeta scientia*), in contrast to the overwhelming sadness of sin.[63] Issuing from the Holy Spirit, it allows man "to distinguish within him all the ways, all the means which God deems useful, so that none of the forces He sets to work will be lost by dispersion of the spirit. God has distinguished the terrestrial needs and the energies of the celestial virtues bestowed by the Holy Spirit each time man rises, thanks to them, towards contemplative life."[64] *Discretio* serves, in fact, as an intermediary between active life and contemplative life; it is the light of the second day of creation which allows the accomplishment of good works. In contrast, Hildegard depicts a lively image of the vagabond, the wanderer who knows no measure, who seeks on all sides, led exclusively by the whim of the moment and refusing to analyze the causes of his instability.[65]

Thus *discretio* permits the individual man to choose consciously his role in the universe and to live it. Although this choice is personal, its effects concern the salvation of the whole world, which is also involved in the strife between the antagonistic forces of Good and Evil.[66] "For the elements drink up all that belongs to the nature of man, just as man absorbs the elements."[67]

In a similar way, illness is considered less as a pathological process than as a deficiency in the sick man, who can be cured only by a sympathy which reestablishes the interrupted current of good creation. The best of all remedies remains the doctor's compassion and his participation in the suffering, instead of the indifference shown by that somber figure who refuses to take any interest in his patient.[68]

These considerations touch our modern sensibility, even if they are expressed in a cosmological and clinical frame of thought which is no longer ours. Our epoch is ready to listen to the complaint of the elements so strongly pronounced in *Liber vitae meritorum*: "We can no longer operate and accomplish our tasks, as we were appointed to do by our Master. For men have upset us by their wicked actions, churned us as in a mill."[69]

These words seem prophetical with regard to today's world, but, with Hildegard, they express at the same time the pessimistic outlook of her epoch and an eschatological vision inspired by apocalyptical patterns. There is no doubt that the image is somber but, at the same time, she shows that negative cosmic influence can only go as far as God allows in His justice, proportionate to the degree in which man has trespassed beyond the limits established by *discretio*; for man, whose body is in correlation with the cosmos, possesses an elementary knowledge of this relationship, as well as of the spiritual forces and moral rules which derive from it. He must develop this innate knowledge by studying with wholehearted zeal the Book of Creation, as well as that of Revelation.

Each time that man in his activity does not respect the measure or limit established, not only does he harm himself and his immediate environment, but he also destroys the equilibrium of the elements which play their part in the history of salvation.

The whole of creation, restored thanks to the Incarnation of the Word foreseen from all eternity, is brought back— not without endless struggles—to the welcoming heart of God.[70]

The vision of Celestial Jerusalem embraces the whole of humanity, now summoned to the fullness of life in God, thanks to sanctification, the fruit of grace and virtues, which establishes mankind in a higher state than that enjoyed at the time of original innocence.[71] This "reestablishment," in the sense given to this term by St. Paul (Eph. 1:10) and by St. Irene of Lyon, is expressed in a final celebration where the symphonic choir of angels and men can be heard.[72]

At the same time poet, visionary, and profound theologian, there is no doubt that Hildegard left to posterity a grandiose work, enlivened by flamboyant images which are also deeply significant since they are linked not only to a personal but also to a community experience of the mysteries of God.

Man and the cosmos.

The cosmos is enveloped by the energies of Trinitarian love symbolized by a sphere of fire. The images of the Father and of the Son are united by a diadem, the Holy Spirit. The universe is presented in the form of a wheel with six concentric circles (dense air, subtle air, watery air, etc.). In the center, there is the earth. Man occupies the center of the universe, which he dominates, his arms outstretched, forming a cross. He is pervaded by all the cosmic forces, symbolized by the breath of animals and the rays emanating from the planets and the stars.

(*Book of Divine Works*, Visions I and II)

(*Codex latinus* 1942, Biblioteca statale di Lucca)

Excerpts from Hildegard's Works

Letter to Bernard of Clairvaux

O venerable Father Bernard,[1] you who, in a wonderful manner, hold the great honor of the strength of God, must be much feared by the wrongful foolishness of this world since, with the holy cross as your banner, inspired by an ardent love for the Son of God, you urge men to wage battle in the Christian armies against the ferocious pagans. I beg you, Father, in the name of the living God, to listen to me and to answer my questions. I am very preoccupied on account of a vision that appeared to me in the mystery of the spirit, a vision that I certainly did not see with the eyes of the flesh. I, wretched creature, more than wretched, being a woman, since my childhood have seen great wonders which my tongue could not utter if the Spirit of God had not taught me, so that I should believe. Most reliable and kind Father, out of your goodness, answer me, your unworthy servant, for from the days of my childhood I have never lived a single hour of security; examine these things in your soul, with your piety and wisdom, according to the knowledge you have received from the Holy Spirit, and from your heart send consolation to your servant.

In fact, in the texts of the Psalms, in the Gospel and other books which are shown to me in this vision, I understand the inner sense which touches my heart and soul like a burning flame, teaching me the depths of the explanation without, however, giving me literary mastery in the Teutonic language, of which I am deprived, for I can read only in a simple way, without being able to analyze the text. Answer me and let me know your opinion on this matter, for I am a human being ignorant of all teaching bearing upon exterior questions, but within my soul I have knowledge, and that is why I hesitate to speak. But hearing of your wisdom and piety, I am already consoled, having dared say these things to nobody else—since, according to what I have heard, there are so many schisms among men—except to a certain monk[2] whom I know well enough to be convinced that he leads a life worthy of full approval. And so I have told him all my secrets and he has certainly comforted me by considering them great and redoubtable. For the love of God, Father, I beseech you to console me and then I shall be completely reassured.

I saw you in this vision more than two years ago, as a man looking at the sun without fear, but with great audacity. And I wept because I myself am so timid and have so little courage.

Most good and kind Father, I have put myself in your soul so that you should reveal to me, in your answer, if it so pleases you, whether I must say these things openly or whether I must keep silent, for I experience great torments in this vision, not knowing what I must say of the things I have seen and heard. And sometimes, after the vision, I am confined to my bed by terrible sufferings, because I am silent, and I cannot even stand up. I shed tears of sadness before you because I am inconstant and my nature is like that of a gnarled, twisted tree, born as I am of the seed of Adam who, having followed the Devil's suggestion, was exiled to a foreign land. Now, rising up, I turn to you for aid, for you are not inconstant, but you always straighten the tree and you are victor in your soul, saving not only yourself but the whole world.

You are also the eagle who gazes at the sun. I beseech you, by the serenity of the Father, by His admirable Word, by the sweet tears of compunction, the Spirit of Truth, and by the sacred sound, with which every creature resounds[3] and by the Word Himself out of Whom the world arose, and by the sublimity of the Father Who, in His gentle viridity, sent the Word into the Virgin's womb, from which he drew His flesh, like honey nesting in a honeycomb. And may the sound itself, the Father's energy, be heard in your heart and raise your soul, so that you do not doze distractedly when you listen to this human being who is addressing you—while you ask God all these things, concerning both this creature (that I am) and the secret itself, penetrating through the door of your soul, in order to know all these things in God.

God be with you and with your soul, and be valiant in His combat. Amen.

Bernard's Reply to Hildegard

To his dear daughter in Christ, Hildegard,[4] Brother Bernard, called to be Abbot of Clairvaux, if the prayer of a sinner has any power.

If you consider our littleness quite differently from how we ourselves judge it in our conscience, we believe we must impute this exclusively to your humility. Therefore I have not hesitated to reply to your affectionate letter, although the multitude of matters I have on my hands obliges me to answer you much more briefly than I would wish. We are happy to know of the grace of God which is within you. And, as far as it behooves us, we exhort you and beg you to consider it as a grace and to make every effort to respond to this gift with sentiments of deep humility and devotion, knowing that "God resists the proud and bestows His grace upon the humble" (1 Pet. 5:5). Besides, when inner instruction and the unction which teaches everything already exist, what need is there for us to teach or to warn?

We heartily beg and beseech you to remember in your prayers to God, us, as well as all those who are united to us in spiritual community with the Lord.

Letter to Guibert of Gembloux

. . . O faithful servant,[5] I, a poor wretched woman, in the vision I tell you these words. . . .

Ever since my infancy, when my bones, nerves, and veins were as yet undeveloped, until the present day, now that I am more than seventy years old, I have always had the gift of vision in my soul. And as God wills, in vision my spirit soars upwards into the celestial heights, borne by the various currents; it dilates among different peoples, no matter how remote their countries are. And since I see [these images] in such a manner, I behold them according to the changing forms of the clouds and of other created things. But I do not hear them with my physical ears, nor understand them with my heart's thoughts, nor do I perceive them with any of my five senses, but only in my soul, with my bodily eyes open, so that I have never known loss of consciousness in ecstasy, for I see these images in a state of wakefulness both night and day. And I am continuously afflicted by illnesses and great sufferings which threaten to cause my death, but so far God has sustained me.

The light that I see is not localized, but it is far brighter than a cloud which surrounds the sun. I cannot reckon its height, length or breadth and I call it "the shadow of the living light." And just as the sun, moon and stars are mirrored in water, so the Scriptures, discourses, virtues, and certain works of man take form in my eyes and are reflected in this radiant light.

All the things I have seen or learned in vision, I retain them in my memory in such a way that, since I have seen and heard them for some time, I am able to remember them. At the same instant, I see, hear, and know, and I understand what I know. But what I do not see I do not know, because I am not learned. And the things that I write are those I see and hear in my vision, and I do not use words other than those I hear, and I utter them in unpolished Latin, because in the vision I am not taught to write as philosphers do. And the words I see and hear in this vision are not like those which issue from human lips, but they are like a bright flame, a cloud moving through pure air.

I can in no way recognize the contours of this light, no more than I can see perfectly the sun's sphere. And in this light, sometimes, but very rarely, I see another light called "the living light." When and how I see it I cannot say but, during the time I see it, all sadness and anguish disappear, so that I seem to be an innocent young girl and not an old woman.

Yet, on account of the continuous illnesses I endure, at times I have no wish to express the words and the visions shown to me; nevertheless, when my soul sees and experiences these wonderful things, my mood changes and I forget my sufferings and tribulations (as I have already said) and my soul draws up what I see and hear in the vision, as if from a fountain—a fountain which always remains full and inexhaustible.

And never does my soul lack that light described above as "the shadow of the living light." I see it as a starless sky within a sparkling cloud; there, in the blaze of the living light, I see the things I often declare and the answers I give to the persons who question me.

As regards body as well as soul, I do not know myself and I consider myself as almost nothing; I yearn towards the living God and leave all things in His hands, so that He, Who has neither beginning nor end, may preserve me from evil on every occasion. And so, you, who have asked me to express myself, pray for me together with all those who desire to hear my words with faith, that I may remain unwaveringly in God's service.

Letter to the Mainz Prelates

In the vision that was engraved within my soul by God the Creator before my birth,[6] I am obliged to write to you about the interdict inflicted upon us by our superiors because in our cemetery we had a man buried, under the direction of his priest, and with no guilt on our part. When, a few days after this burial, we were ordered by our superiors to remove the body from the cemetery, seized with fear, I looked towards the true light, as is my custom, and with wakeful eyes I saw in my soul that, if this order were obeyed and the man's body exhumed, this expulsion would be a terrible threat of dark evil for our convent; we should be, as it were, enveloped in one of those black clouds which announce tempests and thunderstorms.

Since then we have dared neither to remove this man's corpse—seeing that he had received absolution, extreme unction and holy communion—nor follow the counsels and orders of those who persuaded us, or commanded us, to do so. Not that we turn a deaf ear to the advice of wise men or the orders of our prelates but so as not to seem—by an act of cruelty perpetrated by women—to be insulting Christ's sacraments which had fortified this man during his lifetime.

However, not to appear entirely disobedient, we have ceased singing the songs of divine praise, in accordance with the interdict, and we have abstained from partaking of the Lord's body as we were accustomed to do almost every month.

Together with all my sisters, I felt deep bitterness on this account and was overwhelmed by great sadness. Filled with a profound heaviness of spirit, I then heard these words in my vision: "It is not good that, by human orders, you should be deprived of the mysteries of the Word clothed in His human nature, your Saviour in a virgin nature, born of the Virgin Mary. . . ."

In the same vision I heard that I was at fault because I had not come before my superiors, in all humility and submission, to ask leave to take communion, since we had done nothing wrong in accepting the body of that man who, from the hands of his priest, had received everything befitting a Christian and had been buried in our cemetery in the presence of all the inhabitants of Bingen, without any objection being raised.

And this, Your Excellencies, is what God has bid me say

to you. I also beheld something concerning the fact that, to obey you, we have ceased to sing the divine office, limiting ourselves to reading it in an undertone. I heard a voice coming from the living light relating the various forms of praise, as David says in the psalm (Ps. 150:3–6) "Praise Him with the sound of the trumpet, praise Him with the psaltery and harp. Praise Him with the timbrel and with dance; praise Him with stringed instruments and organs. Praise Him upon loud cymbals, the high-sounding cymbals. Let everything that has breath praise the Lord."[7]

These words bring us from outer realities to inner ones and teach us how, by imitating these material instruments and their diverse features, we must direct all the élan of our inner being towards the praise of God and how we must express this praise. If we give the matter our careful attention, we recall how ardently man seeks the voice of the living spirit, lost because of the disobedience of Adam who, before his transgression, still innocent, took no small part in the choir of angelic praises. The angels possess such voices through their spiritual nature, and are called spirits by the Spirit, who is God. Adam, then, lost this vocal affinity with the angels which was his when in Paradise and—just as, upon awakening, one is no longer certain about what he saw in his dream—so the knowledge [of God] which was his before the fall lies dormant within him. . . .

But God, Who saves the souls of the elect by sending them the light of truth to lead them back to their original happiness, decided to renew the hearts of a great number [of them] by bestowing on them the prophetic spirit so that, through inward illumination, they might recover part of the gifts lost by Adam when he was punished for his sin.

So that man should not live in the remembrance of his banishment, but rather in the sweet souvenir of that divine praise which Adam had once shared joyfully with the angels, and to encourage him to praise God, the holy prophets, enlightened by the spirit they had received, not only composed psalms and canticles which were sung to stir the devotion of listeners, but they also invented—for the same purpose—the many-toned musical instruments which accompanied the songs with multitudinous sounds. And so listeners, roused and prepared outwardly by the forms and features of these musical instruments and by the meaning of the words sung, also receive inner enlightenment.

Following the example of the holy prophets, other wise and clever men, by their human endowments, have also invented numerous instruments, to be able to express in song the joy within their souls. They adapted their singing to the bending of the finger joints,[8] remembering that Adam was created by the finger of God, the Holy Spirit.

In Adam's voice, before the fall, there was all the sweetness and harmony of musical art. And if he had remained in the condition for which he had been created, mortal man's frailty could never have endured the force and resonance of that voice. When the Devil learned that man had begun to sing through divine inspiration and would be urged to remember the sweet music of his heavenly home, seeing the failure of his perfidious plans, he became so frightened and tormented that he has never ceased to hinder, and even destroy, the utterance, beauty, and sweetness of divine praise and hymns of the spirit. He does this not only in man's heart, by wicked insinuations, impure thoughts and various distractions, but also in the very heart of the Church, wherever he can, by causing discord, scandals, and unjust oppressions.

And so you, and all other prelates, must be extremely wary before issuing a decree which closes the mouths of a community singing to God and forbids them to celebrate and receive the sacraments. Beware in your judgments not to be deceived by Satan who drags men away from celestial harmony and the joys of Paradise. . . .

Ponder on this matter: just as the body of Christ took flesh from Mary's intact virginity, by the power of the Holy Spirit, so the songs of praise—echo of celestial harmony— are instilled into the Church by the Holy Spirit. The body is the raiment of the soul which gives life to the voice. And so it is fitting that the body united to the soul should sing God's praises out loud. . . .

And since, when hearing certain melodies, man sometimes sighs and groans, recalling heavenly harmony, the prophet David, considering deeply the profound nature of man's spirit, and realizing that his soul is symphonic, exhorts us in his psalm to give praise to the Lord on the lute, on the ten-stringed psaltery (Ps. 32:2, 91:4): the lute, which has a lower sound, is meant to urge man to bodily control; the psaltery, which draws its sound from above, to elevate his spirit; its ten chords are a reminder to contemplate the Law.

It follows that those who, without having sufficiently reflected, impose silence upon the Church singing God's praises, unjustly rob God of the beauty of these earthly songs and will themselves be deprived of taking part in the angelic choirs in heaven, unless they remedy their fault by true repentance and humble penitence (Wisd. of Sol. 11:24). Let those who hold the keys of the kingdom of heaven take good care not to open what should remain closed and not to close what should be opened. For those in charge will be submitted to the more severe judgment, unless they "rule with diligence" (cf. Rom. 12:8). And I heard a voice saying: "Who created Heaven? God. Who opens Heaven to His faithful ones? God. Who is like unto Him? Nobody." And that is why, O ye faithful, none of you must resist Him, or oppose Him, lest He should come down upon you with His power and you should have nobody to defend or protect you on the day of judgment. . . .

Scivias: Second Vision of Book II

Then I saw a very bright light and, in this light, a human form of sapphire color which blazed within a very suave rutilant fire.[9] And this bright light penetrated all the rutilant fire, just as the rutilant fire penetrated the bright light, and light and fire penetrated the entire human form, so that they were one single light and one single strength and power.

And once again I heard the same living light saying to me:

1. Of the Meaning of the Mysteries of God

"This is the meaning of the mysteries of God, so that we should clearly discern and understand that plenitude without beginning whose force, which makes the rivers of the strong gush forth, never fails. For if the viridity of God were to fail, what then would His work be? Truly it would be void. Thus it is in His perfect work that we recognize the Worker."

2. The Three Persons

"Thus you see the very bright light which, without stain of illusion, defect or error, represents the Father and, in the sapphire-colored human form, without stain of imperfection, envy, or injustice, we recognize the Son, born of the Father in His divinity before the centuries began but, in His humanity, born into the world, in time. This whole form blazes in a bright and gentle fire which, without stain of aridity, mortality, or obscurity, manifests the Holy Spirit by whom was conceived the Son of God, according to the flesh, born of the Virgin Mary, in time, to illuminate the world with the true light. But although this bright light penetrates all the rutilant fire, and the rutilant fire penetrates all the bright light, and the bright light and rutilant fire penetrate the whole human form, nevertheless all three constitute one single light in one same force and power. This is because the Father, Who is most equitable justice, is not without the Son or the Spirit, and the Spirit, who kindles the hearts of the faithful, is not without the Father or the Son, and the Son, the plenitude of fecundity, is not without the Father or the Spirit. In the majesty of the divinity they are indivisible. . . . So these Three Persons are one God in the majesty of one single and same divinity and the unity of this divinity persists inseparably in the Three Persons. For the Divinity cannot be split, remaining always inviolable, without any change.

But the Father is manifested by the Son, the Son by the birth of creatures and the Holy Spirit by the incarnation of the Son. In what way? The Father who, before the beginning of time, begot the Son, the Son, through Whom all things were made from the Father at the beginning of creation and the Holy Spirit Who appeared in the form of a dove at the Baptism of the Son of God, for the end of time."

3. Man Must Never Forget to Invoke Ardently the One Single God in Three Persons

"Man should never forget to invoke Me, the only God, in these Three Persons, for I have purposely shown Them to him so that he should love Me more ardently; it is for the love of man that I sent My Son into the world, as John, My beloved, proclaims:"

4. John, on the love of God

"By this has the charity of God appeared to us, because God has sent His only begotten Son into the world, that we may live by Him. In this is charity: not as though we had loved God, but because He has first loved us and sent His Son to be a propitiation for our sins" (1 John 4:9–10).

What does this mean? Because God loved us, there resulted another salvation than the salvation we had at the time of creation, when we were heirs of innocence and holiness: the Heavenly Father showed us His love for us, when we were exposed to dangers and punishment, sending, through His almighty power, His Son—plenitude of holiness—to the children of man in the darkness of this world. There the Word accomplished all things to perfection, by His gentleness bringing back to true life those who were cast down by the impurity of their transgressions and were not able to return to the state of sanctity they had lost.

For through the Son the maternal love of God came to

embrace us, to make us grow in true life, and to sustain us in dangers, a most intense and most suave charity which urges us to repentance. . . .

Salvation given by charity did not issue from us, for we are not capable of loving God for our salvation; but since the Creator and Master of all things has so loved His people, to save them He sent them His Son, Prince and Savior, who has "washed and dressed our wounds" (Jer. 30:17, Ezek. 16:9); a very sweet balm issued forth from Him and all the gifts of salvation flow from this balm. And you, man, understand that God is not subject to any change, for the Father is the Father, the Son is the Son and the Holy Spirit is the Holy Spirit; these Three Persons remain truly undivided in the unity of the Divinity.

5. The Three Forces of Stone

There are three forces in stone, three in fire, and three in speech.

In stone there is a force of humid viridity, a palpable consistency and a rutilant fire. It possesses humid viridity so that it will not be dissolved or broken, a palpable consistency so that it has a shelter and a rampart, a rutilant fire so that it is warmed and strengthened in its hardness. The humid viridity signifies the Father whose strength never dries up or dies, the palpable consistency represents the Son Who, born of the Virgin, can be touched and comprehended, while the rutilant fire stands for the Holy Spirit Who "kindles and illumines the hearts of the faithful."

Sometimes man, when a part of his body touches the humidity of stone, catches an illness which weakens him; in the same way, a man who, in the instability of his thoughts, considers the Father superficially, loses his faith.

As men, thanks to the consistency of stone, build dwellings to defend themselves against their enemies, so the Son of God, "the true cornerstone" (Eph. 2:20), is the shelter of the faithful and their protection against enemies.

As the rutilant fire illuminates the darkness, burning up

everything it touches, so the Holy Spirit puts everything to flight, removing all stains of iniquity. . . .

6. The Three Forces of Flame

Just as the flame has three forces in one single ardor, in the same way there is one God in Three Persons. How? Flame is composed of a splendid light, a vermilion viridity and an igneous ardor. . . .

In the splendid light recognize the Father Who, in His paternal love, spreads His light over the faithful and in the vermilion viridity that is in Him as cause, and in which the flame shows its strength, see the Son Who took flesh of the Virgin, and in Whom the Divinity has manifested its wonders; in the igneous ardor, perceive the Holy Spirit Who kindles the hearts of the faithful. But where there is no splendid light, no vermilion viridity, no igneous ardor, no flame is to be seen. In the same way, where neither Father, Son, nor Holy Spirit is honored, God is not venerated as He should be.

Just as in one single flame we can distinguish three powers, it is to be understood that there are Three Persons in the unity of the Divinity.

7. The Three Elements of Human Speech

Just as three elements are to be found in human speech, so the Trinity must be considered in the unity of the Divinity. How? In speech there is sound (*sonus*), expressive force (*virtus*), and breath (*flatus*). Sound so that it may be heard, expression so that it may be understood, breath that it may attain its purpose. In sound recognize the Father Who, in His indescribable power, manifests all things; in expression see the Son, born of the Father in a marvelous manner; in breath, the Holy Spirit Who gently burns within Them. But where the sound is not heard, the expression is not manifested; where the breath does not rise, speech is not understood; in the same way, Father, Son, and Holy Spirit are not separated but perform their work in unison. So just as these three elements are united in speech, so is the supreme Trinity in supreme Unity. . . .

Understand, O man, that God is One in Three Persons. But you, in the weakness of your mind, think that God is not powerful enough to be in Three Persons, but only in One. But the God in Three Persons is the true God, "the First and the Last" (Rev. 1:17).

8. The Unity of Essence

But the Father is not without the Son, nor the Son without the Father, nor the Father and Son without the Holy Spirit, nor the Holy Spirit without the other Two Persons, because these Three Persons are inseparable in the unity of the Divinity. In what way? Speech sounds in the mouth of man, but there is no mouth without speech, nor speech without life. And where does speech reside? In man. And from whence does it issue? From man, from living man. In the same way the Son is in the Father, He Who was sent by the Father to the tenebrous earth for man's salvation, having been conceived by the Holy Spirit in the Virgin's womb. The Son is unique in His divinity, just as He is unique in His virginal birth and, as He is the Only Son of the Father, so He is the Only Son of His Mother, for just as the Father begot Him before the centuries began, so the Virgin Mary gave birth, in time, to Him alone, since she remained a virgin after this birth.

Therefore, O man, consider your God in Three Persons, the God Who created you by the power of His Divinity and has saved you from perdition. . . .

Of Man and Woman

When God created him, Adam felt a deep love within him during the sleep into which God had plunged him.[10] And God gave a form to the image of man's love and so woman became the love of man. And the very moment woman was formed, God gave man the power of creating so that, through his love—that is, woman—he should procreate children. When Adam beheld Eve, he was filled with all wisdom for he saw in her the mother who was to bear his children. And when Eve beheld Adam, she seemed to be looking towards Heaven, just as the soul desirous of celestial things gazes upwards, for her hopes were centered in man, and that is why there must be one single love between man and woman, and no other love.

But the love of man for the love of woman is as ardent as a volcanic fire which can be extinguished only with great difficulty, and he turns towards a wood fire, easily quenched. The love of woman for the love of man is like a gentle warmth, coming from the sun and bearing fruits; it goes towards a very ardent wood fire and that is why it bears a sweet fruit, the child.

But after the transgression, the great love which was in Adam when Eve rose from his body and the sweetness of that first sleep have changed their nature. And because man still feels a great sweetness within him, he hastens swiftly to woman "as the stag to the living waters" (Ps. 41) and she to him—she like a threshing floor heated by the strokes that detach the grains of wheat.

The Complaint of the Elements

From *Scivias I, 2, c.27*

And all the elements of the world[11] in which formerly there reigned complete calm were agitated by terrible phenomena. Now, creation was destined for man's service and nurtured no hostility for him, but after man's disobedience and his revolt against God, overwhelmed with confusion, it lost its equilibrium and inflicted many great tribulations upon man, so that he, having turned towards evil, was punished by creation itself. Since man, in the garden of Paradise, had rebelled against God, creation, which was originally under man's dominion, revolted against him.

From Liber vitae meritorum

And I heard the elements of the world[12] addressing the Man of God with a wild cry: "We can no longer operate and accomplish our tasks, as we were appointed to do by our Master. For men have subverted us by their wicked actions, churned us as in a mill. We already stink in our pestilence and die of hunger awaiting full justice." The Man answered them: "With my broom I am going to purify you and torment men until once more they turn towards Me. I am going to prepare many hearts and attract them towards My heart. By the same torments used by those who have besmirched you, I shall purify you, each time that you are polluted. And who could equal my power? At present all the winds are filled with rotten foliage, the air spits forth filth to such an extent that men cannot even open their mouths as they should. The force of viridity has dried up on account of the folly of blinded human crowds. They follow only their good pleasure and cry: "Where is our God whom we never see?"

I answer them: "Do you not see Me day and night? Do you not see Me when you sow and when the seed is born, watered by My rain? Every creature is drawn towards its Creator and clearly understands that One alone created it. Man alone is rebellious and splits up his Creator in the multiplicity of creatures. Who, in His wisdom, composed the Holy Books? Open them, to find out Who made you. As long as one single creature acts only to satisfy your desires, you will not have perfect joy. But when worn-out creation has disappeared, the elect will contemplate the highest joy in a life of happiness. . . ."

The Restoration of Creation at the End of Time

Once the judgment is terminated,[13] fear will cease to agitate the elements: thunder, lightning, and tempests will calm down; everything that was transient and perishable will disappear, never again to return, like snow melting in the sun. Absolute peace and tranquillity will reign everywhere by divine order. When all is finished, the elements, as you see, will sparkle with a peerless brightness and beauty, all traces of grime and filth having disappeared. For fire will shine without burning, like the dawn, the air will glitter in complete transparency, the waters will be limpid and calm, without flooding or devastating the land, and the earth will appear strong and even, without fragility or defects. There will be calm and beauty everywhere.

And the sun, the moon, and the stars will shine in the sky with all their light, like precious stones set in gold. Their troubled course to separate night and day is ended. Since the world disappeared, they have become changeless. The shades of night will no longer descend and day will never end as John, My beloved, affirms: "And night shall be no more, nobody shall need the light of the lamp or the light of the sun, because the Lord God shall spread His radiance upon all (Rev. 22:5).

Symphony

Ceaselessly we must praise the Heavenly Creator with the voice of both mouth and heart,[14] for, by His grace, He receives in the celestial dwellings not only those who stand erect, but also those who fall and those who are bent.[15]

And so behold, O man, that very luminous air which betells the radiant joy of the heavenly citizens, an air which, in a marvelous manner, transmits to your ears (in accordance with the symbols explained above) the different kinds of music by which those of the faithful who have courageously persevered in the way of truth sing the joys of Heaven, together with those who, with lamentations of repentance, have been led back to the praise of these celestial joys.

In fact, just as the air embraces and sustains all that is beneath Heaven, in the same way—as you understand in all

God's wonders shown to you here—a sweet and gentle symphony makes resound in joyful key the miracles [performed for] the elect dwelling in the Celestial City, after persevering in their loving devotion to God; and through the lamentations, you perceive the sufferings of those who are bent, those whom the old serpent tried to destroy and whom God's strength has nevertheless vigorously brought back to the company of those who enjoy heavenly happiness, proclaiming through them those mysteries unknown to human spirits inclined towards the earth. . . .

This is why that sound, the voice of a multitude, sings in symphony the praises of the Divine Kingdom, for symphony repeats, in unanimity and harmony, the glory and honor of the heavenly citizens, carrying aloft what speech offers aloud.

Just as speech stands for the body, so symphony manifests the spirit, for celestial harmony announces the Divinity and speech proclaims the humanity of the Son of God.

Viridity

> O, most noble viridity,
> You who have root in the sun,
> You shine in the limpid brightness,
> In the movement of a wheel
> Which escapes human intelligence.
> You, viridity, are enveloped
> In the force of the heavenly mysteries.
> You redden like the dawn,
> You blaze in the ardor of the sun,
> O, most noble viridity![16]

PART II

Mechthild of Magdeburg

(ca. 1207–ca. 1294)

The Trinity
The concentric circles represent the Father and the Holy Spirit. In the center, the Man-God. (Cf. Vision 2, BK. II)
(From: Hildegard von Bingen, *Wisse die Wege*, (*Scivias*), Otto Müller Verlag, Salzburg, 1976, plate II, with the kind permission of the publisher).

Introduction

Life

Mechthild was born between 1207 and 1210 in the diocese of Magdeburg, of a family that was certainly well-to-do and that surely provided her with a good education, as is proved by her style of writing and her knowledge of the courtly ideal. It is unlikely that she was of noble origin, as medieval authors make no mention of this fact.[1] "Hailed" by the Holy Spirit at the age of twelve, she left her family about 1230 to respond to God's summons in "exile"; that is to say, in the town of Magdeburg, where she asserts she knew only one person at that time. She entered a community of Beguines and for many years concealed the exceptional graces which had been bestowed on her. Finally she decided to confide in her confessor, the Dominican, Henry of Halle, and, encouraged by him, in 1250 she sat down to the task of writing her one book: *Das Fliessende Licht der Gottheit* (*The Flowing Light of the Godhead*).[2]

It is composed of a series of poems, both long and short, interspersed with pieces of rhymed narrative prose. In a lyrical vein, Mechthild expresses her mystical experiences, writes dialogued scenes between God and the Soul, between Lady Soul and Lady Love and other allegorical figures, such as Fidelity, Constancy, Pain, and Withdrawal of God. She also evokes Purgatory, Hell, and the demons, as well as the ineffable joy of union. In the name of the Church she so bitterly criticizes the decadence of the clergy, of the Empire, and even of the Dominican Order to which she is nevertheless deeply attached that, in spite of admiration in certain spheres, she seems to have attracted considerable clerical antagonism. It is thought that it was, in fact, in order to escape from calumny and persecution that in her later years she decided to retire to the Cistercian convent of Helfta, where she was received by the Abbess Gertrude of Hackeborn. The latter asserts that she prayed, but in vain, for divine signs to be shown on the occasion of Mechthild's death around 1294, in the hope of silencing her critics. The abbess and her younger sister, Mechthild of Hackeborn, as well as another Gertrude (later called the Great), were strongly influenced by the personality and the writings of our Beguine, and strangely enough their works knew greater fame than that of Mechthild herself. These later works, although less original, bear witness to the high level of these nuns' religious instruction, which included study of the scriptures, the Fathers, and the theologians. It was an almost clerical instruction, which Mechthild ceaselessly complains is lacking her, but this fact is certainly to the advantage of the direct inspiration of her book, "flowing from the very heart of God."[3]

We shall now translate a few passages from the very fine essay of Hans Urs von Balthasar: "The Ecclesial Mission of Mechthild."[4] In our own times it is he who has best spoken of her, following in the steps of the medieval scholars, Henry of Halle and Henry of Nördlingen (the former translated her work into Latin and the latter into Middle High German), and perhaps also in the steps of Dante who, in his *Divina Commedia*, describes a Matelda who might very well be our *Mechthild*.[5]

"As a Beguine, she may be placed somewhere between religious and secular life. She decided to leave all for God but without seeking the shelter of a convent. She carried out her mission without enjoying any protection, as regards both her person and her inner life; she was persecuted, slandered, suspected by a powerful clergy and by the religious, of whom only a few, hesitatingly, lent her an ear. She criticizes men of religion most severely, often even bitterly, and demands perfection of them (III,8), she herself never retreating before any exigency. She prays for all those who cause Christ pain (*alle meine Christenpeiniger*) (V,35), for the person she calls 'her pharisee' (VI,36), for the 'liars under holy appearances' (VII,41), and for the lascivious canons whom she treats as 'stinking goats' (VI,3). But when she sees her tormentors in the fires of purgatory, she does not hesitate for a moment to take upon herself their terrible punishment. 'Ah, dear Lord, let me render good for evil!' (VII,41). Her messages, which she declares have 'flowed into her heart from the Living Deity' (VI,43) and, as she says, must be read nine times to be understood (I,Prol.), are passed from hand to hand. But she is playing with fire and she is aware of it. 'I have been put on my guard about this book and certain people have warned me that, unless I have it buried, it will be burnt.' Although she humbly protests that she lacks learning, she places upon God the responsibility for what she writes, she prays, and continues.

She enters the convent only at an advanced age (about 1270). The cultured and refined women of Helfta welcome the elderly weather beaten sibyl with veneration and awe. . . . But the forces which had sustained her in the world have now abandoned her. The last part of her book, written at Helfta, contains many texts which are only a mere echo of her former writings and sometimes no more than weak doggerel suitable for conventual occasions. She feels this herself and complains to God that the forces of her body and mind have deserted her, that her life continues to drag on in a useless fashion, that she is 'cold in graces' and can no longer bear 'the burning love of God known in her young days' (VII,3). While to the very end she is filled with a sense of unworthiness at having been entrusted with the mysteries of God (VII,8), she grows inwardly to the highest dimension and truly becomes (as God tells her) 'in your old age a companion (*Hausfrau*) of My Deity' (VII,3). The accents of 'holy fear' become more and more precise: just as the beginning of her way was marked by the suffering she felt

because all things were not good (VI,5), so its end was bound
to resemble its commencement. Love and desire, remorse
and fear, characterize it, but now in a universal and catholic
manner. 'The sins of all men cause me remorse, so that I
am like a sick person' (VI,6). . . . She trembles beneath the
rod to the very end (VII,4), she desires neither honor nor
security (VII,7), and in her humble and merciless way of
accusing herself, she resembles the aged Augustine (VIII,38).
The visions disappear, God is silent: 'Ah, my Lord, how
silent you are now! I thank you for not having shown
yourself for so long' (VII,46); she wraps herself in Christ's
garments of shame (VII,27)."[6]

Thus we find in Mechthild a striking parallel between the
experience of our biological life, which passes from the
exuberance of youth to the decline of old age, and that of
the spiritual life. On both human and spiritual planes she
accepts this decline, the apparent withdrawal of the forces
of life and of Love.

Mechthild's Work and Inspiration

Of the *Flowing Light of the Godhead*, we have only one manuscript, in the Alemanic language (a fourteenth-century
transcription in High German which seems to follow closely
the lost original manuscript in Middle Low German). This
manuscript gives the complete text in seven books: the first
six were compiled by Henry of Halle, the seventh at Helfta
after the latter's death. There exist also two manuscripts
which give a Latin version, but they are less complete and
weakened by translation. Lastly, there remains a series of
fragments which bear witness to the diffusion and fame of
this work during the Middle Ages. It seems to have been
particularly appreciated in the famous circle of the "Friends
of God" which had centers at Bâle and in the Rhineland in
the fourteenth century. One of this circle's best-known
members, the secular priest Henry of Nördlingen, mentioned
above, wrote in one of his letters to Marguerite Ebner, a

Dominican of Medingen, that he was going to send her a book entitled *Light of the Deity.* "It is," he says, "written in the most wonderful German and is the fruit of the most perfectly appeasing love that I have ever read in German." But it is a German alien to him (Middle Low German) and that is why it took him two years to translate it into his own language (Middle High German). He asks his spiritual daughter, Marguerite, to read the work with great respect.[7] W. Preger has shown that this translation, done in the years 1344–45, was, in fact, the codex rediscovered in the nineteenth century at Einsiedeln and edited by Fr. Gall Morel in 1869.[8]

There is a gap of several centuries before we can find judgments which agree with that of Henry of Nördlingen. According to Alois Haas, Mechthild expresses herself "with the indisputable guarantee of an incomparable language," a language so spontaneous, so independent of all genres and all rhetorical figures that this work supplies "the phenomenology of religious experience in its pure state."[9] As for Balthasar, he considers that Mechthild represents the second apex of charismatic theology in the Middle Ages, after Hildegard and before Eckhart, and he adds that it is to be deprecated that, in seven hundred years, theologians have not produced any serious study on *The Flowing Light of the Godhead.* In actual fact, Mechthild is the link between Hildegard and the *Minnemystik,* just as she connects the feudal, sacral Medieval period, now on the decline, to the successive courtly and individualistic part of the Middle Ages.

"What unites her to Hildegard, but only as regards part of her work, is the cosmic and symbolic vision of the epic of the first beginnings in the heavens, of the fall [of the soul, which is a cosmic event] and of the order of salvation which responds to this fall: Christ, Mary, the Church, and the amply structured representation she gives of the end of time. For our visionary, the end of time has the same concrete and colored character as sacred history, past and present. In these parts of her work, Mechthild is prophetess and sibyl in the same sense as Hildegard. We misunderstand fundamentally the importance of what these two women say if we apply to them the gauge generally used, from St. Augustine to St. Theresa of Avila, to measure mystic visions, a gauge according to which 'imaginative' visions are far beneath those that are 'purely spiritual and intellectual.' "[10] According to Balthasar, this intellectualistic superstition could partly explain why the theologians have underestimated these two women. Perhaps the present-day rehabilitation of the imagination will help to make the value of their message better understood.

In any case, with Mechthild, the hierarchical structure of the old order increasingly gives way to the modern accents of *Minnesang*, but her song of love, even when, following the Fathers, St. Bernard, William of St. Thierry, and the Victorines, it takes up once more the images of the *Song of Songs*, is not satisfied with merely repeating them. These images appear again, in a new form, after a spiritual processing which is that of Mechthild's personal love experience, an experience of desire brimming over with impatience, a desire which, despairing of the inanity of created things, flees the *icht*, or the something, and seeks the *niht*, or the no-thingness of created things, that is, the desert (I,35).

While she lives this experience in an intense and personal manner, it is nevertheless the language of the Greek Fathers and of the tradition they created that Mechthild employs. The return of the soul to its original being in God—that is what motivates her desire and is the underlying theme of her work: the Flowing Light of the Godhead in which it is her true nature to live, just as a bird's nature is to fly in the air and a fish's is to swim in the water. Even if the influence of the "metaphysics of Essence" is less marked than in the works of her Flemish sisters, Beatrice and Hadewijch, or in Marguerite Porete's book, this theme of returning to her true original nature constitutes a strong link with them. Apart from the general influences mentioned in the Introduction, one must probably recognize that of the Dominicans established at Magdeburg since 1224, particularly of Albert the Great whom Mechthild venerated (V,28).

"Beyond the world and time, she depicts in grandiose

frescoes the birth of the soul originating in God the Father, the natural appurtenance of the soul to God by reason of this divine birth, her original destiny to be the betrothed of the Son in a precosmic nuptial mystery, so that she feels that her true nature is a super-nature that she yearns to recuperate, aching with irresistible nostalgia for her homeland: 'God has given to all natures to live according to their nature. How then could I resist mine? I must leave all to go towards God, Who is my Father by nature. . . . my Betrothed by love and I am His from before time' (I,44, and VI,31). 'Having emanated from the heart of God,' she trembles amidst other creatures and before her own sensuality, like a humiliated princess, and in her dialogue with the senses she speaks, in proud and veiled terms, of an original secret which they cannot understand or even guess. God is pure fire (VI,29) to which she wishes to return; beyond all terrestrial and human virtues, she tries to rediscover her shameless nakedness before God and in God: 'Lord, now I am a naked soul!' (I,44). The secret of betrothal essential to this soul, a secret that 'leads her to the Holy Trinity' (I,22) raises her above the angels (I,9; II,3; II,22; IV,14; VII,1)."[11]

In fact, as with our other Beguines and nuns, for Mechthild the mysteries of love are enclosed in the mystery of the Trinity: "God the Father is the cup-bearer of this inebriating life, the Son is the cup, the Holy Spirit is the wine" (V,24). The friends of God "are completely consumed in the Trinity" (I,16; VI,25) and, inversely, God's desire for man is described in accordance with this mystery: "Allow me to refresh in you the furnace of My Deity, the desire of My Humanity and the joy of My Holy Spirit" (IV,2).

In contrast to the "objective" teaching of the theologians, her soteriology is completely existential. It is what she has lived personally that becomes the subject of her "revelations": "I myself must announce myself if I wish to be able to show truly the goodness of God." (III,15). "I neither wish nor am able to write anything, unless I see it with the eyes of my soul and hear it with the ears of my eternal spirit, feeling in all the parts of my body the strength of the Holy Spirit"

(IV,13; cf.V,12). This is why it has been said that, in a certain sense, her book could be included in the Augustinian tradition of the *Soliloquies* and the *Confessions*. In fact, in all the genres that Mechthild employs—tales, dialogues, poems, visions, prayers, ecstasies, liturgical and, more particularly, lyrical reminiscences—"what is decisive is always, and almost exclusively, the *I* which is responsible for the ensemble of these revelations."[12] "The last of the foolish Beguines" (*minste . . . torheten beginen*) (III,15), as she calls herself, becomes one with the grace and knowledge bestowed upon her. She says this very clearly in the first lines of her Introduction: "This book must be received willingly, for it is God Himself Who speaks the words therein: 'I send this book as a message to all religious persons, to the bad as well as to the good, for when the pillars fall, the work cannot survive and, in praising Me, it indicates Me alone and announces My secret.' All those who wish to understand this book must read it nine times" (I,Introd.).

Her experience of God, which is love, but also knowledge, leads her to mistrust the mysticism of unknowing. Although one constantly finds in her work the patristic theme of the abyss of God and of the soul, Mechthild certainly does not appreciate "the blind saints who love and do not know" (I,2). The last stage of spiritual life is, however, for her also, night, but it is the night of love which is sacrificial death (I,21):

> Love without knowledge
> seems darkness to the wise soul.
> Knowledge without fruition
> seems to her infernal pains.
> Fruition without death
> she cannot sufficiently deplore.

". . . Like a burglar she breaks into the deathly region of love, where 'the infinite God draws to Himself the depthless soul,' and where she, 'face to face with this wonder, forgets the earth' (I,2); where the Prince and the servant-maid embrace and unite 'as water mingles with wine' (I,4); where the fiancée longs to love to death, without measure, without interruption (I,28). 'He who dies of love must be buried in God' (I,3). The Eros who urges Mechthild towards God has something of violence, a sort of cruel brutality and this is because, for her, he comes from God's eternal nature. While the Platonists and Aristotelians saw, above all, in Eros the restless heart of the creature striving to attain the repose of the Eternal Mover of all love, Mechthild introduced the anguish of desire (*gerunge*) in God Himself. It is God Himself Who, 'with great desire, shows His flaming heart to the soul and places her therein' (I,4). He is 'God burning with His desire (*Sehnsucht*)' (I,17) Who looks upon the soul as 'a stream in which to cool His ardor' (I,19). 'The intensity of My love for you comes from My desire (*Sehnsucht*), for it is My longing (*Begehr*) to be loved intensely' (I,24). 'God desires (*gelüstet es*) the famished soul' (III,1); He is 'sick with love for her (*minnesiech nach ihr*)' (III,2). 'A desire (*Verlangen*), more than sweet, joyful, hungry, and full of love, flows from God without measure, deeper and deeper within the soul, (VI,22), in a flux which—since it is eternal life—is beyond hunger and satiation. 'Cover me with the cloak of your long desire (*Verlangen*),' the soul prays (VII,35), 'for where two burning desires encounter, there love is perfect' (VII,16)."[13]

But Mechthild knows and often repeats that this accomplishment of the *Minneweg*, or way of love, is transitory in this life: "This cannot last long" (I,44). "When the game is at its best, one must leave it." (I,2). Such was her experience, that of one who has known divine consolations for several years, only to find later that they were denied her. Here we have the important theme of *Goetzvroemdunge*; the withdrawal of God.

"It is here that we approach the central point of Mechthild's experience of God and discover the completely new element it contains. Already in the *Song of Songs* there is a passage where the fiancée, apparently abandoned, seeks in tears her lost Beloved. The Fathers of the Church had interpreted these tenebrae of love in a very Platonic manner, that is to say, they explained them by the absolute nature of the Divine

Being Who dwells in His inaccessible eternity above the creature and Who, for this very reason, when one has already seized, possessed, and tasted Him, disappears into the lofty heights and, by His Ab-solute, keeps awake the insatiable Eros emanating from Him, even in eternal contemplation. Origen, Gregory of Nyssa, Augustine, Denys, and Maximos all deal with this theme, although each in his own particular manner. It is important to note that, even in the new mysticism of St. Bernard and the Victorines, this conception does not change fundamentally. It is always a question of theologians reflecting, writing, and projecting all their personal experiences into this Platonic schema. Mechthild, the unlearned, is not fettered by this model: it is in an entirely spontaneous manner, in accordance with her own experience, that she describes ecstasy as an 'ascension,' a 'flight of love' from the creature to God, as a supreme moment, but one which cannot last long and separated from it she 'precipitates,' she 'becomes cold' (V,4), finding herself cast back once more into her excruciating desire. However, the essential fact is that, for her, it is not merely a matter of faith or doctrine, but an experience she makes in an absolute manner and she expresses this experience as she conceives it: God is infinite *Freedom*; He is free to come and to go away. 'I come to you according to My pleasure, when I wish to' (II,25). For the soul who, in order to adhere to God, gives up everything, has left all, and has betaken herself to the desert of God, this experience is absolutely incomprehensible. Did not God call her? Did she not obey? Does she not follow Him 'with the voice of a hungry lion?' (II,25). And although Mechthild's pages have no chronological order, either in the German or in the Latin version, we consider it is possible to trace the development of her central experience in this way: from the first shock of this possibility (of God's withdrawal), through the repetition of the mystical 'night,' until the tremulous conviction that such is really the case, and that God so wills it, and therefore the soul must bear it. Then, very slowly and with indescribable resistance, comes the acceptance of the return of this possibility. Finally,

in an almost incomprehensible manner, there comes a desire
for this return (of withdrawal), a realization that this possibility corresponds to the most inward will and law of Love,
that the soul-in-love will choose precisely this possibility and
none other, when God puts it before her. And, at the very
end, we find her familiar with this 'withdrawal of God,'
which she now grasps as a mode of the Flowing Light itself:
the void of what flows, the uselessness of emanation. This is
doubtlessly the center."[14]

It is then that God's plan is revealed to her: this hell of
love which she must undergo, a precipitated love which
makes her follow the destiny of Christ in His Passion and
His Descent into Hell, conditions of the Resurrection for
Him, as for the soul who henceforth accepts and even desires
this withdrawal of God, which alone can draw her close to
Him forever. That is why she is happy to sink into Hell
"even beneath the tail of Satan" and why she begs in her
"profound humility" to be the last of all creatures (VII,18).

"And so her final plea is for night (VI,15), for gall and
bitterness (II,24). And love does not reach the plenitude of
its growth until the soul has descended with the Son below
the earth and has risen above all the heavens, so that all
things shall be accomplished (Eph. 4: 8–10). The soul
becomes adult when she has been raised to the very highest
summit she can reach while she is still within the body, and
when she has fallen to the lowest level, into the most profound
depths she can find (V,4); then she has the full dimension
of the history of salvation. And thus, by her personal
experience of the soul's three stages, Mechthild corrects the
traditional Platonic formula of the purgative, illuminative,
and unitive ways, when she says: 'It is the nature of Love to
flow first in sweetness, then She becomes rich in knowledge,
and thirdly She demands and desires to be rejected'
(VI,20)."[15]

In numerous texts, Mechthild describes to us her experience in the worlds of corruption and of suffering, from
which she would like to deliver the whole of Christianity,
not only from the "city whose name is Eternal Hatred"

(III,21), but also from Purgatory, from which place of suffering she ceaselessly strives to free souls. God counsels her to bathe them in the tears of love and after this ablution they become as bright as the sun (II,8).

This is one of the reasons why it has been suggested that Mechthild could very well be Dante's Matelda who, in the earthly Paradise, immerses souls in a purifying bath and then leads them towards the water which makes them remember the good they have accomplished in their lifetime.[16] But there are other parts of Dante's poem which seem to evoke Mechthild's work:

"One perhaps remembers that page where fervor is expressed by such an ardent symbolism, where Mechthild tells of her desire to walk with the Son of God among the flowers of holy knowledge (IV,12), or that dialogue in which the soul learns that her Betrothed will come to meet her when the dew falls, when birds' songs resound; and when the Betrothed arrives, the virgin dances to please Him (I,44). Do not these symbols remind us of the Enamored Lady who, with light step, goes gathering the flowers of Paradise in the pale morning light?"[17]

These comparisons are based on serious studies initiated by Wilhelm Preger and Hubert Stierling and then continued by Jeanne Ancelet-Hustache. In the famous *Life of St. Dominic* by Dietrich of Apolda, Stierling discovered long passages taken from the Latin version of Mechthild's book, in praise of St. Dominic and his order. The author says these fragments are borrowed from "very secret and very true" revelations received by a person who greatly loved St. Dominic.[18] One of these passages was certainly taken up again by Dante.[19] Moreover, ". . . We can recall (in Mechthild's work) certain scenes, evocations of Hell, the ascension of purified souls from purgatory, the idyllic landscape of the Earthly Paradise—all of which, when confronted with corresponding pages of Dante's, are found to be extraordinarily similar, even in the opinion of those critics least in favor of Mechthild. Her prophecy of the New Order and her apocalyptic spirit also remind us of certain mysterious pages of Dante."[20]

In fact, one of the features common to Dante and Mechthild is the millenarianism inherited from Joachim of Fiore who prophesied the coming of a New Era, that of the Spirit, which was to be realized by a new order of priests.

For Mechthild, it is the attacks against the Dominican Order which herald the arrival of the last days. Her perception of this event opens with these words: "The Order of Preachers was formerly attacked by false clergy and also by many covetous sinners." (IV,27). The marginal note that accompanies these lines—doubtlessly written by Henry of Halle for the German manuscript (and reproduced on the Latin manuscript)—is significant: "In the year 1256." We must recall the fact that it was in 1255 that the Inquisitor William of Saint-Amour gave free rein to his hatred of the Mendicant Orders, in a book entitled *The Dangers of the Last Days*. This book was directed against the *Introduction to the Eternal Gospel* written by the Franciscan Gerardo of Borgo San Donnino who, in his own manner, interprets the doctrine of Joachim of Fiore. The religious order which the latter asserted was destined to preach the Gospel at the dawn of the New Era was, according to Gerardo, that of the Franciscans. A commission assembled at Anagni by Pope Alexander IV condemned the *Introduction* in November 1255. But the Pope, whose partiality for the Mendicant Orders throughout these vicissitudes cannot be doubted, ordered William of Saint-Amour's book to be burned, a fact which must have pleased Mechthild if, as is probable, news of this event reached her ears. For she, too, announced the coming of a Religious Order which was to take part in the combats at the end of the world, but according to her it would be a reformed and renewed Order of Dominicans. The most interesting passage is the one in which she evokes the prince destined to be the first master of this Order. His name, she says, means *vor got*, before God. As J. Ancelet-Hustache has suggested, it is easy, for those conversant with the fantasy of medieval etymology, to recognize the name of Conradus or Conradin (*coram deo*), the grandson of Frederick II. In fact, Mechthild wishes to remain at the same time faithful

to the Pope and to the trust the German people had placed
in the Emperor Frederick II. She dreams of a better future
in which the Pope will hold the chief role but which would
assure Frederick's descendant of his legendary mission. In
this way, the promised reconciliation of the last days would
come to pass.[21]

If, to conclude, we attempt to situate Mechthild in the
history of Western Christianity, we must remember particularly her experience of the night, lived in a way that might
be termed modern. This primacy of experience, together
with her creation of an original language, underlines her
freedom from stereotyped religious patterns. Nevertheless,
this religious experience was expressed within a precise
cultural framework. It was, in fact, the Cistercian, Victorine,
and doubtlessly the Albertinian tradition which taught
Mechthild the great Neoplatonic and patristic theme of the
return to our original nature in God. It is true that this
experience is much less subject to a philosophical and
scholastic interpretation than that of her contemporary
theologians. At the same time we must note that in her work
it is impossible to find a doctrine stripped of all sociological
influence, although this aspect (due to the status, or lack of
status, of the Beguines) is much less marked than in Hildegard's works. But today we have become aware of the
sociocultural influences which nobody escapes. This is why,
for example, we cannot consider as a divine revelation, as
Mechthild claims, the attitude which she says should be
adopted towards the Jews. One is ready to admit that she is
moderate when we think of the exactions and persecutions
against the Jews which disgraced Medieval Germany and
which Mechthild must have known about at Magdeburg
where she stayed until 1270.[22] However, she may be considered to be among those who have helped history to advance
towards a modern and respectful attitude to the individual
person, since her conception and her experience of God are
an expression of the transition from a sacral and hierarchical
establishment, towards one that became liberal and individual. Thus, in a certain sense, she prepares the way for the

change in medieval thought and the development of modern spirituality: that is, the primacy of freedom and of the will, which is destined to overthrow, in God as well as in man, the traditional primacy of the intellect.[23] In fact, for the thirteenth-century theologians, will, instead of intellect, becomes the predominant factor in attaining beatitude. This is shown in the dispute on the nature of beatitude which, around 1300, divided the voluntarist Franciscan school from the Parisian scholastics. The famous Franciscan scholar Duns Scotus asserted, in contradiction to Thomas Aquinas, that understanding is not more intimate to the divine Being that will is, and that it is in the will that man's salvation is accomplished. This primacy of the will, reaffirmed by Luther and other Reformers, and later on by Descartes, has led the modern world further than its initiators could possibly have imagined. Goethe summed up this evolution in a striking manner in his second *Faust*, showing that we have substituted the capital dogma of the modern world, "At the beginning was *Action*" for the biblical Revelation, "At the beginning was the Word."

However, this development of voluntarism cannot be attributed to Mechthild or, for that matter, to any other of our Beguines. She gave importance to the will, but to a will essentially passive to the Divine Being. She prepared the way for a deeper comprehension of feminine values in the description of this passivity of the soul, and of the feminine aspect of God, by her so often identified with Lady Love.[24]

Excerpts from Mechthild of Magdeburg's "The Flowing Light of the Godhead"

Of This Book and Its Author (II,26)

I have been warned about this book
And this is what I have been told:
That unless I had it buried
It would become a prey to fire!
And so, as had been my wont since childhood,
Being sad, I began to pray.
I addressed myself to my Beloved
And said to Him: "Ah, Lord, behold me afflicted
For the sake of Your honor.
Will you leave me without consolation?
For it is You Who have led me here,
You Who ordered me to write this book."
Then, without delay, God showed Himself to my
   saddened soul,
Carrying the book in His right hand.
He said: "My Beloved, do not despair like that,
Nobody can burn the Truth.
He who wishes to take this book from My hand
Must be stronger than I am.
This book is threefold

And refers to Myself alone.
The parchment that envelops it
Is the image of My humanity, pure, unsullied, just,
That for love of you suffered death.
The words signify My marvelous Deity:
They flow hour by hour
From My divine mouth into your soul.
The sound of the words proclaims My Living Spirit
And expresses with Him the just Truth.
See how all these words
Announce My secret in praiseworthy manner.
In no way must you doubt yourself."

THE SOUL.

"Ah, Lord, if I were a spiritual and wise man
In whom you had worked this unique great miracle,
You would receive glory from it for all eternity.
But, Lord, who could believe
That upon a foul slough
You have built a house of gold,
In which You really live
With Your Mother and all creation,
And with all Your heavenly servants?
Lord, in this place earthly wisdom cannot find You."

GOD:

"My daughter, more than one man has lost his precious gold
Through negligence, on the highway of the armies,
When his intention was to use it for higher studies.
Now, somebody must find this gold.
By nature I have withheld it so many days:
Whenever I decided to bestow extraordinary gifts,
Each time I have sought out the lowest place,
The humblest, the most hidden spot.
The highest mountains cannot assume the burden
Of revealing My graces,
For the flood of My Holy Spirit

By its very nature flows towards the valley.
One encounters many a wise master of Scripture
Who in My eyes is no more than a fool!
And I can tell you more:
Before them, it does Me great honour
And greatly reinforces Holy Christianity
That a mouth deprived of instruction
Through My Holy Spirit, teaches the instructed tongue."

THE SOUL:

"Ah, Lord, I sigh and yearn
And implore You in favor of the copyists
Who have transcribed the book after me,
That you should give them also, as reward, the grace
Which has never been refused to man.
For Your gifts, Lord, are a thousand times more
    numerous
Than Your creatures who are able to receive them."
Then Our Lord spoke thus:
"They have written the book in letters of gold:
Henceforth all the words thereof
Will be stamped upon their outer garments,
And forever manifested in My kingdom
In brilliant, celestial gold;
Inscribed on all their attire.
For Love in its freedom must always be what is
    highest in man."

And while the Lord was saying these words,
I saw the Lordly Truth
In its eternal elevation.
"Ah, Lord, I beseech You
To preserve this book
From the glance of hypocritical attention
Which from Hell has come towards us,
For never could it issue from Heaven.

It has been conceived in the heart of Lucifer
And born of spiritual pride,
Nurtured in hatred
And in violent anger has so greatly swollen
That it thinks no virtue can equal it.
That is why the children of God must waste away
And be shamefully enslaved
So that with Christ they may win the highest honors."
It is a holy attention that we must pay to ourselves
And bear it within us at all times,
To preserve us from faults.
It is an attention full of love
That we must pay to other Christians
With kindness showing them their failings.
Thus we can spare ourselves much useless talk.
Amen.

Of the Soul's Journey to Court, where God Reveals Himself (I,4)

When the poor soul comes to court, she is wise and courtly, and so she looks upon her God with joy. Ah, with what great love she is received there. She is silent, intensely longing that He should praise her. Then with great desire He shows her His divine heart: it is like reddish gold, burning in a large charcoal fire. Then He places her in His ardent heart so that the Noble Prince and the little servant girl embrace and are united, as water and wine. Then she is brought to nought and abandons herself, as if she had no strength left, while He is sick with love for her, as He has always been, for (in this desire) there can be neither growth nor lessening. Thus she speaks: "Lord, You are my consolation, my desire, my flowing fountain, my sun, and I am your mirror." Such is the journey to court of the loving soul, who cannot be without God.

The Love of God in Five Points (I,17)

O God, You Who pour Yourself out in Your gift!
O God, You Who flow in Your love!
O God, You Who burn in Your desire!
O God, You Who melt in union with Your beloved!
O God, You Who rest on my bosom, without You I
    cannot be![1]

Of Seven Things Concerning the Way of Love (I,44)

....

THE SENSES:

Lady, if you wish to refresh yourself lovingly[2]
Lean over the Virgin's breast
Towards the newborn babe; see and savor
How He, the joy of angels, sucks the celestial milk
    of the Eternal Virgin.

THE SOUL:

That is a childish love
To feed and nurse an infant;
I am an adult fiancée;
I wish to follow my Betrothed.

THE SENSES:

O Lady, if you go thither,
We must become completely blind,
For the Deity is a burning fire,
As you yourself well know.
All the fire and all the live embers
Which light up Heaven and all the saints,
This blaze has all flowed
From His divine breath,

From His human mouth
And from the counsel of the Holy Spirit.
How could you remain there, were it but one hour?

THE SOUL:

The fish in the water cannot drown,
The bird in the air cannot fall,
Gold is not destroyed by fire,
But there receives its shine and glow.
God has given to all creatures
The way to follow their own nature.
How then could I resist my nature?
I have perforce left all to enter into God
Who is my Father by nature,
My Brother by His humanity, my Betrothed by
    love,
And I am His since before time began.
Do you believe I do not experience this?
He can do both: burn with His strength and refresh
                        with His consolation.
But be not over-sorrowful:
You can again teach me, when I return;
Then I shall surely need your counsels,
For the earthly kingdom is full of pitfalls.[2]

Then the Most Beloved goes toward the Most Beautiful in
the hidden chambers of the invisible Deity. There she finds
the couch and the pleasure of Love, and God awaiting her
in a superhuman fashion. This is what Our Lord says:—
Stay, Lady Soul.—What is your wish, Lord?—That you
should be naked.—Lord, how can this happen to me?—Lady
Soul, you are so "co-natured" in Me that nothing can be
interposed between you and Me.[3] Never for one single hour
was any angel given the honor that is bestowed on you for
all Eternity. That is why you must cast off these two things:
fear and shame, as well as all exterior virtues. It is only those
that you carry within you by nature that you must desire to

feel eternally: these virtues are your noble desire and your insatiable hunger which I shall satisfy eternally with My infinite superabundance.[4]

Lord, now I am a naked soul,
And You, in Yourself, a richly adorned God.
The communion between us
Is life eternal, stripped of death.
Now there is a blessed silence
According to their mutual will:
He gives Himself to her and she to Him.
What befalls her now, she knows,
And therein lies my consolation.
But this cannot last long,
For when two lovers unite in secret tryst,
They oft must part without adieu.
Dear friend of God, for you have I written this
                  Way of Love.
May God concede it to your heart. Amen.

The Desert Has Twelve Things (I,35)

You must love no-thingness,
You must flee something,
You must remain alone
And go to nobody.
You must be very active
And free of all things.
You must deliver the captives
And force those who are free.
You must comfort the sick
And yet have nothing yourself.
You must drink the water of suffering
And light the fire of Love with the wood
                of the virtues.
Thus you live in the true desert.

How the Fiancée Who is United to God Refuses the Consolation of All Creatures, Desiring Only That of God, and How She Sinks into Suffering (IV,12)

This is what God's fiancée says, she who rests in the secret chamber of the treasure of the entire Holy Trinity:
Ah, all you creatures, stop and leave my path, you do me harm and have no power to console me!

THE CREATURES:

Why?

THE FIANCÉE:

My Beloved has fled far from me while I was sleeping, while I was resting with Him in union. (Song of Songs 2:4)

THE CREATURES:

This wonderful world, with all the good things it possesses, cannot that console you?

THE FIANCÉE:

No, I see the serpent of Falseness who, with his deceitful trickery, steals into all the joys of the world. I also see sweetness without nobleness capturing many human beings, thanks to the baits of desire hidden in her enticements.

THE CREATURES:

Can Heaven console you?

THE FIANCÉE:

No, as to Heaven, it would be dead
If it wasn't for the living God.

THE CREATURES:

Let us see, Lady Fiancée, the saints,
Cannot they console you?

THE FIANCÉE:

No, for if they were to be separated
From the flux of the living Deity
Which traverses them,
They would weep more than I do,
Because they dwell high above me and far,
And live more deeply in God.

THE CREATURES:

The Son of God, cannot He console you?

THE FIANCÉE:

This I ask Him earnestly, when we go
Among the flowers of holy knowledge;
And I beg Him, brimming over with desire,
To reveal to me, in His pleasure, the flux
Which flows in the Holy Trinity,
And on which alone the soul lives.
If I must be consoled according to my nobleness,
The breath of God must draw me to Him
And there must be no weight detaining me,
For, in its splendor, the sun of the Living Trinity
Shines through the clear water of humanity,
And the sweet joy of the Holy Spirit
Issues from these two together,
And has taken from me all
Of what lives beneath the Deity.
Nothing attracts me except God alone;
And so, in a most wonderful way, I am dead.
This attraction too I would joyfully renounce
So that He should be celebrated in a marvelous manner.
For since I, unworthy human being,

Cannot, with my own strength, praise God,
I send all creatures to the Court
And order them to glorify God for me
With all their wisdom,
With all their love,
With all their beauty,
With all their desire,
As they were created by God in their integrity,
And also with all their voices,
As they sing now.
When I contemplate this great praise,
Then no part of me suffers.

But I cannot bear that one single consolation should touch me, unless it comes from my Most Beloved. I love my earthly friends as companions in Eternity, and I love my enemies with a holy suffering for their salvation. God has sufficiency of all things, but as to union with the soul, never has He sufficiency.

When this wonder and this consolation had lasted eight years, God wished to console me too much, more than befitted the degree of nobleness of my soul. Then this unworthy soul said: "Ah, my dear Lord, raise me not too high! The lowest part is still too good for me; it is there, in your honor, that I wish to remain forever." Then the poor soul was cast down among the awaiting and the damned souls, and even there, it seemed too good a place for her. Then Our Lord followed her in a way reserved for those who have experienced only the lowest spiritual joys. For God's beauty shines on everyone but to the extent that he or she has, here below, become sanctified in love and ennobled by the virtues. St. John says in his Epistle: "We shall see God as He is" (John 3:2). That is true. But the sun shines according to the weather which changes here on earth under the sun—just as there are different dwellings in Heaven (John 14:2). Consequently, according to the way in which I am passive to Him and see Him, so He is for me.

Then Our Lord said: "How long do you want to dwell here?" The fiancée replied: "Ah, withdraw from me, dear Lord, and let me descend even lower in your honor!"

Thereupon, my body and soul entered such darkness that I lost consciousness and no longer knew anything of God's intimity, and most blessed Love also forsook me. The soul then said: "And where are you, Lady Fidelity? I am now going to entrust to you the function of Love and in me you shall defend God's Sovereignty." This Maid-in-waiting then took charge of her lady with such holy patience and such gay indulgence that I lived without sufferings. Then came Unbelief, wrapping me in such darkness and howling after me in such a wild and vehement manner that his voice made me tremble with horror. And he said: "If this grace had come from God, He wouldn't have abandoned you in this way!" Then the soul said: "Wherever are you, Lady Constancy? Bring true faith to me!" Then the Heavenly Father spoke to the soul: "Think of what you felt and saw when there was no-thing interposed between you and Me!"[5] Then the Son spoke: "Think of how much your body endured My torments!" And the Holy Spirit thus spoke: "Remember what you have written!" Then the soul and body replied together, firm in the stability of the true faith: "As truly as I have believed, loved, experienced, and known, I shall depart from here intact."

Afterwards came Constant Withdrawal of God, and enveloped the soul so completely that the latter, in her happiness, said: "Be welcome, most blessed Withdrawal of God! How happy I am to have come into this world, since you, O Lady, will henceforth be my maid-in-waiting! For you bring an unaccustomed joy, incomprehensible wonders, as well as an unbearable sweetness. But, Lord, You must take away from me the sweetness and let me keep only Your Withdrawal. Ah, what joy for me, intimate God, to be able to receive it in virtue of the variations of love." How that happened to me I dare not say, but I can assert: "In the palace of my soul, gall was transformed into honey." Then I wanted all the creatures to glorify God singing "Te Deum

laudamus." They did not wish to do so and turned their
backs on me. The soul rejoiced exceedingly and said: "That
you despise me and turn your backs on me, you see, this is
salvation for me! This glorifies Our Lord immensely. Henceforth the Sovereignty of God is accomplished in me; for at
present God proceeds with me in a marvelous manner
because His Withdrawal is dearer to me than His Very Self."
The soul well knew that God wished to console her in this
most great Withdrawal. That is why she said: "Consider,
Lord, who I am and abstain from me!" Then Our Lord
said to me: "Allow Me to refresh in you the furnace of
My Deity, the desire of My Humanity and the joy of My
Holy Spirit." To this the soul replied: "Yes, Lord, but in
such a way that the pleasure may be for You alone, not for
me!"

Thereupon, the fiancée entered such darkness that her
body sweated and writhed in pain. Then someone begged
Pain to act as messenger to God, and I said:

"Lady Pain, this I order you:
  That you should set me free now
  For at present you have power over me."
Then Pain left the body and the soul
Like a tenebrous ray
And went towards God with wisdom
Calling out in a loud voice:
"Lord, You know well what I want!"
Then the Lord came towards Pain before
              the gates of the kingdom,
And said: "Welcome, Lady Pain!
You were to My body, on earth,
Nearer than what I wore, My closest garment,
And the shame of the whole world
Was My most precious cloak.
But, although there below you were welcome to Me,
Here you cannot enter.
But upon the virgin who wants to do two things,
I am going to bestow two things.

If this virgin is constantly collected within,
                              and wise,
Then she helps to make of you her messenger,
And I shall grant her My embraces
And union with My heart."
Then Pain thus spoke:
"Lord, I procure bliss for many people
And yet I myself am not happy;
I devour many holy bodies
And yet I myself am wicked;
I lead many to the kingdom of Heaven,
And yet I myself never enter there."
And this is how the Lord answered her:
"Pain, you were never born in the kingdom of Heaven,
That is why you cannot return there.
Far worse, you were born of the heart of Lucifer,
It is to him you must return
And live enternally with him."
Ah, blessed Withdrawal of God,
How lovingly am I bound to you!
You strengthen my will in pain
And make me love the long and heavy waiting time
                              in my poor body.
And the more I am in your company
The more completely and wonderfully does God
                              invade me.
Oh Lord, I cannot be engulfed far from You
For even if I escape you easily in pride,
The deeper I sink
In the depths of pure humility,
The greater is the sweetness which appeases me.

The Good Man Must Have Three Children
for Whom He Must Pray (V,8)

Nobody knows what consolation, pain, and desire are, unless
he has been touched by these three. I seek help because,

alas, I suffer too much. I have three children in whom I see great distress.

By the first I mean poor sinners who are in eternal death; my only consolation is that they are still in their human bodies.[6] Alas, it is with a bleeding heart that I look upon this child, and my eyes are full of tears when I clasp him lovingly in the arms of my soul and carry him to the feet of his Father, from whom I received him. Thus I look upon this child and beg his faithful Father, Jesus, to awaken him with the voice of His divine mercy, that same voice with which He roused Lazarus.

To this God replied:

> I will transform the illness of this child.
> If it is his will to sink no more into this death,
> Then he shall be always like unto Me
> In My beauty, in My nobleness,
> In My richness.
> Surrounded and inundated
> With all joys in everlasting eternity.
> Rise up, dear child of mine, you are healed,
> Convert [towards me] the free will that I gave you,
> And that I shall never take from you.
> For your free will is the gauge
> Which measures all your worth
> In the splendid kingdom of Heaven
> Where you become like unto the saints.
> Alas, this child still remains rigid
> In his own will!

By my second child, I mean the poor tormented souls in purgatory, to whom I must give my heart's blood to drink. When I plead for them, and when I consider the multiple aspects of their wretchedness and the bitterness they taste for each one of their sins, I feel the pains of a mother, and yet I am happy they suffer just punishment for their transgressions, in God's honor.

They bear their sufferings with great patience
Because they clearly see their sins,
Enduring their misery with well ordained wisdom,
They carry within them profound heartache.
If this child is to recover quickly
The mother must be most faithful and merciful.

By my third child I mean imperfect religious persons. When I look upon all my sick children, I see none that makes me suffer as much as this one, for, alas, having turned his senses towards the outer world, and having plunged into transient things, he has drifted so far from celestial matters that he has completely lost his noble manner of being and the sweet intimacy with God to which God Himself had drawn him by special choice. Such persons then become so warped that no word can convert them; it is thus that they insult the inner life and turn aside God's sweetness, and all they see and hear they receive with malevolence. Outwardly they seem wise but, alas, they are all fools within! This child has the most difficulty to recover, for he sinks first into obstinate quarrels, then into inertia, then into false consolations, followed by despair and finally, alas, he is deprived of all grace. And so it is very difficult to say which direction this strayed soul will take.

PART III

Beatrice of Nazareth

(1200–1268)

The Abbey of Florival (Bloemendael) at Archennes near Wavre, from the engraving by J. Harrewijn (seventeenth century). (Cabinet des estampes, Bruxelles). Reproduction from: *Vita Beatricis. De autobiografie van de Z. Beatrijs van Tienen O. Cist., 1200–1268*, ed. L. Reypens (Studiën en Tekstuitgaven van *Ons Geestelijk Erf* XV) Antwerpen: Ruusbroec-Genootschap, 1964, plate VIII. With the kind permission of the publisher.

Introduction

Life

The Cistercian nun, Beatrice of Nazareth, has left us only one short work, written in Middle Dutch and entitled *The Seven Manners of Love*. On the other hand, her life, known at least until she became prioress of the Nazareth Convent, is, in itself, an exemplary oeuvre which we can trace thanks to the biography written by a "brother and servant," confessor of the Nazareth Convent.[1] This priest, whom it has not been possible to identify so far, did not know Beatrice personally, but he had at his disposal her *Book of Life* (or diary) written in Dutch, as well as memories furnished by her sisters in religion and by her own sister, Christine.[2] He asserts that he modified this diary very little, merely "polishing the style of a stuttering tongue" and enhancing it with the figures of style of Latin rhetorics. He sometimes added moral considerations to the original text or, on other occasions, summarized passages which to him seemed far above the heads of the average reader (III,par.275,p.185ff.). In spite of these modifications, this biography—which doubtlessly respects the rules of hagiographical narration—must be considered as authentic, and its veracity can be proved by other documents.[3]

Beatrice's was certainly an exceptional family, constituting a real religious community. Gertrude, her mother, was renowned for her holiness and charity; her father, Barthélemy, after his wife's death, accompanied his daughters,

Beatrice, Christine, and Sibylle, to their various convents which he helped to found (I,pars.8–15; pp.17–21,193–196). Together with his son, who like him had become a lay brother, he followed the Cistercian Rule but still found time to look after the practical affairs of the convents of Florival (Bloemendael), Val des Vierges (Maagdendael), near Oplinter in Brabant, as well as Nazareth, near Lierre. Two other children of his had also entered religious orders.

Born in 1200 at Tirlemont (Tienen) in the Liège diocese, Beatrice was a serious little girl, attentive to others, and it is said that at the age of five she knew by heart the Book of Psalms, which in those days served as a first reading book (I.par.19,pp.23–24). After her mother's death, when she was seven years old, her father entrusted her to the school of the Beguines at Léau where she received the rudiments of knowledge.[4] For once, it is possible to follow the scholastic career of a cultured woman of those times. Although it is not really known whether there were other girl-students attending these classes, it is certain that Beatrice followed the courses of liberal arts of the Latin school. She returned home without having finished the *trivium*, which included grammar, rhetoric, and dialectic (I,par.21,p.25). Following her desire, she entered as an oblate, the Florival Convent, which had adopted the Cistercian Rule about 1210. There she had to follow the classes of the convent school, where she completed the *trivium* program, as well as that of the *quadrivium* with a syllabus of music, geometry, arithmetic, and astronomy (I,par.23,p.26).

From this time onwards, with a friend with whom she had made a sort of pact of spiritual emulation, she was most scrupulous about observing the convent rules and even used to get up at night, in secret, to sing the Holy Office (I,par.28,p.29).

This was the age of terrible, self-inflicted punishments, which left no part of her body intact: among other penances, she would sleep on thorns, scourge herself, deprive herself of food, and wear uncomfortable garments.[5]

At the age of fifteen, Beatrice wished to become a novice.

In spite of hesitations on the part of the abbess, who "turned pale with amazement" at the request, which she wished to refuse on account of the girl's weakness and bad health, (I,pars.45–48,pp.38–41), Beatrice managed to convince the Chapter and was authorized to take the habit on Holy Thursday, 1215. She took her vows a year later and was then sent to the convent of La Ramée[6] to learn the art of calligraphy and manuscript illumination at the *scriptorium* (copyist workshop) there. It was here that she formed a close friendship with Ida de Nivelles who was still a novice but, being more mature than Beatrice, guided her young friend devotedly. It is to be noted that the whole of Beatrice's life is studded with these friendships, which are typically Cistercian. On this point we have only to recall Aelred de Rievaulx's treatise: *Of Spiritual Friendship*.[7]

Beatrice remained in touch with Ida de Nivelles; she sought her in a moment of depression and actually fell ill when her friend died.[8]

She stayed at Florival until 1221; then, with her father, her brother, and sisters, as well as several nuns, she went to the Val des Vierges convent at Oplinter where she pronounced her final vows in 1225. From 1236 onwards she lived at the Nazareth Convent[9] where she was prioress from 1237 until August 29, 1268, the date of her death. These events are briefly described in the *Life* but we have no record of what happened while she was prioress at Nazareth, apart from the narration of two visions and the fact that she accomplished her duties "in a perfect manner."

Beatrice's Spiritual Evolution

The author of the *Life* of Beatrice gives us a spiritual biography rather than a record of exterior events.

Beatrice's spiritual development is in accordance with a traditional schema and her biographer describes the initial, progressing, and perfected stages of this evolution. The same kind of events—penances, ecstatic manifestations, and visions—happen at each stage, but at a different level.

She certainly exaggerated her penances, even when we remember the strictly ascetic atmosphere of a Cistercian convent. The motivation of these mortifications lies in the awareness of being a sinner; in other words, there is a conviction that one is absolutely incapable, by one's own efforts, of attaining union with God, the perfectly good Being.

Desire is the motive power of this attitude and is described as being "fervent," "very impellent" and even "demented."[10] The mystic feels the *attraction* of God and this gives rise to a vehement wish to follow Christ and to be united to God; the result is an almost unbearable tension of the will, whether it is a question of mortifying oneself, scrupulously performing pious practices, or imitating the virtues of one's co-religious.

The force of this desire leads almost to folly, that folly of love described by Richard of Saint-Victor in *Les quatre degrés de violente charité* (*The Four Degrees of Violent Charity*).[11] Strange exterior manifestations are symptoms of the violence of this love, a love which is laden with graces but at the same time confronted with the limits of human nature.

There is no doubt that Beatrice was ecstatic, but so were her friends, Ida de Nivelles, Ida de Léau, and many others; they fall into a state of ecstasy, even of catalepsy or, on the contrary, they begin laughing or clapping their hands (pp.224–226). Beatrice actually goes as far as to feign complete madness, to be all the more despised; her spiritual director, however, convinces her that such behavior would cause serious trouble to the community and so she gives up her idea. (III,pars.208–212,pp.134–135). With few exceptions—that is, when they upset the liturgical order[12]—these manifestations were tolerated by the community, a fact which probably explains their frequency and doubtlessly accounts for a certain contagiousness.

However, all these exterior signs of an affective life—often overwhelmed by the very movement of love which at times seems to draw her close to God and at others cast her far from Him—do not prevent Beatrice from examining her spiritual state with lucidity and from reflecting upon her place in God's designs. At this stage, the light of reason plays an essential role in self-knowledge, as is also witnessed in the spirituality of St. Bernard and William of St. Thierry.[13] At this point the biographer inserts into the *Life* (treating them in a rather allegorical and moralistic manner) some of Beatrice's meditations, which were doubtlessly "points of meditation" drawn up for the benefit of her sisters in religion.[14]

While realizing she is a sinner, Beatrice also discovers the noble quality of her nature hidden in the very depths of her soul. In the light of grace, she sees what she has received from God: natural gifts, a "noble pride" which seeks the highest things, subtlety and acuity of spirit which lead towards contemplation, generosity and largesse, qualities which are all attributes of a soul created in the image and likeness of God (II,par.121,p.87). Henceforth the aim of her combat is to re-form her nature, wounded by sin, and to rediscover the purity of the state in which she was created. This search for purity involves a shedding of everything which is not God and a quest for integrity and freedom, signs of the restoration of the divine image within herself.[15]

These reflections are accompanied by meditations on the Scriptures, where she seeks enlightenment, now moral, now mystic, for herself and for others, and when she does not understand, it is the Holy Spirit Who illuminates her intelligence and in her trials it is He Who consoles her (II,pars.85–86,pp.67–68).

This stage of lucidity and reflection was followed by three years of indescribable sufferings, this time passive trials and no longer penances chosen by herself. Now she is subjected to temptations of the flesh, shameful images, loss of faith, despair, and a disgust of life, considered as a dark prison (II,pars.130–132,pp.92–94; par.156,p.105).

Beatrice fights with all her strength against these assaults, attributed to the devil and manages to remain steadfast in her battle.

Such trials of love are destined to be repeated throughout Beatrice's life. We must note, however, an important, even decisive, turning point in her spiritual development. Already at a previous stage she had become aware she was counting too much on her own strength and that she must let God act within her (I,par.67,p.54).

Little by little, meditating on Christ's passion and the mystery of the Trinity, she reaches another dimension. First of all, during Mass, after the elevation, she sees Christ on the altar, with arms outstretched. She is literally united to Him, heart to heart, and all Christ's spirit pervades her. By means of a love pact, she agrees to do everything the Lord asks of her and He impresses His image upon her, as upon soft wax, to make her similar to Himself.[16]

In the light of contemplation, she is stripped of her own will, all her forces are unified by the same élan, so that all her acts participate in the service of God. There is no longer any distinction between active and contemplative life: "She ordered at the same time all her acts and sentiments, both inner and outer, to comply to the decision of her reason, so that none of her faculties remained idle, but she dedicated them entirely to the service of her Creator; her spirit devoted to holy affection, her mouth to divine praise, her hands to works of charity and every part of her body to the duties which behooved it." (II,par.181,pp.117–118).

Two Trinitarian visions confirm this state and widen her field of understanding. In one of these visions, which took place about Christmastime 1232, she saw God as the source of a river from which flowed streams and rivulets: the river is the Son of God, the streams His stigmata, marks of our redemption, while the rivulets represent the gifts of the Holy Spirit. Beatrice now understands the judgment of God, the procession of the Persons within the Trinity and within the Divine Essence itself. There is a kind of conversion within her and she becomes aware of the universal dimensions of charity. Before, she sought perfection in an ascetic life and in pious exercises, whereas she now perceives that, to do God's will, we must concern ourselves with our neighbor, in a material as well as a spiritual sense. (III,pars.213–218, pp.137–140).

Lastly, in a transforming union, her will merges completely into the divine will, so that she can desire only what God desires. She has now reached inward peace; she feels indifferent towards trials and at the same time she becomes physically stronger (III,pars.222–227,pp.143–146). Between the pacified spirit and the suffering body there is established an equilibrium which the Cistercians of the twelfth century had perceived and described.[17] Beatrice's tense, forceful willing is transformed into a serene acceptance of God's will.

Of Beatrice's life at Nazareth, her biographer has reported only two of her visions. He is, in fact, more concerned with relating the manifestations of her charity, which henceforth will always be her guiding principle. Like the mother of a family (obeying the head of the family, God, presented here as mistress, *magistra, domina*), (III,par.264,p.180), she provides for the needs of all those who come to her for aid or for advice, whether they are her daughters in religion or others, of "every age, every condition and profession" who look upon her as their "patroness," their helper and counselor (III,par.266,p.182). The sick, the poor, as well as sinners and troubled souls, return home healed or consoled. In serious cases, she goes as far as identifying herself with the sinner, until he is freed by her prayer.

And, as with St. Francis, her compassion embraces the animal kingdom, the birds, and small creatures whose sufferings she shares (III,par.242,p.155). Without having the cosmic dimensions of Hildegard's visions, we can nevertheless say that Beatrice includes the whole of creation within her love.

Beatrice's Visions

Her visions are all linked to liturgical life: they are introduced by the verse of a psalm, the words from a sermon, by the celebration of the Eucharist and they follow on her conscious meditation. They are experienced in a state of ecstasy or else are followed by this state, to the point of total loss of movement and use of her senses.[18]

In contrast to Hildegard and her brilliant, animated universe, the outward *visual element* is very slightly marked. The description of space is lacking and the visions evolve in an abstract setting, without any indication of time. Extremely stereotyped, they do not go beyond the patterns of traditional imagery: Jesus on the altar with outstretched arms; the nine angelic choirs and their glorious home; the wheel of the world.

On the other hand, *tactile* sensations play an important part in Beatrice's visions: she *feels* God's presence passing through her whole body; the Lord pierces her soul with the fire of His love, as with the point of a flamboyant sword, drawing her heart to His (II,par.170,p.113). The blood of Christ's wounds flows into her soul (III,par.238,pp.152–53).

Beatrice insists on the profound affective turmoil caused by her visions, which stimulate her love and let her "savor" the sweetness of divine love, *taste* being another of those spiritual senses that bring her joyful experience of God's grace in her (II,par.163,pp.108–109).

Hearing intervenes in the same way: Jesus speaks to her "not in the vernacular, but in Latin," suggesting to her a pact of union which Beatrice promises to respect (II,par. 165,p.110). On another occasion she hears the Lord's voice crying out to her that she has been chosen and her name has been inscribed in the Book of Life. This is the beginning of a conversation between the two and Beatrice asks the Lord how she has earned this favor "without any previous merit on her part." Jesus answers that she has committed no mortal sin and has followed Him, urged on by the force and violence of her love for Him (II,par.171,pp.113–114).

With Beatrice, it is true that the element of the senses united to the will is extremely important, but there is no doubt that the intellectual element (intelligence enlightened by love) is also strongly marked. Throughout the account of the visions we notice the frequent use of the verb *to understand* and, at the same time, the increasing abstraction in the visions. The biographer tells us that Beatrice possessed a quantity of books on the Trinity, although he does not indicate which books they were.

There is no doubt that she is profoundly aware of the final incomprehensibility of God, but He comes to her aid, infusing His own light within her.

With Beatrice there is convergence between, on the one hand, the act of intuitive intelligence which accedes (as far as it is possible) to the knowledge of God's mysteries, and, on the other hand, the fruitive love which joyfully assimilates the gifts received. But finally all this experience leads her to active charity, as we have already seen.

The Seven Manners of Love

In one of the last chapters of the *Life* of Beatrice, the biographer gives a Latin adaptation of her work (III,pars. 246–261).[19] It is thanks to this translation that it has been possible to identify the author of the Middle Dutch (thiois) text contained in the *Limbourg Sermons* which were rediscovered in 1895.[20]

The text itself has posed great problems for scholars, particularly the *Seventh Manner*, which would seem to be a repetition of the previous stages. Was it perhaps added later on? It is not our task to resolve this problem here. It is sufficient to admit that the problem exists and that various solutions can be given to it.[21]

There is no doubt that with Beatrice's little treatise, we have an original work in which mystical language appears for the first time in the Brabant dialect. It may thus be called a creation, written in a prose that is rich and often rythmic. If, in the biography written by the Cistercian confessor, we have an approximate chronological record of Beatrice's spiritual life, this life is presented according to a traditional schema, in a convent setting and reflecting her monastic theology. *The Seven Manners* are doubtlessly guaranteed, authenticated by the Cistercian's account and we can find many parallels between the *Life* and Beatrice's treatise.[22] However, her book is not a chronological account, but a synthesis of everything she lived: her exaltations, even her excesses, are expressed in this work in a perfectly controlled way, as regards both form and thought.

The basic, structural element of this little book is love, *Minne*. In the subtitle, in one line, all the dynamic of fundamental experience is shown: "Love takes seven forms which come from the apex (*uten hoegsten*) and return to the summit (*ten oversten*)."[23] Love starts from what is highest and comes back to this height: it is the Neo-Platonic movement of exit and return. We may well wonder whether, for Beatrice, the apex and the summit are God or the apex of the soul, since the expresson remains imprecise. It is up to the reader to enter into this very movement of love: Beatrice's personal love for God which makes its richness felt throughout her body, heart, and soul, and overwhelms her with its gentle or cruel effects. But this happens within an exchange of her love with a transcending Love, an abyss of love drawing the soul so that she may reach her profound being in God Who is "High and supreme nobleness in His essence" (I,p.7,l.61), and Who gives Himself to those who abandon themselves to Him. This gift arouses desire which, in its turn, is nourished by the gift. "To render love to Love" surely presumes the encounter of two subjects.

The First Manner shows the desire to love and to follow the Lord as a potent magnet towards the rediscovery of purity, nobleness, and freedom, the signs of our creation in the image and likeness of God, constitutive elements of our ultimate perfection. This desire gives no respite, for it creates a tension between her present being, what she is (which must be recognized clearly by both heart and intelligence) and her ideal being, what she should be; between her natural gifts and acquisitions and, on the other hand, what she lacks in order to be in the image of love, "in the proximity of likeness." Whatever may be its painful effects, this tension banishes fear at once, as it is at a level beyond fear of judgment and punishment.

This First Manner may be considered as an apprenticeship, fundamental because its final aim is love: union with God, freedom of conscience, purification of the spirit and lucidity of the intelligence. At the same time it indicates the means of removing obstacles found on the way, means such as reflection upon self and the progressive subjection of the *heart*, impulse to the ceaseless quest for love.

The Second Manner, which is very short, is devoted to the gratuitous character of love: Beatrice wishes to serve God gratuitously, "with no [reason] why,"[24] a formula which, appearing now for the first time, will meet with great success among later mystics. Gratuity and serving go hand in hand and Beatrice here employs the vocabulary of the troubadours, inverting the relationship, since it is now the lady who wishes to serve her lord, having in mind no idea of reward except that of "rendering love to Love," in a way which is without measure and above all measure,[25] and beyond all human intelligence. The necessity for totality is emphasized by the repetition of the word "*all*," which will be used even more forcefully in the Third Manner: "to serve in all fidelity . . . with all that she has she wishes to please Him."

In the *Third Manner*, the predominating note is *suffering*. She would like, in fact, to do more than all human and celestial creatures; the necessity for totality becomes obsessive. In fact, in ten lines, the word *all* appears ten times. The desire to serve love comes up against the finite quality of the human being whose limited nature cannot satisfy the boundless exigencies of love and therefore remains her insolvent debtor. The soul is overwhelmed by this inability to meet her obligations, by this lack (*ontbliven*) within herself.[26] However, she does all that is possible: praises, actions of grace, labors, but nothing brings her repose. She seems to be trapped in a "living death," to be suffering the torments of hell. She will remain in this condition until the Lord consoles her, giving her a more intimate knowledge of Himself.

The Fourth and Fifth Manners form, as it were, the two panels of a diptych, as the first lines indicate: "at times Our

Lord lets the soul savor great delights, at other times great sufferings."

The first panel is that of sweetness. This free gift of God puts the whole creature in ferment, in movement . . . to the point of total absorption. A beautiful hymn to Love shows the various degrees of this process: "And the heart is touched by Love, irresistibly attracted by Love, tightly clasped by Love, subjugated by Love; the soul is so lovingly embraced by Love that she is conquered by Love." Her whole being participates in this blessed state: her spirit is illuminated and freed by this intimacy with God, her senses are overwhelmed, her will transformed. In this "engulfing," "she has become Love."[27]

Consolations are frequent in the *Life* of Beatrice. They always coincide with a precise event: prayer, meditation, holy communion. In the *Fourth Manner*, she emphasizes the unexpected, gratuitous character of these consolations and she gathers all her experiences of spiritual joy in a hymn to Love, whose qualities she then enumerates: beauty, purity, justice, nobleness (IV,pp.14–16).

The repercussions of these overwhelming experiences are described in the *Fifth Manner*. There is an increase of energy within this state of well-being created by the embraces of love and the fruition of her gifts: whether the soul is in action or at rest, the same force takes hold of her. But the sweetness which urges to the accomplishment of great works is sometimes followed by tempests, leading even to folly. Hence the return to the theme of desire, absent in the previous "manner." Beatrice's impotence to satisfy Love causes sufferings which ceaselessly repeat themselves and are described in a way both concrete and symbolic: her veins open up, her blood is in ebullition, her marrow dries up, her bones weaken, her chest burns and her throat is parched. Sometimes an arrow pierces her bosom: she is wounded, heartrent by Love. However, within this rage of Love (*orewoet*), a feeling of security arises. Even if the soul desires to untie the knot which grips and oppresses her, nevertheless she does not wish to renounce union. The more she begs for—in her distress—the more she receives and the closer she draws to purity, nobleness, and the fruition of love. Her very lack of satisfaction heals her and the wound gives her health. Absence already contains the promise of presence.[28]

Parallels between the Fifth Manner and the *Life* are numerous, although the descriptions of somatic phenomena are much more condensed in the latter. Moreover, events presented as exterior in the *Life* are here considered from the interior aspect. For example, the arrow that pierces Beatrice's bosom is a visionary image in the *Life*.

In the *Sixth Manner*, all contradictions and conflicts are eliminated: Love has become her master and has established her in a condition of well-being and freedom. She has received the gifts she longed for: purity, spiritual sweetness, knowledge, equality with the Lord.[29] All the levels of her person are touched: her conscience is liberated, she has become "free of herself," her senses are orientated and regulated, and her soul links up with its primitive noble condition. The theme of systematic *detachment*, which will become of such great importance among the later mystics, is absent here. Freedom appears rather as the fruit of love, the result of a dynamic, as a victory over her interior obstacles, as mastery over her profound being (*wesen*).[30]

Whereas in the Fifth Manner her heart was oppressed, conscious of its narrow limits, it now enjoys a sense of spaciousness, and Beatrice here employs the traditional images of the fish and the bird, each frolicking in its element, certainly concrete images, but at the same time related to St. Paul's words (Eph. 3:18) on the infinite dimensions of God's love: the length, the breadth, the height, and the depth. This freedom makes her so bold that she no longer fears creature or angel, the devil or God Himself (insofar as she cannot be dissociated from Him).

A corollary of her freedom is her sovereignty over her whole exterior and interior life, with the image of the housewife who carries out her tasks according to the inspiration of Wisdom (Prov. 31:10–31). Action and contemplation go hand in hand and do not hinder each other. The phrase "She lets in and she lets out"—a discrete reminiscence of John 10:9—is in line with the Christian tradition of harmony between contemplative and active life, introversion and extroversion.

The Sixth Manner constitutes a summit, "an angelic life" which corresponds well to perfect adhesion to God's will, followed by a durable mastery of self and a great readiness to serve others, as described in the *Life*.

As already mentioned, the *Seventh Manner* has posed certain problems. As it seems to take up once more all the previous stages, it has been thought that this text should have been inserted before the Sixth Manner, or that Beatrice may have added it later on, at the end of her life, as a sort of summary of her experiences.

One might also venture to suggest that it is a question of another degree of love which repasses through the previous stages, but at a different level, like climbing a spiral and always getting closer and closer to the top. What allows us to make this conjecture is the fact that there is a change in vocabulary: the notion of *heart*, which until now was at the center of all sentiments, of all live forces, the place where desire arises, is replaced by the word *being* (*Wesen*); at the same time there appears a new term, *nostalgia* (*verlancnisse*), linked to that of *fatherland* (*lantscap*), opposed to *exile* (*ellende*) in the region of unlikeness.

As vehement as ever, desire is expressed by the paradoxes already evoked: suavity and suffering, life and death, joy and sadness. The passive element seems to dominate: the soul is drawn into another sphere, where the positive attributes of God "all-powerful, understanding all, etc. . . ." have as counterparts the negations "incomprehensible wisdom, inaccessible height. . . ." To sink into the "profound abyss of the Divinity," Beatrice must be attracted beyond time, beyond all human ways, above her own *nature*, in order to enter a state, a different being (*ein hoger wesen*) where her true being (*hare wesen*) is to be found, the most intimately linked to God (*dat naeste wesen*); in other words, a state of the greatest likeness.[31]

For Beatrice, fruition is the vision of the Divinity in the Trinity, as well as participation in the love and the knowledge of the blessed spirits. This love encompasses creatures in love for God. For the first time in the Middle Dutch tongue appears the expression "common love" (*gemeenre minne*) which had been previously defined by the Victorines and the Cistercians and would be so deeply developed later on by Ruysbroeck.[32]

The *Seventh Manner* unveils a new space and also a new time. In the *Sixth Manner* Beatrice moved in what one might call a "final time," her being having reached its finality through union with God. Now, she must still await "plenary time." The desire for death, due to excessive suffering, returns on several occasions during Beatrice's lifetime, but after the great Trinitarian vision of Christmas 1232, God promises her that she will never again suffer in a way that makes her desire death; the wish to die will be provoked exclusively by a longing for heavenly joys. Is it not to this experience that the *Seventh Manner* refers? The pains of exile, the aspiration to "depart and to be with Christ" (Phil. 1:23), to go towards the fatherland of eternity and fruition in glory, whereas she is now in an intermediate situation between this world and the world beyond. This thought gives rise to the nostalgia accompanying her desire.

The treatise ends with a peaceful expectation of eternal beatitude: having sought and served Love so long, she will be received by the Beloved and henceforth will be "one spirit with Him." On the note of this nuptial hope, Beatrice's quest is terminated.

Beatrice and the arrow of divine love—a baroque vision.
Engraving by Liska, in A. Sartorius, *Verteutscht Cistercium bis-tercium,* (Prague: 1708). From: *Vita Beatricis. De autobiografie van de Z. Beatrijs van Tienen O. Cist., 1200–1268,* ed. L. Reypens (Studiën en Tekstuitgaven van *Ons Geestelijk Erf* XV) Antwerpen: Ruusbroec-Genootschap, 1964, plate XIV. With the kind permission of the publisher.

Excerpts from Beatrice of Nazareth's "Vita" and "The Seven Manners"

A Trinitarian Vision—How, in Her Desire, Beatrice Aspires to the Knowledge of the Holy Trinity

Par. 215:[1 and 2] "As for a certain time she had been pervaded by a desire for this comprehension, it happened that on the day of the Most Holy Nativity of the Lord, applying all her heart's powers to meditation, she began to ponder deeply on the mystery of Our Lord's Incarnation, when, all of a sudden, in ecstasy, she was carried up into the celestial spheres, borne aloft by the Divine Spirit, her own spirit being in an instant raised to the contemplation of an admirable vision. What did she see? From the omnipotent and eternal Father there came forth a great river from which flowed in all directions numerous streams and rivulets which offered water to drink 'springing up into life everlasting' (John, 4:14). Some drank from the river itself, others from the streams, while others quenched their thirst at the rivulets. But she who was privileged to see these things was able to drink at all the waterways. While drinking, she immediately grasped, with the innermost point of her mind (*acies mentis*),[3] the meaning of all these images.

Par. 216: The river was the Son of God Himself, Our Lord Jesus Christ, eternally engendered by the Father, born in time of His Mother for the redemption and salvation of mankind. The streams were the signs of our reestablishment, the stigmata of the Lord's Passion which He deigned to suffer on the wood of the Cross for us sinners. Then the rivulets are the graces which the Giver of all good things never ceases throughout the centuries to bestow upon His faithful ones, to enable them to do His will.

Those drinking at the river are those who, outstanding for their more perfect lives, followed the Redeemer's footsteps with unwavering zeal; those drinking at the streams are those who, thanks to compassion, progress by remembrance of the Lord's Passion. And those drinking at the rivulets are those who strive to transform the graces they have received into works of charity, thus accomplishing God's will. The crowd of persons drinking, with their different manners of doing so, is disposed according to the hierarchy of merits, for Christ gave drink to the first from His very person, He restored the second category with the sweet chalice of His passion and He satiated the others with the delightful gifts of His graces and with the celestial sweetness of His consolations.

She also saw that some refused to drink, wishing to approach neither the river, nor the streams, nor the rivulets, thus remaining parched and empty on account of their stubbornness. These are the persons who, by the stains of grave sins and the practice of evil works, have voluntarily separated from the community of the elect, despising the Lord Who does not despise them. Parched and empty and knowing nothing of celestial delight, they remain attached exclusively to their earthly pleasures and desires.

Par. 217: After seeing all this, the Lord's handmaid, having carefully followed with the keen eye of contemplation the course of the river back to the source of eternity whence it began, had the privilege of understanding what she had wished to understand of the mystery of the Holy Trinity: how the Lord, the Son of God, was generated eternally by the Father and, in the accomplishment of time, born in time of a mother; how the Holy Spirit proceeds equally from the Father and the Son, how the difference of the Persons was englobed in one single Essence of divinity, eternity, and majesty, as well as all the other holy and sacred mysteries of the Divine Trinity, venerated in perfect faith on this earth by our Holy Mother Church. All this, thanks to the revelation of the Holy Spirit, Beatrice's soul was able to seize fully, at one and the same time."

Coming back to herself (after the ecstasy), with her own strength, Beatrice would like to continue meditating on these mysteries. The Lord dissuades her from this and orders her to devote her cares and attentions to others.

Par. 218: ". . . Having accepted as a divine gift this task of charity, it seemed to her that, in a most admirable manner, her heart dilated and expanded, as if it should cover the whole world, at the cost of bursting. From then onwards, she clasped to her heart the whole human race, as if she had captured it in an enormous net.[4] I think that this term of capturing signifies nothing other than the breadth of charity, so that she became debtor—as the Apostle says (Rom. 1:14)— 'towards both the wise and the foolish.' According to the grace she had received, in all purity of faith and heart, she dedicated herself to the service of each one, according to his needs. And she undertook these duties of charity with devotion, and with even greater devotion she carried them out."

Vision of the World as a Wheel—How She Saw the Whole World Placed Beneath Her Feet, Like a Wheel

Par. 234: "After she had spent a long time in the accomplishment of her duties as prioress,[5] it happened one day that she heard a nun reading those words of St. Bernard in which he says that 'Many are those who suffer torments for Christ but few are those who love themselves perfectly for Christ's sake.'[6] She kept in her memory the words of this holy man and for two days she often pondered over them. But by herself she was not at all able to discover their correct meaning, wondering how man's love applied to himself could in some way be more important than bearing the sufferings of the Passion for Christ. As man, whether he be good or evil, naturally loves himself for 'no man hates his own flesh' (Eph. 5:29), this brief addition 'for Christ's sake' seemed to her to give special significance to these words, because experience alone, and not the subtlety of the human intelligence can discover the meaning of this addition.

Par. 235: Realizing that, through the efforts of meditation, she did not succeed in finding the deepest sense of these words, God's servant then turned to prayer, ardently beseeching the Lord to illuminate her on this matter. In His goodness, what could He refuse His chosen handmaid, in her arduous search and fruitful zeal? The grace of divine love not only gave her what she asked for, that is, the meaning of the words quoted above, but it also enlightened her, revealing to her the manifold secrets of the divine mysteries.

Par. 236: As soon as she was raised aloft into ecstasy, she saw placed beneath her feet the whole machine of the world as if it were a wheel. She saw herself placed above it, her eyes of contemplation magnetized towards the incomprehensible Essence of the Divinity, while the innermost point of her intelligence, in an admirable manner, considered the eternal and true God, the uncreated Most High, the Lord, in the majesty of His substance. She was so adequately positioned between God and man that, below God, but higher than the whole world, she trampled upon terrestrial things, remaining inseparably united to the Divine Essence by the embraces of charity.

In this union in which she became 'one single spirit with God' (I Cor. 6:17) she realized that she had reached that purity, freedom of spirit and glory for which she had been created from the very beginning. And as if her spirit had been transferred entirely within the Divine Spirit, she thus understood that, for a short while, she was united to the Most High Deity and rendered entirely celestial.

Par. 237: Coming back to herself, she retained in her

memory the sweetness of this contemplation, delighting in it, without, however, experiencing it again. And remembering what she had seen and understood, comforted by the indescribable divine sweetness, she reposed peacefully in the arms of the Beloved, burning with the fire of love. Then she understood the sense of the words cited above, but less by intelligence than by experience, with the purified eye of the spirit, and she became aware that she loved herself perfectly for Christ's sake, but that there are few who reach this summit of perfect love."

The Seventh Manner of Holy Love

There are seven manners of holy love: They come from the Most-High and return to the summit.[7]

The Betrothed knows still one more manner of sublime Love which submits her to a hard inward toil:[8] attracted by a Love which is above her humanity, above human reason and intelligence, above all the heart's operations, drawn exclusively by Eternal Love in the eternity of love, in the incomprehensibility, in the inaccessible breadth and height, in the profound abyss of the Divinity Who is "all in all things" and Who remains unknowable above all things, unchangeable, the plenitude of Being Who embraces all in His power, intelligence and sovereign work. The blessed soul is so tenderly engulfed in love, so strongly drawn by desire, that her tormented heart is gnawed with impatience and her infatuated mind is overwhelmed by the strength of these desires. All in her is strained towards the fruition of Love in which she wishes to settle (*wesen*). This is what she demands insistently of God, what she begs ardently of Him, in the strength of her desire. For Love leaves her neither peace, nor respite, nor rest. Love raises her up and casts her down, suddenly draws her close only to torment her later, makes her die to bring her back to life again, wounds her and heals her, drives her to madness and then makes her wise again.

It is in this way that love draws her to a higher state (*in hoger wesen*).

In spirit, she is raised above time into eternity, above the gifts of love, which is outside time, above human modes of loving, above her very nature in her desire to overpass it. Such is her being (*wesen*) and her will, her desire, and her love: to enter the certitude of truth, the pure light, the high nobleness, the exquisite beauty—to enter the sweet company of the higher spirits who are engulfed in overflowing Love and who know clearly their Love and possess Her in fruition.

Her wish is to be up there; in her desire she goes there, she comes amidst these spirits, particularly the burning Seraphim; but it is within the Great Divinity, the Most-High Trinity that she hopes to find sweet repose and lasting fruition.

She seeks [the Lord] in His majesty, she follows Him up above, contemplating Him with her heart and her mind. She knows Him, she loves Him, she desires Him so strongly that she can consider neither saint, nor man, nor angel, nor creature, unless it is in that common love in which she loves everything with Him. It is He alone Whom she has chosen in love, above all else, at the heart of everything and in everything, with all the aspirations of her heart, all the strength of her spirit, it is He Whom she desires to see and to possess in fruition.

That is why her life on the earth is henceforth a complete exile, a narrow prison and excruciating suffering. She despises the world and the earth disgusts her; all that is terrestrial can neither satisfy nor appease her and it brings her great torments to be a stranger in a distant land. She cannot forget her exile and she cannot satisfy her desire, while her nostalgia distresses her. Hers is merciless passion and torment, beyond all measure.

Thus she feels a great desire and a great longing to be liberated from this exile, to be freed from this body and, with bleeding heart, she ceaselessly repeats the words of the Apostle: *Cupio dissolvi et esse cum Christo*, that is, "I desire to be dissolved and to be with Christ." (Phil. 1:23). And in her violent desire and excruciating impatience, she wishes to be delivered in order to be with Christ, not because she is weary of the present, nor on account of future sufferings, but it is by reason of a holy love, an eternal love, that she ardently and vehemently longs to reach the land of eternity and the glory of fruition. Her nostalgia is strong and immense, her impatience pressing and painful, her suffering overwhelming beyond words, so violently does her desire torment her. However, she must live in hope and this very hope makes her sigh and languish. Ah, holy desires of love, what force you have in a loving soul! It is a blessed passion, a raging torment, a lasting suffering, a brutal death, a dying life. Up above, the soul cannot arrive; here below, she cannot feel at peace. She cannot bear to think of the Beloved, so great is her longing for Him; not to think of Him fills her with pain on account of her desire; this is why she must live tortured and torn apart.

And so she cannot be, nor wishes to be, consoled, as the prophet says: *Renuit consolari anima mea*, that is, 'My soul refuses to be comforted' (Ps. 76:3). She refuses all consolation from God Himself and from creatures, for all the joys which she might thus obtain stimulate her love and draw her towards a higher state (*in een hoger wesen*), increasing her yearning to be united to Love and to reach fruition, thus making this exile unbearable. In spite of all God's gifts, she remains unsatisfied, unappeased, far from the presence of her Love. It is a hard, painful life, for she does not wish to be consoled as long as she has not received what she is seeking for relentlessly.

Love has drawn her and guided her, has taught her Her ways; the soul has followed Love faithfully, in great toils and countless works, in noble aspirations and violent desires, in great patience and great impatience, in suffering and in happiness, in numerous torments, in quest and supplication, loss and possession, in ascent and in suspense, in pursual and in embrace, in anguish and cares, in distress and in troubles; in immense trust and in doubt, in love and in affliction, she is ready to endure everything. In death or in life, she wishes to devote herself to Love; in her heart she endures endless sufferings and it is for Love alone that she wishes to reach her Fatherland.

When she has tried everything, in vain, in this exile, she finds her only refuge is in celestial glory. For love's work is this: to desire the most intimate union (*dat naeste wesen*), the closest adhesion to that state in which the soul abandons herself to Love. She wishes to follow Love, to know Love, to reach the fruition of Love—an impossibility in exile; so she wishes to migrate to the land where she has established her home and where she rests with Love. This she knows: every obstacle will be removed and she will be tenderly welcomed by the Beloved. She will contemplate the One she has loved so ardently and Whom she will possess for all eternity, for her eternal happiness, the One she has so faithfully served. In all plenitude she will enjoy her Beloved Whom her soul has so strongly embraced in love. Thus she will enter into the joy of her Master,[9] as St. Augustine says: *Qui in te intrat, in gaudium domini*) etc., that is to say, "He who enters into you, enters into the joy of his Master," and he will no longer fear but will enjoy beatitude in the Sovereign God.

It is then that the soul will be united to her spouse and will be "one single spirit with Him" (I Cor. 6:17) in an indissoluble fidelity and an eternal Love. And those who have devoted themselves to Love in the time of grace will enjoy her in eternal glory where there will be nothing other than praise and love.

May God deign to lead us all thither! Amen.

PART IV

Hadewijch of Antwerp
(13th Century)

The Bruges Beguinage (thirteenth century)
(A. Van Mieghem, Ostende, Belgium).

Introduction

Life and Works

After having been acclaimed and quoted in the fourteenth century by John Ruysbroeck and his disciple, John of Leeuwen,[1] Hadewijch's works, of which only four manuscripts remain, were more or less entirely forgotten until they were rediscovered in the nineteenth century by medieval specialists, as well as by the great poet Maeterlinck.[2] Her writings appeared in a critical edition in 1920, thanks to the arduous labors of J. Van Mierlo.[3]

In our own times, each year brings in such a harvest of studies, both literary and spiritual, that we can say that Hadewijch is much better known today than during her lifetime.[4] On the other hand, the exterior facts of her life remain obscure for, unlike Beatrice, she did not find a biographer, doubtlessly because, being a Beguine, she lived outside the monastic milieu. Only one manuscript has preserved her name, together with a geographical indication: "Blessed Hadewijch of Antwerp."

It is thought that the period of her literary production can be included in the second quarter of the thirteenth century. In the *List of the Perfect* which follows on the fourteenth *Vision*, she mentions a Beguine who had been condemned to death by Robert le Bougre "on account of her just love." Now this inquisitor was responsible for persecutions in Flanders from 1235 to 1238.[5]

As regards other biographical details, we can glean them

only in her *Letters* and in certain poems where she appears as "mistress" or spiritual guide to an unorganized group of Beguines whom she addresses with authority. According to certain allusions she makes, she was exposed to opposition coming from both outside and inside her community of Beguines. Threatened with banishment and even imprisonment (if we take her assertions literally), she realizes she must leave her beloved friends: Sara, Emma, and Marguerite, from whom attempts are made to separate her, although she still manages to correspond with them.[6] At the same time, she has devoted herself to a charitable activity, probably care of the sick, as was the custom of the Beguines of her time.[7]

It has been thought that Hadewijch was of noble lineage, since she used so many courtly expressions in her poems. To what extent was she formed and influenced by a certain cultivated social milieu? It is impossible to give an answer to this question, but there is no doubt that she had an astonishing degree of culture, both profane and theological. She knew Latin and was conversant with the rules of prosody and rhetoric as well as with the art of letter writing. The use of numerous French words is certainly the result of her familiarity with the poetry of the trouvères of Northern France. From the religious point of view, she gives proof of an extensive knowledge of the Scriptures, liturgy, and theology. She cites, without mentioning their names, Richard of St. Victor (*L.X*) and William of St. Thierry (*L.XVIII*) and also quotes from a Trinitarian hymn attributed to Hildebert of Lavardin (d.1134) (*L.XXII*). In *Vision VIII* she is led by a guide who is a scholastic theologian; he cannot accompany her to the summit of union because he has put intellect before love. This tells us that Hadewijch moves in a spiritual universe very close to that of Beatrice, the Cistercian, although she gives a more important place to intelligence. In fact, to her friends she recommends attention to their intellectual progress as a source of spiritual progress. They must seek information, pose questions and study! All this presumes they lived in a cultured setting, in communities, with priests capable of answering their questions, as she herself says, "In Latin and in Flemish" (*L.XXIV*).

Hadewijch's works, the chronology of which is difficult to establish, is composed of *Poems, Visions,* and *Letters,* literary forms very different from one another but all showing the richness and variety of her literary genius.[8]

Poems

With her poems, Hadewijch may be considered one of the creators of Dutch lyrical poetry. They are divided into two groups: forty-five *Poems in Stanzas (Strofische Gedichten)* and sixteen *Poems in Couplets* which are often rhymed letters (*Mengeldichten*).

In her poems, Hadewijch uses an infinite variety of rhyme schemes. We find this also in courtly poetry, with its traditional forms and its repertory of recognized clichés.[9] Hadewijch follows the patterns of this courtly poetry and initiates the majority of her poems with a stanza on the seasons, generally the Spring, following the "reverdies" of the trouvères in which they sing of the rebirth of nature, either to identify themselves with her, or else to flee her, so strongly does the poet's suffering clash with the joy of earth's renewal.[10]

Her stanzas are divided into three parts, with two or three alternate or enclosed rhymes; the last stanza, the *envoi*, sums up the whole poem, or stresses the main idea. In this rather conventional framework, Hadewijch is capable of handling lines, which are sometimes long and sometimes short, in order to express the intensity, the emotion and all the existential drama of her relation to herself and to God, a relation that is described, exalted, and repeated with many variations.[11]

Love (*Minne*) is sung of from many aspects which reflect the multiple attributes of this denomination. Love (feminine in Dutch, as in German), is presented as a person to whom one can speak: a lady, a queen whose strength and richness are praised and who imposes laws. To this theme of personified love are added images of chivalrous life: adventure (*avonture*), horse riding, jousting,[12] as well as hunting, when love pursues and at the same time is pursued. There also appear enemies whom courtly poetry calls *losengiers*, scandalmongers who try to destroy love and who, with Hadewijch, have a deeper meaning, being considered aliens (*vremde*) who refuse to recognize love and wage battle against those who serve Her.[13]

But as Lady Love is also Divine Love,[14] Hadewijch's experience will evolve within her own human quest, love of Love and the transcendence of a Love who gives Herself wholly but at the same time escapes from the grasp of the lover. At the beginning of her spiritual discovery—as is the experience of all those who seek for God—she is as if inebriated by the gifts which are offered her in such abundance (*S.G.XVI*):

> In the days of my youth
> When Love first fought against me,
> She showed me a wealth of advantages:
> Her goodness, her wisdom, her force, and her riches;
> ....
> Thus Love deceived me,
> Showing me a table laden
> With many a dainty dish
> By which novice youth is nourished
> And finds renewed delight. . . .

Then arrives the moment when she comes into conflict with her own insufficiency. From consolation, she passes to desolation: her lack (*ghebreken*) clashes with the hope of fruition (*ghebruken*) and causes all kinds of suffering and rebellions which had already been a prominent feature of Beatrice's spiritual way. Hadewijch often reaches the point of the "madness, or rage of love" (*orewoet*) and of those brutal antitheses, signs of man's inherent impotence and insufficiency, stirred up by desire (*S.G.V*):

Sometimes burning and sometimes cold,
Sometimes timid and sometimes bold,
The whims of Love are manifold. . . .
Sometimes gracious and sometimes cruel,
Sometimes far and sometimes near. . . .
Sometimes light, sometimes heavy,
Sometimes sombre and sometimes bright. . . .[15]

One of the features of Hadewijch's quest is the constant "recharging" caused by the novelty of love (*nuweheit*). There is convergence of several themes: eternal creation coming from the Father, the renewal of life in Christ, the re-creation of man according to Ephesians 4:24, as well as the theme of grace considered as a perpetual rejuvenation. We might say that Hadewijch's *nuweheit* is not very far removed from Hildegard's *viridity*. However, it is mingled with a more subjective element: associated with desire, this novelty of love reveals the infinite dimensions of spiritual life; at the same time, there is suffering delving always deeper and an urge to penetrate into a mystery becoming more and more profound.[16]

Novelty and freedom are associated with other notions, such as dignity and nobleness, and all these qualities are features of the "fine amour" of the trouvères of Northern France or the *hoghe minne* (high Love) of the *Minnesänger* (love singers). Among various definitions, we might mention this one: "*fine amour*—I am led to understand *fine* in virtue of a certain alchemical connotation: affined, refined, purified of all which is not of this love, brought back to its quintessence."[17]

The troubadours and trouvères sing of an inaccessible love which demands of the lover an unreserved pledge which governs his moral life,[18] and this corresponds closely to Hadewijch's conception of *Minne*. However, if we give credit to recent interpretations concerning the troubadours and trouvères, it is not so much the woman loved as the song itself which sustains the poet's love, for the sentiment expressed passes wholly into the poem.[19]

In Hadewijch's poetry, metaphors can be interpreted at several levels, as can be seen in *Poem XVI* of the *Mengeldichten* in which love is successively called Bond, Light, Charcoal, Fire, Dew, Living Source, Hell.[20] Her songs express an experience which allows Hadewijch to give enthusiasm and enlightenment to those who wish to follow her along the path of her spiritual "adventure."[21] This adventure leads to something beyond the poem, in a transcendence experienced as a loss, darkness, abyss, as expressed in these admirable lines:

> Her deepest abyss is her highest form. . . . ,

followed by the image of silence as the end of the experience:

> Her deepest abyss is her highest song.[22]

The Visions

The Visions[23] would seem to belong to Hadewijch's youth (in one of them she makes mention of her nineteenth year) when she must have been more marked by paranormal phenomena. What here appears most "juvenile" or rather, let us say, less stripped of all else, is the acute awareness that she has of herself and of her vocation, an attitude which gives way to a greater sobriety in the *Letters*.[24] However, the composition of the Visions might be dated much later if we consider, on the one hand, their depth and maturity and, on the other, the numerous similarities which can be found with the *Letters*.

Of the fourteen texts contained in the collection, only eleven are actually visions and in them the visual element is relatively slight and not very original: the lamb, the eagle, New Jerusalem, all of which symbols are borrowed from the Apocalypse. In *Vision I* there is the allegorical theme of the gardener and his trees. One of these trees is upside down and constitutes a symbol of the knowledge of God.

Hadewijch is often led by an angel (*Vis.I,IV,V,VI*) or by the guide already mentioned.

As with Beatrice, each of the visions is linked to a liturgical event: Easter, Pentecost, or one of Our Lady's feasts.

Hadewijch describes three stages in her visions. First of all there is the affective turmoil before ecstasy; she feels as if a force were drawing her towards her inner being, just before she is snatched away. On one occasion she says: "During the Epistle, my senses were attracted towards my inner soul; an awe-inspiring spirit, like a strong tempest, made me retreat from the exterior to within myself. And from this inward self I was carried upwards in spirit" (*Vis. IV*). And again: "I drew close to God (in the Eucharist). He enveloped me from within, in my powers, and took me away in spirit" (*Vis.III*).

This stage of introversion is followed by the vision itself and its message, which is the essential part. Then the visionary is raised up "beyond her spirit" (that is, into ecstasy), "far from myself and from everything I had seen of Him, beyond all concepts, all knowledge, all intelligence, apart from that of being united to Him and of having fruition of Him" (*Vis.VI*). Then she returns to herself, once again delivered to normal life.

The visions deal with three themes. Like Beatrice, Hadewijch is invited to become aware of God's action in the world. Always with an implicit reference to Eph. 3:18, our mystic enters the dimensions of divine love. God's countenance is surrounded by three pairs of wings: "The higher wings fly in the height where God enjoys the highest power of love, the two middlemost ones fly in the vastness of Love's perfection while the two lowest ones fly in the fathomless deep, there where He engulfs all beings" (*Vis.XIII*). Divine love is here described as the principle of *ad extra* works, of the perfection of virtues, while the dimension of depth englobes essential union.

In the depths of the abyss, she sees all beings in their truth: "I saw an infant being born within those souls who love in secret, those souls hidden from their own eyes in the profound abyss of which I speak, to whom nothing is wanting, but that they should lose themselves in You" (*Vis.XI*). Here we have the theme of the "birth of God within souls" which, for Hadewijch, is more often than not associated with Mary's maternity and her own spiritual maternity. The nuptial union ("your blessed soul," God says to her, "is the bride in the City") is fecundity. The soul is "spouse and mother" (*Vis.X*).

The different stages of union are described in *Vision VII*: Christ gives Himself to Hadewijch under the Eucharistic species, then He comes to her as a person, with His heart and His humanity, and she feels Him in all her body. Then this beautiful form fades away and she cannot perceive it outside of herself. As He has become entirely and inwardly hers, she is now assimilated to Christ: "It is as if we were one, without any difference."

Even if the depth of the Divine Essence appears to her to be an abyss in ebullition, God nevertheless remains for her Being and Love. She unites the definitions of Exodus 3:14 and 1 John 4:8, in a striking formula: "You shall have fruition of Me as the Love that I am". (*Vis.III*). Ecstasy is merely a passing moment, whereas in daily life she will be marked by the humanity-divinity of Christ. In suffering and in toil, she will feel the most intimate presence of Christ Who refused consolations. As she is a human being, she must live as a human being and, in the perfection of virtues, "one becomes God and remains so for all eternity" (*Vis.I*).

It is in the very midst of life upon this earth, in exile and misery (the two meanings of the word *ellende*) that one can possess Love in fruition, expressed by the beautiful metaphor which concludes the *First Vision*. After describing the upside-down tree with all its branches, Hadewijch reaches the quintessence of the message. Christ says to her: "If you want to do [what I have told you], take away with you the leaves of this tree, for they symbolize knowledge of My will. And if you are saddened, pick a rose from the top of the tree and pluck one of its petals: that symbolizes Love. And if you can no longer bear things, take the heart of the rose: then you will feel My presence. Continuously you will know My will, you will feel My love and, in your distress, you will enjoy fruition."

The Letters

Of Hadewijch's thirty-one *Letters*,[25] some are personal missives addressed to those she directs and whom she calls affectionately "dear child, sweet child," while others are little treatises on spiritual life as, for example, *Letter XV* on the nine Pilgrimage Rules or *Letter XX* on the "Twelve Nameless Hours." It is in her *Letters* that Hadewijch puts to best use all her linguistic resources and her wealth of spiritual theology.

Whence comes the soul and whither is she going? The whole of life evolves between these two questions. According to the exemplarist doctrine which Hadewijch shares with Beatrice, the soul has been in God from all eternity and in this consists all her nobleness and freedom, her very wealth. The task of man is to find once again that fundamental being that he has in God, the presence which he feels (even if only in an obscure manner) in the depths of his soul: "If you wish to possess finally all that is yours, give yourself entirely to God and become what He is" (*I.II,ll.* 163–165). It is necessary to let oneself be "re-created" by God (*L.XI,l.* 15). "If you wish to attain your being in which God created you, in all nobleness, you must not refuse any difficulty; with all hardiness and pride you must neglect nothing, but valiantly seize the best part, I mean the Totality of God, as your own wealth." (*L.VI,ll.* 191–196).

The soul is summoned by an inner commandment (*manen*) to find again this original dignity in accordance with the model of Christ: "And so it is that He has raised us up and drawn us by His divine power and His human justice towards our original dignity, rendering us the freedom in which we were first created and loved by God, thus confirming His call and establishing our election in which he had foreseen us from all eternity (cf. Gal. 5:13, Eph. 1:4–5) (L.VI,ll.338–343).

Man's response to what is authentically predestination, or eternal vocation (Eph. 1:5) is manifested in him by "unspeakable desires" which thrust the soul into the infinite space of divine life. There is no doubt that it is in her *Poems* that Hadewijch has best evoked the agony of this desire which clashes with human finiteness,[26] while what she longs for is nothing less than the Totality of God, the plenitude of Love which demands in return the totality of the person.

If spiritual experience is first of all marked by a kind of illumination, love needs time to attain its perfection. The word "growth" (*wassen, volwassen*) appears on many occasions in Hadewijch's writings. In them we can trace a gradual development, a real pedagogy of time. This spiritual growth is continuous and, using a very feminine metaphor, she says that, if it was interrupted, it would be like "stopping the labour of a woman in confinement" (*L.XXI*). In one of her poems has she not compared spiritual life to the nine months' gestation, in this case referring to the growth of Jesus in Mary's womb? (*MD XIV*)

The path of this growth is through suffering: "Unless you suffer, you do not grow" (*L.II*) "All misery, all exile that one bears willingly for the love of God is agreeable to Him and draws us close to the totality of His nature" (*L.II*).[27]

Inward suffering, outward suffering provoked by the incomprehension of "aliens," must not hinder the practice of the virtues. Ceaselessly Hadewijch insists upon the necessity of devoting oneself to works of mercy towards one's fellow men, of living in harmony with the rest of one's community.[28] But as all virtuous acts are not necessarily the expression of a pure love, she lays down a few rules about discernment of spirit and clearly unmasks the counterfeits of virtue. By reason of the exceptional psychological insight she shows here, she well deserves to be called "mistress." To give an example: she tells us that a zeal to devote oneself to others may be untimely and may upset everybody (*L.V*). In human relationships one must not expect from others what they cannot give: fidelity, for example (*L.VI*). In all cases we must avoid fear, anger, and preferences. Knowledge of oneself must not give rise to a false sense of shame, but rather to sincere recognition and acceptance of one's weaknesses (*L.XXIV*) and this is Hadewijch's personal goal (*L.XV*). Moreover, the search for spiritual sweetness, for graces that can be felt, also takes us farther from our final aim (*L.X*). Prayer for others, especially for sinners, must be detached! Its efficacy will be in relation to the love one has for God (*L.VI*).

In this search for detachment, reason plays an important role, at several levels of conscience. First of all it must keep our discernment in a state of wakefulness and give us knowledge of the virtues.[29] Then it intervenes to stir up the soul's ardor when it is in a state of abandonment. With Hadewijch, reason is tied to metaphors of light:[30] it is *reason enlightened by love* that "lights up all the paths along which we follow the cherished will of Love" (*L.XII*). It is illuminated reason that enables contemplative life to perceive in some obscure manner how admirable God is and how "He is all things to all, and wholly in all" (Cf. 1 Cor. 15:28), and to glimpse at His mystery which is fascinating and terrifying at the same time. (*L.XXII*). In *Letter XVIII*, she takes textually a piece from William of St. Thierry's treatise *Of the Nature and the Dignity of Love*[31] which deals with the "two eyes of love," integrating this text perfectly with her own thought. Love and reason go hand in hand: the latter teaches the former which, in turn, enlightens reason. But reason can touch God only in what He is not (that is, reason sees by means of images, arguments, and symbols, all of which can express His Being only in an imperfect manner). Love, on the other hand, touches the very Being of God, insofar as it abandons itself to Him, plunging into the abyss hidden from each creature, where fruition is reached. By adding this word "abyss," Hadewijch extends William's reflection in a sense that will be developed by later Rheno-Flemish mystics.

The rest of this letter, although concerned more specifically with Love, nevertheless contains a sapiential knowledge in which vision plays the chief part. This is perhaps a continuation of her meditation on the two eyes of Love. In fact, her advice is to fix one's gaze on the Beloved and to read

His judgments on His face, and this presumes an activity that is as much intellectual as affective.

This vision of the Divine Countenance, a mystery which is at the same time overwhelming and fearful, revealing as well as concealing, leads to a penetration of God's depths, there where all reason must be abandoned, for at this stage it remains powerless (*L.XII,L.XX*).

"The eighth nameless hour is when the nature of Love makes itself known, in the most marvellous manner, in Her countenance. Faces are what generally reveal most but, in the case of Love, it is the face that remains most secret, for this is Love Herself in Herself (*L.XX,ll.*81–85)."[32]

It seems that, as one gradually progresses in the reading of the *Letters*, one becomes aware that Hadewijch delves more and more deeply into mystery. Before "becoming God with God," she has still to experience despair (*wanhope*), a paradoxical unfaith (*ontrouwe*) lanced like a sort of challenge: "This unfaith is above a too easy faith, or a trust which rests on its laurels before reaching pure knowledge and is satisfied by the present moment. . . . This high challenge is such that it constantly nourishes the fear either of not loving enough or of not being loved" (*L.VIII,l.*33ff.).

Her Spiritual Doctrine

So that the soul should find her being in God, Hadewijch tells us to love Him with the love with which He loves Himself, in order to become one single being with Love, "one single spirit" (1 Cor. 6:17), that is, "To become God with God".[33] Hadewijch's concept of this union is the same as William of St. Thierry's, that is, total adhesion to God's will: "When the soul has nothing else but God, when she has no other will than that of God alone, and when she is brought to nought and wills all that God wills with His will, when she is engulfed in Him and reduced to nothing—then He [here Christ] is raised above the earth and draws all things to Him and the soul thus becomes with Him all that He Himself is" (*L.XIX,ll.*52–61).[34]

Union does not make the person disappear but, through divine action, instead of being dissimilar, God and the soul are equal in oneness (*L.XXII,l.*73). It is from God Himself that we receive our being, absorbed, but not destroyed, by divine light, as Hadewijch explains with a beautiful image: the soul can be compared to the moon which, receiving all its light from the sun, disappears from the sky at sunrise (*L.XIX,ll.*64–74; cf. 2 Cor. 3:18).

The preparation for union involves a stripping of everything else. Hadewijch rarely uses the words *naked* (*bloet*) and *intact* (*ongherijnleect*) which, with Hadewijch II, are signs of a refusal of forms and images, but she employs much more often the word *gheheel*: whole, integral, referring rather to a reintegration of the powers—"the searching mind, the thirsting heart, the loving soul"—in the abyss of Love (L.XX) through the elimination of everything that is not Love. In spite of this negative ascetic phase, Hadewijch's mysticism seems to us to be more a mysticism of plenitude than of void: "I have integrated all that was divided within me" (*L.XXVIII,l.*252). It consists of a widening of the soul to the dimensions of God.[35] In *Letter XXII*, she refers to a hymn attributed to Hildebert of Lavardin[36] who sings of the paradoxes of divine nature: "God is above everything without being raised up; below everything without being lowered, in everything without being circumscribed, outside everything and yet wholly comprised." That is where proud souls are invited to enter and Hadewijch is only too anxious to accept. It is from a Trinitarian point of view that she comments on the plea contained in the Lord's prayer: that His kingdom may come (within us). We ask the Father to let us participate in His "power and rich essence," to make us love the Son with the Father and be the Son Himself with the Spirit. (*L.XXII,*1.47ff.).

Taking up again the Augustinian ternary of memory, intelligence, and will, Hadewijch applies it in a dynamic manner to the relationship between the One and Trine God and the human soul. We must love each of the Persons with the faculty which corresponds to the other Persons: the Son with the memory (attributed to the Father); the Father with enlightened reason (that is, the Son); the Holy Spirit with the "high inflamed will," which refers to the love uniting Father and Son.

Hadewijch's life reflects this fundamental experience of participation in the intra-Trinitarian mysteries. With their apparent paradoxes, *Letters XVII* and *XVIII* show, at the same time, the consequences of union with the Trinity and the necessity of an overpassing into Unity. With the Father and His all-powerful work, the merciful Son and the Holy Spirit— the source of virtues—one must remain in the service of Love in all circumstances of life. But on the other hand, just as the Father, considered as the Origin and Essence of the Persons in Unity, so the soul must refrain from all action other than repose—or fruition—in Love.[37] Although at the end of *Letter XVII* Hadewijch seems to dissociate repose and activity, we notice that in the opening couplets of the same letter she shows that these two phases must be simultaneous; to act, but with detachment; to repose in God without ceasing to be active, to the image of a God Who is "manifold in His unity and onefold in His multiplicity" (*L.XXVIII,l.*82).

It is in this sense that we can speak of an overpassing of the virtues. As does Marguerite Porete later on, Hadewijch talks of "abandoning the virtues," because Love overpasses these virtues and activities and nourishes them, She Herself receiving no other sustenance than Her own plenitude. In *Vision I* we pass from the multiplicity of virtues (represented by the lowest of the three highest branches of the tree of wisdom) to the unique and total virtue (represented by the very highest branch): "The third branch means being constant and thus wholly united to Love, beyond the multiplicity of virtues in the unique and total virtue that engulfs the two lovers together and casts them into the abyss where they will seek and find eternal fruition" (*ll.*170–175).

Union with the Trinitarian Persons in active and contemplative life leads to fruition in Unity. While developing the same spirituality as the previous ones, *Letters XXVIII, XXIX,* and *XXX* are more strongly marked by abstraction. In *Letter XXVIII*,[38] having announced the divine names: Presence in the Son, Overflow in the Holy Spirit, Totality in the Father, and having stated the attributes of each Person (power, wisdom, goodness, etc.), Hadewijch describes the ultimate experience of her union with God. Beyond what she has felt with her spiritual senses—sight, hearing and taste—she is now swept above all intellectual or affective perception. In excess (*verweentheit*), she is led to *repose* and *silence* "in accordance with the nobleness of my overpassing into Unity." And so, when one is gathered inwardly, away from multiplicity of gifts, one becomes "all that *That* is and it is then that Unity has what it demanded." The One, Being, and Love are here wedded in the unification of the soul. In this secret place, the soul finds her true freedom,[39] having overpassed inner conflicts and dominated the whole universe, as a king rules his kingdom.

Let us notice how admirably Hadewijch's language expresses this superabundance of spiritual experience, through the alternating use of negation and hyperbole: "without God because of an excess of God, unstable because of an excess of stability, ignorant because of an excess of knowledge" (*L.XXVIII,ll.*227–230). Words can do no more than show the abyss between the experience of spiritual plentitude and the manner of expressing it. That is why such words must not be uttered or, at the most, communicated only to those who are capable of receiving them.

Although she has experienced the highest stages of union with God, Hadewijch admits she does not possess this union in a lasting manner. As in the case of Mechthild, her most precious treasure is "the suffering of being deprived of fruition" which is far dearer to her than "the blessedness of being lost in the fruition of Love" (*L.XXIX,ll.*80–82). As long as she does not possess in her very being the fruition of Love which belongs to her in her eternal being, she will remain a "human creature who must suffer in loving with Christ, until death" (*L.XXIX,ll.*89–90).

This state between eternity and time, so admirably evoked by Beatrice in her *Seventh Manner,* is compared to Hell in Hadewijch's *Poem XVI* (*MDXVI,ll.* 160–164):

> To see oneself devoured, engulfed
> In Love's abyssal essence,
> Ceaselessly to founder in ardour or in coldness
> In the profound and lofty darkness of Love:
> This indeed surpasses the torments of Hell.

Excerpts from the Works of Hadewijch I and Hadewijch II

Hadewijch I:
Stanzaic Poem V

However cheerless the season and little birds[1 and 2]
The noble heart must not be sad,
But ready to suffer for Love's sake.
    It must know and experience all:
    Sweetness and cruelty,
    Joy and pain,
    All that belongs to the service of Love.

The proud souls who have advanced so far
That they can bear loving without satisfaction,[3]
Must be in everything
    Both strong and courageous,
    Ever ready to accept
    The consolation or affliction
    That Love deals out to them.

The ways of Love are strange,
As those who have followed them well know,
For, unexpectedly, She withdraws Her consolation.
    He whom Love touches[4]
    Can enjoy no stability

And he will taste
Many a nameless hour.[5]

Sometimes burning and sometimes cold,
Sometimes timid and sometimes bold,
The whims of Love are manifold.
    She reminds us all
    Of our great debt[6]
    To Her lofty power
    Which draws us to Herself alone.

Sometimes gracious and sometimes cruel,
Sometimes far and sometimes near[7]
He who grasps Her in faithful love
    Reaches jubilation.
    Oh, how Love
    With one sole act
    Both strikes and embraces!

Sometimes humble, sometimes haughty,
Sometimes hidden and sometimes revealed;
To be finally overwhelmed by Love,
    Great adventures must be risked[8]
    Before one can reach
    The place where is tasted
    The nature of Love.

Sometimes light, sometimes heavy,
Sometimes somber and sometimes bright,
In freeing consolation, in stifling anguish,
    In taking and in giving,
    Thus live the spirits
    Who wander here below,
    Along the paths of Love.

Stanzaic Poem VII

1. At the New Year[9]
   We hope for the new season,
   Bringing new blossoms
   And manifold new joys.
   Who suffers on account of Love
   Can now live happily,
   For She will not escape him!
   In Her richness and Her power
   Always new and always gentle,
   Always gracious in Her ways,
   Love sweetens with a recompense
   Each new pain as it comes.

2. How new to my eyes
   Is he who serves new Love
   With renewed fidelity,
   As a novice should rightly do
   As soon as Love reveals Herself to him.
   Even if he had few friends
   That would matter very little
   As long as he clings to Love.
   For Love offers new gifts:
   An entirely new spirit
   That renews itself in all,
   And Her new touch.

3. At every moment Love is new
   And is renewed each day,[10]
   Those who are renewed, She causes to be reborn[11]
   To a goodness which is ever new.
   Alas, how can one remain old,[12]
   Renouncing Love's presence,
   Old in sadness
   And without gain?
   For such a one has strayed from the new path
   And the newness escapes him,

That newness of a new Love
In the essential love of new lovers.

4. Alas, where is new Love
   With her renewed gifts?
   For my distress brings me
   Many new woes;
   My senses abandon me
   In the rage of Love;
   The abyss into which She hurls me
   Is deeper than the ocean,
   For Her chasms ever deeper
   Open my wound anew.
   Never shall I be healed
   Unless I find again all Her fresh newness.

5. But the wise, the old who have been renewed,
   Who give themselves anew to Love,
   Abandoning themselves to Her entirely,
   These I call young and old.
   They live in exalted mood
   For they cling to Love,
   Gazing upon Her ardently.
   Their power in Love grows,
   For they must be as novices
   And, as old, lean upon Love
   And be led where the Beloved wishes them,
   Their spirit renewed by a new yearning.

6. Those who attend Love's new school,[13]
   With new love,
   Following new Love's counsel
   In honor of a new fidelity,
   Seem to be wandering aimlessly,
   And yet they are deeply engulfed
   In Love's disfavor
   While they are yearning for Her.

And then there comes new clarity,
With all new truth,
Bringing new revelation
Confided to me in secret.

7. Oh, how sweet are the tidings
Though they bring new vicissitudes
And many new sufferings;
Yet there is a new security,
For Love will amply repay us
With great new honors.
Love shall raise us up
To Love's highest council
Where newness shall be in plenitude
In renewed and glorious fruition.
"New Love is wholly mine!"[14]
Ah, rare is this new favor!

Both new and newly reborn
Must distrust and condemn
All those who fear this [true] newness
And renew themselves with alien novelties.

Eleventh Vision

One Christmas night,[15] when I was lying in bed in a very
depressed frame of mind, I was suddenly taken up in the
spirit. There I saw a very deep whirlpool, wide and extremely
dark. And in this vast abyss all things were included, packed
together and compressed. The darkness illuminated and
penetrated everything. The unfathomable abyss was so deep
and so high that nobody could reach it. I shall not describe
it now, for it is not the moment to speak of it, and I cannot
put into words what is indescribable. Moreover, I would not
have time to do so, for I saw many other things: all the
omnipotence of our Beloved. I saw the Lamb take possession
of our Loved One. In the vast spaces I looked upon festivities,

such as David moving his fingers over the harp strings. Then I saw a Child being born in the secret part of loving souls, souls hidden from their own eyes in the deep abyss of which I speak, and lacking nothing, except to be lost forever in this abyss. I perceived the forms of many souls, according to what the life of each had been. Those I saw and had already known [in life] remained familiar to me and those I had not known before became known to me; I received interior knowledge about some and also exterior knowledge about a great many. And some I knew inwardly, although I had never seen them outwardly.

Then I saw a bird arriving, the one called phoenix.[16] It swallowed up a gray eagle that was young and an old eagle with young yellow feathers.[17] These eagles were ceaselessly flying about in the depths of the abyss. Suddenly I heard a voice like a clap of thunder saying: "Do you know who these different-colored eagles are?" And I replied: "I should like to know them better." And when I had expressed this wish, I saw all things as they were, in their essence. For all that is seen in the spirit, when one is ravished by Love, is wholly understood; it is tasted, seen and heard into its very depths . . .

As regards the eagles who were swallowed up, one was St. Augustine and the other was myself. The eaglet with gray feathers, old and young at the same time, was myself, commencing and growing in Love. The old eagle with the young yellow feathers was St. Augustine, old and perfect in the Love of our Beloved. The "oldness" is me came from the perfect nature of my eternal being, although I was young as regards my created nature. The young feathers of the old eagle were the new splendor he received from my great love for him and my desire to be united to him in the single Love of the Trinity, where he himself burns so totally with an unextinguishable love. And this youthful color of the old eagle's feathers also stands for the eternal youth of Love which continuously grows in Heaven and on earth.[18] The phoenix that swallowed up the two eagles is the Unity of the Holy Trinity where both of us were lost.

When I returned to myself, finding myself poor and wretched, I reflected upon this union with St. Augustine which I had experienced. I was not happy about what my Beloved had allowed, in spite of my consent and my inclination. I was overwhelmed by the thought that this union with St. Augustine had made me perfectly happy, whereas before I had known union with God alone, far from saints and men. And I understood that, neither in heaven nor when taken up in the spirit, can one enjoy one's own will, unless it is in accordance with the will of Love. After pondering on this matter, I asked my beloved God to deliver me from this imperfection. For I wished to remain in fruition only within His deepest abyss. And I also understood that, since my childhood, God had attracted me to Himself, far from all others whom He gathers to Himself in different manners. I also understood that all beings in Him are eternal glory and perfect enjoyment, but I wished to dwell alone in Him. And I realized that, by praying for this, desiring and suffering for lack of this, that I was free. But I remained only God's, even when I was united to this man [St. Augustine] in Love. But the freedom I gained then (shunning all to belong to God) brought me something extra which neither St. Augustine nor others possessed.

I do not claim to be more privileged than St. Augustine but, having known the truth of Being, I did not want to be consoled or have my suffering alleviated by him, a human creature; neither did I want to rely on the security given me in this union with St. Augustine, for I am a free human creature and partially pure[19] and I can, through my will, freely desire and will as high as I wish and seize and receive from God all that He is, without encountering contradiction or refusal on His part, and this is what no saint can do. In fact, in the other world, the will of the saints is perfectly accomplished and they cannot wish for more than they possess. As for me, I have rejected many wonderful experiences and states because I wanted to belong to Love alone and because I could not believe that any human creature could love God as much as I did. However, although it is certain [that there are people who love God as much as I do], still it is hard for me to realize it and accept it, so strongly have I felt the touch of Love.

In many wonderful encounters I have belonged to God alone in Pure Love, just as I have belonged to my saintly friend and to all the saints, each one according to his dignity, and to all according to the degree of their love, and also according to what they were and what they are. But I have never experienced Love as repose, so much have I been overwhelmed by the weight and disfavor of Love. For I was a human creature and the Deity is so terrible and implacable, devouring and consuming without mercy. The soul, contained in a narrow riverbed, when flooded, soon overflows and her dikes quickly burst, and thus the Divinity rapidly engulfs her (the soul) within Itself.

I loved the intimate being of the saints, not without envying them. What repose God enjoyed in them! What inquietude for me was their quietude which brought me forty pains for one single pleasure! To know that they were smiled upon while I wept; that they were jubilant while I was groaning; that in every land they were honored by God and God was honored because of them, while I was derided. All this was nevertheless my greatest repose since I knew it was His will. Mine was the repose that comes to all those who seek love and union and, in this search, reap such woes as I do.

As regards persons, my repose lay in loving each of them in what was proper to him and wishing for each what was good for and dear to him; but whether this good came from his own will or from the Divine Will was a matter I was not concerned with. But what each one had in Love, *that* I loved for God, so that He might strengthen this love and help it reach perfection: such was my desire. I loved God's being loved: that was the only pleasure I asked of Love.

But as for persons who failed God and were strangers to Him, they weighed heavily upon me. For I was so full of His Love, so absorbed in it that I could hardly bear it that anyone should love Him less that I did. My charitable compassion made me suffer so terribly when I considered that He had left these souls as strangers to Him, deprived of all the good that He Himself is in Love. At times I was so crushed by these thoughts that I felt as Moses did on account of his love for his sister. My wish was that he should withdraw love from me to give it to others; I would have liked to be hated by God, if this could have been the price of His loving them. Sometimes, as this bargain was not possible, I would willingly have turned away from His Love and loved them in spite of His anger. Seeing that these unfortunate souls could not know the sweet and ardent love that dwells in His holy nature, I would gladly have loved them, had I been able to do so.

Ah, charitable compassion towards persons has wounded me more than all else, except Love Herself. And what is this Love? It is a divine power that must come before everything else, as it has done in my case; for the power of Love spares nobody, in hatred or in love. It restrained me when it was my desire to deliver all men in the twinkling of an eye, in opposition to God's decisions. To turn against Him would have been, for a human creature, both beautiful and free indeed: I could desire whatever I wished to. But to refrain from doing so made me participate in a closer and more beautiful way in the divine nature.

Thus in tranquillity I have lived as a human being, finding my repose neither in men nor in saints. I have lived in sufferings, outside Love, in the love of God and of those who belong to Him. For I have not received from Him what is mine: God still withholds what I nevertheless possess and will remain mine. I never felt Love, unless as a renewed death, until the time of my consolation came and God allowed me to know the perfect nobleness of Love, and how we must love the Humanity in order to reach the Divinity and to recognize them in one single Nature. This is the noblest life that can be lived in the Kingdom of God. This rich peace God bestowed on me, when it was the propitious moment.

Letter XVII

Be prompt and zealous in every virtue,[20]
But do not apply yourself to any single one.
Do not neglect any work,
But do not devote yourself to any particular one.
Be kind and compassionate towards every need,
But do not give your special care to any.

For a long time I have desired to impart these counsels to you, for I consider them of great importance. May God help you to understand what I mean, in the sole and simple essence of Love.

The things I order you in these verses are those ordered me by God Himself. Therefore, in my turn, I wish to pass them on to you, because in all truth they belong entirely to the perfection of Love—and because in a just and perfect manner they are proper to the Deity. The modes I have just mentioned refer, in fact, to the Divine Being. "To be prompt and zealous" is the nature of the Holy Spirit, through which He is a subsistent Person, while *"not to apply yourself to any single one"* is the nature of the Father [that is, of the Essence considered as origin of the Persons].[21] Through this, He is the one Father [Essence], without distinctions. This pouring out and keeping back is the Deity Itself and the total nature of Love.

Do not neglect any work,
But do not devote yourself to any particular one.

The first line refers to the power of the Father (as Person), whereby He is God Almighty; the second refers to His just will (as the Unique Essence), by which His justice accomplishes His mighty and secret works in the profound darkness, works unknown and hidden to all those who are below the pure Unity of the Godhead. However, they serve the Persons, as befits each One, with all loyalty, as I say in the first line of each couplet: "Prompt and zealous in every virtue"—"Not neglecting any work"—"Compassionate towards every need." That indeed seems to be the most perfect life one can lead on this earth. This you have always heard me recommending to you above all else, and you also know that I lived such a life, rendering service accordingly and working loyally (*overscone*), until the day I was forbidden to do so.

The second lines in each of the three couplets express the perfection of Union and of Love and, according to justice, Love attends to Herself and to nothing else: one single Being, one single Love. Ah, how tremendous is that Essence which engulfs in the unity of its nature so much hatred and so much love!

"Be kind and compassionate towards every need" corresponds to the Son in what is proper to His Person (for He was purely this and did purely this), but: *do not give your special care to any*; this again means the Father (the Unique Essence) Who engulfs the Son. This terrible great work is always His. This is the Unity of the love of the Deity, and it is more beautiful than anything else; this Unity is so just with the justice of Love that it absorbs zeal and humanity and the virtue which would not like to fail anyone in need. And it absorbs the charity and pity one feels for those in hell, and in purgatory, for those unknown to God, or [those who,][22] though known to Him, stray far from His beloved will, for those loving souls who suffer more than all others, because they are deprived of what they love. Justice[23] absorbs all this in itself. Each of the Persons, however, does not fail to give out what is proper to Him, as I have said. But the just nature of the Unity, in which Love belongs only to Herself, and is perfect fruition only of Herself, does not apply itself to the accomplishment of any virtuous act, or to any particular good work, however pure, or of whatever pure authority it might be—Unity takes no need under Her charge, no matter how capable She is of bringing relief. For in this enjoyment of Love there never has been and never can be other work than that unique fruition in which the one almighty Deity is Love.

What was forbidden me (as I told you) was to nurture any injustice of Love on this earth; that is, I was ordered to heed nothing of what is outside Love, to devote myself to Her so intimately that I should hate and avoid everything outside of Love. As regards those outside of Love, I should have no inclination, employ no virtues, perform no special works to help them, use no mercy to protect them, but remain constantly in the fruition of Love. However, when this fruition diminishes or lacks, one does well to devote oneself to these works previously forbidden, for then it becomes a question of justice and duty to do so. When anyone seeks Love and wishes to serve Her, he must do all things for Her honor, for during all this time he is human and needy. We must act generously in all things, love our neighbor personally, serve him and be merciful towards his sufferings, for everywhere we feel lack and need. But in the fruition of Love, one has become God, powerful and just. And then one's will, work, and power are equally just, as the Three Persons are in the one God.

These prohibitions were made known to me on Ascension Day, four years ago, by God the Father Himself, at the moment His Son came upon the altar. At His coming I was embraced by Him and by this sign I was chosen: United to Him, I came before His Father Who took me to Himself together with the Son and took the Son to Himself together with me. And in this Unity into which I was taken and in which I was enlightened, I understood this Essence and knew it more clearly than, by speech, reason, or sight, one can know anything that is knowable on this earth.

This seems truly wonderful but, although I say this, I am sure it does not astonish *you.* For divine words are something this world cannot understand. Enough words in Dutch can be found for all things on earth but, for what I want to express, there are words neither in Dutch nor in any other language. Although I have as good a knowledge of the Dutch language as anyone can have, for this matter, I repeat, it is not possible to find words or expressions which are suitable, to the best of my knowledge.

I forbid you certain things and command others, but you must serve for a long time still. I forbid you that *particular application*, as was forbidden me by God. But you must still toil at the works of Love, as I myself have done for a long time, as Love's friends have done and still do. I devoted myself to this in my time and since then have not ceased to remain faithful: to seek after nothing but Love, work nothing but Love, protect nothing but Love and dwell in no place except in Love. How you are to do, or refrain from doing, each of these things, may God, our Lover, teach you!

Letter XVIII

Ah, dear, sweet child,[24] may you be wise in God, for you have great need of wisdom, as has anyone who wishes to become like God. Wisdom, in fact, leads us well onwards into the divine depths. But we are living in an age when nobody desires, or is able, to recognize his needs in the service of Love he owes to God. Oh, you have much to do if you wish to live the Humanity and the Divinity, to reach that full growth which behooves your nobleness, in accordance with God's Love and designs for you. Stand firmly in wisdom and strength, undaunted (like a knight) in all that is yours, in the way of life that behooves you and in keeping with your nobleness and freedom.

He Who is powerful and rich beyond all riches gives enough to all of us out of His omnipotence and grace. This He does not by his own exertion, or by offering gifts with His own hand, but through His rich power and mighty messengers, the perfect virtues, who serve Him and govern His kingdom. They give to all souls what they need, in accordance with the honor and power of their Master. These virtues confer upon each one what is fitting for his nature and his function. Mercy sustains with her gifts the indigent people who are utterly naked, prisoners of the vices, deprived of honor and all possessions. Charity protects the common people against the rich and provides everyone with what he lacks. Wisdom arms the noble knights who, in their ardent desire, engage in mighty combats for noble Love. Perfection gives to the peers of the kingdom its rich domain, sovereign endowment of the soul I am speaking of, who, with a perfect and sovereign will and with perfect works, always remains nobly true to Love's will. Justice, whose task is to condemn or to commend, dispenses these four virtues, And so the Emperor Himself[25] remains free and at peace, because He commands His ministers to see that His rights are respected and invests the kings, dukes, counts, and princely peers with the noble tenure of His domain and the precious rights of His Love. His Love is the crown of the blessed soul, always ready to help others according to their requirements but, in her works and undertakings, seeking nothing for herself, except the Love of her Beloved. This is what I meant to convey to you when I last wrote to you about the three virtues:

> Be kind and compassionate towards every need;
> *But do not give your special care to anyone*

and the other things I wrote to you [in my previous letter].

And so give all your care and attention to the perfection of your soul which is [by nature] noble and perfect. But understand well what that means: dwell in Unity; refrain from getting involved in any work, good or bad, high or low; let things go their way and keep yourself free to devote yourself to the task of seeking union with your Beloved and to content those [souls] whom you love in that Love. This is your real debt, what you owe to God, in all justice, according to your true nature, and also to those souls with whom you share His Love: to love God solely and to seek after nothing but this sole Love Who has chosen us for Herself alone. Understand also the deep nature of your soul and the real meaning of this word: soul. Soul is a being beheld by God and by whom, in return, God can be beheld.[26] The soul is also a being who wishes to satisfy God; she keeps the sovereignty of her being as long as she does not fall into

alien things, beneath her dignity. Then the soul is a bottom-
less abyss in which God suffices to Himself and ever finds
His plenitude in her, just as the soul ever does in Him. The
soul is a free way for the passage of God from His profound
depths; again, God is a way for the passage of the soul into
her freedom, that is to say, into the abyss of the Divine
Being, which can be touched only by the abyss of the soul.
And if God does not belong to the soul in His totality, He
does not truly suffice her.

The sight with which the soul is endowed by nature is
Charity.[27] This sight has two eyes: Love and reason. Reason
can see God only in what He is not; Love rests not except
in what He is. Reason has safe paths along which to proceed;
Love feels Her failure, but this failure makes Her advance
more than reason does. Reason proceeds towards what God
is by what He is not; Love sets aside the things that God is
not and rejoices in Her failure, as regards what God is.
Reason is more easily satisfied, but Love has more sweetness
and bliss. However, these two are of great mutual help to
each other, for reason instructs Love and Love enlightens
reason. When reason is carried away by Love's desire, and
when Love accepts to be guided by reason, within reason's
limits, together they can accomplish a wonderful work. But
you cannot be taught this except by experience. For wisdom
does not intervene here, nor does it penetrate this abyss
hidden from all beings and reserved exclusively for the
fruition of Love.[28] Nothing alien, no alien soul can share
this blessedness.[29] To gain it, the soul must be nursed with
motherly care, in this joy, in the delights of this great Love
and curbed by the discipline of fatherly mercy. Moreover,
this soul must cling closely to her God, reading His designs
for her in His countenance, and thus she abides in His peace.

Now when this high soul comes back among men and
human affairs, her face is so overspread with joy and
wonderful sweetness, as if embalmed by the oil of Charity,
that in all she does her goodness is apparent and because of
the truth and justice of the designs she has read in the Divine
Countenance, she seems strange and awesome to un-noble

men. And when they see that all in her conforms to truth, they are obliged to flee before the power of Love, so dangerous and fearful it is to them. As for those who are chosen for the state, for union with Love, and who have not yet reached full growth, they have in their grasp the might of Eternity, but this power is not yet known, neither to them nor to others.

Such is the secret illumination of Love. This sight of the soul constantly enlightens Her as regards God's true will. He who reads God's designs for him in His countenance does everything in accordance with the truth of Love's laws. Now it is the law and custom of Love to be perfectly obedient and that is often contrary to the ways of aliens. He who truly wishes to observe the precepts of Love must work, not as others work, but according to the truth of powerful Love. He is subject to nobody except to Love alone, Love Who holds him fettered in love. No matter what anyone else might say, he speaks only according to Love's will. He serves Love and performs Her works, according to Her will, night and day, in all freedom, heedless of cost, without delay or fear, in accordance with the designs read on Love's countenance. These designs remain hidden from all who, on account of alien persons, and alien things, forsake the works of Love, so as not to be criticized by those who consider it better than their own will, rather than Love's will, should be done. This is because they have not reached the heights of that lofty Countenance of powerful Love which allows us to live free, even in the midst of all kinds of distress.

You must know this freedom and also those who serve for its sake. People pronounce all kinds of personal judgments; they scorn the works of Love and they do so under the pretext of greater freedom and apparent wisdom. They issue contrary orders and prohibitions, so that Love's orders will be abandoned. But a noble soul who wishes to be faithful to Her rule, following what enlightened reason teaches Her, fears neither alien commands nor counsels, no matter what torments will be caused to Her by slander, disgrace, accusations, insults, isolation, ostracism, even nakedness and the lack of all human necessities. None of these things does She fear: whether She be called good or bad, She will never fail for one instant to obey Love in all that Love wills. She devotes herself to Love in all things, according to truth, with all the power of Love, and, in spite of sufferings, She never loses the joy of her heart.

Living exclusively for this aim, then, you must gaze fixedly at God with the sweet glance of single affection, freely devoting yourself to the One Beloved. You must contemplate God wholeheartedly, even more than wholeheartedly, so that your unified gaze remains clinging to your Beloved's countenance, attached by the piercing nails of burning, ever-renewed desires. Only then can you rest with St. John who slept on Jesus' breast,[30] as still must do those who serve Love in freedom. They rest on that sweet, wise breast and see and hear secret, ineffable words[31] whispered by the Holy Spirit—words which can in no way be heard or perceived by ordinary men.

So fix your eyes steadfastly upon the Beloved Whom you desire, for whoever looks upon whom he desires is ceaselessly enkindled anew, and his heart soon becomes faint beneath the sweet burden of Love. He is drawn within the Beloved by his life of constant gazing, of never-interrupted contemplation. And Love makes Herself felt to him in such a sweet manner that he forgets everything on earth.[32] And whatever befalls him at the hands of aliens, he feels that he would deny himself nine hundred times rather than neglect one single item of the works ordained by noble Love whose servant he is and whose foundation is Christ.

The "New Poems"—Hadewijch II

Although contained in three of the four Hadewijch I manuscripts, poems XVII to XXIX of the *Mengeldichten* (which, following Dom Porion, we shall call *New Poems*), are not the work of the Antwerp mystic, but of an unknown author, or authors (poems XXV to XXIX might well be of a still different pen) whom we shall refer to as Hadewijch II. There also exists an isolated collection of these poems in another manuscript. This is of a later date: the end of the thirteenth or the beginning of the fourteenth century, a fact which becomes evident if we notice the use of a particular form of verse typical of that period.[33]

The *New Poems* probably come from an unidentified Beguine setting, more influenced by the scholastic trend and by a mysticism more intellectual than that of Hadewijch I. Words of foreign origin, such as *contempleren, reveleren, speculieren, questie* (MD XXIII) bear witness to this fact.

Although Hadewijch I and Hadewijch II have a great number of themes in common, such as that of *Minne*, with its courtly metaphors and its antitheses, and the return of the soul to its origin (exemplarism), the general tone is more abstract with Hadewijch II, although there is a wealth of fine poetical expressions. To give just one example: While Hadewijch I speaks of the dilation of the soul to the dimensions of God, the author of the *New Poems* says the same thing using a more metaphysical formula: "The circle of things must shrink and be annihilated so that the circle of nakedness can grow and extend in order to embrace the All." (MD XVIII,ll.25–30.) It is when the soul has grown and has been extended by love that it can find the light (ll.34–35).

The general theme of these poems is the conquest of a freedom which is not considered as simply moral, but rather consists of *nakedness (bloetheit), void (ledicheit)*; that is to say, a shedding of the will, of forms and images, which are no more than accidents *(toeval)* encumbering the spirit. This shedding allows the soul to attain the "pure and naked Nothingness," that is the Deity beyond all human representation. Union appears less as fruition—the highest stage of beatitude with Hadewijch I—than as a plunge into a boundless unknowing, into the "wild desert" of the Divine Essence. We recognize here themes which were developed by Eckhart.[34]

However, it is difficult to assert whether these poems should be dated before or after Eckhart's works. Dom Porion has shown the more important parallels, mentioning a certain number of more or less contemporary texts (such as the Old German hymn on the Trinity: *Dreifaltig Keitslied*) which characterize a whole current of thought of the late thirteenth century.[35]

Leaving aside these reciprocal influences, it is certain that John Ruysbroeck (1293–1381) took inspiration from the Beguines, including both Hadewijch I and Hadewijch II. At the beginning of his book *The Twelve Beguines*, he puts into the mouths of these holy women verses composed by both our mystics. We can also trace this influence in his use of a whole series of images, expressions, and even literal quotations, taken from our Beguines.

As regards doctrine, the influence of these two mystics on Ruysbroeck has been a subject of considerable discussion.[36] However, there is no doubt that the latter presented the intuitions of these Beguines in a more systematical, more theological manner. Nevertheless, even if Hadewijch I and Ruysbroeck drew from common sources—particularly from William of St. Thierry—it is certain that the Prior of Groenendael owes much to the Antwerp mystic. This is particularly true as regards his conception of spiritual freedom and "common life," of participation in Trinitarian life in the flux of the Persons, the reflux in the Essence, ordaining the unity of active and contemplative life.

But it is to the author of the *New Poems* that he is indebted for a more abstract vocabulary: such expressions as "overpassing" and "the plunge into the abyss of unknowing." We have an example of this debt in the "Words of the Twelfth Beguine":

> If I desire something, I know it not,
> For in a boundless unknowing
> I have lost my very self.
> In His mouth I am engulfed,
> In a bottomless abyss;
> Never could I come out of it.[37]

Poem XVII

It neither pains me
Nor troubles me
That I must write,[38]
Since He Who lives in our midst
Upon us bestoweth
His precious gifts,

And by a new teaching
With His clarity
He will enlighten us.
Blessed may He be
At all times,
And in everything!

In naked knowledge
It is certainly great
What the mind receives,
But it is as nothing
When one considers
What is lacking. (*ontblivet*).

Our desire must be plunged
Within that lack,
So that all that we do
May be good,
No matter how imperfect
It might be.

Those who in that high knowledge
Of naked Love,
Speechless Love,
Strive to go ever deeper,
Find that their lack
Always increases.

A new knowledge
In the light-darkness
They find,
Of high price,
Modeless,
In the far-nigh.

In the immense eternity
Boundless in all dimensions,
The soul is separated,
Dilated, saved,
Engulfed in the One.

Her thought,
In its silent chase,
Which makes it boundless,
All in all,
Will find again
the uncircumscribed Whole.

There it seems that,
In the obscurity,
Appears a simple Thing (*simpel iet*)
Which seems to recede from her
And which she must learn to recognize
In the nakedness of No-thingness (*bloet niet*).

In that nakedness
Live the strong souls,
Satiated
By their vision;
They feel lack
When He [God] flees them.

Between what is received
And what is lacking
There is no doubt to my mind,

We can make no comparison,
The lacking is the greater.

Therefore they go on,
Those who recognize this truth,
And they follow
The tenebrous,
The trackless,
The wholly inward paths.

Their greatest gain,
Their most rewarding loss
Lies in this lack.
And how is that?
Be sure:
Nothing can be written of this.

But we must detach ourselves
From the agitation of reasons,
From forms and images,
If we wish
Inwardly to know,
Beyond understanding.

Those who do not stop on the way
To give themselves to other work
Than this here spoken of,
They are unified
In their first Origin,
In Eternity.

There they become
With Him so One
In their first origin
That no earthly union
Of two beings
Could be compared to this.

In the intimity of Unity
They are pure
And wholly inward,
Wholly naked,
Without images,
Without forms.

As if freed
In eternal time,
Uncreated,[39]
Boundless,
Uncircumscribed
In the silent vastness.

And here I can find.
Neither end nor beginning,
Nor any comparison
By which to express
In a worthy manner
This union.

And so I leave this task
To those who live it;
For to speak any further
Of such inward thoughts
Would wound the tongue
For having dared do so.

Poem XIX

Above all that is written[40]
And above all creatures
The spirit can learn
And see clearly
And follow closely
The way of Our Lord.

If knowledge is lacking you,
Seek inwardly
Your simplicity;
There you will find
Your mirror,
Always ready for you.

It is a great thing to see
In nakedness, without intermediary!
Well for him who is capable of this.
With one glance
He is alive
And can take his élan.

Abandoning what is behind him,
Looking only ahead,
To choose the One,
Leaving all for Him
And grasping Him eternally,
Without risk of ever losing Him.

A soul so disposed
Suffers great pains,
At every hour,
When she understands
That she assumes
The weight of sins.

She remains naked
And in anguish
Until the time when,
According to her conscience,
She has made satisfaction,
Such as she can.

And she will not be delivered
Until she has received
The inward testimony

That her offences
Have been forgiven in love.

To desire and love
Without the aid of the senses;
This is what is needed.
Outwardly and inwardly
To be without knowledge,
Like someone dead.

Learn to know
What Love commands;
Heed the love of nobody,
For Love covers
Those She teaches
As if with seraphim wings.

A foretaste
He must first have
And then be transformed,
He who, without turning back,
Desires to be anchored
To the beautiful Deity.

To praise God
On high,
Joyfully here below,
To be true to Him,
Without betrayal,
This is a noble work indeed!

....

Ah, noble praise offered,
Soar to the heavenly court
And embrace the Beloved there:
His comings and goings
Have taken from me
Consolation and pain.

Fear and love,
Desire and knowledge,
Intelligence,
Hope and aspirations
Joy and taste,
All have left me.

My knowledge has soared above me
Beyond intelligence,
Beyond the senses;
But of this I must keep silent
And still stay where I am.

It is like a desert
To be here below,
For here,
Neither sense nor words
Can reach or penetrate.

Poem XXVI

Most willingly would I draw closer to Love[41]
If I could do so inwardly,
But those who mingle much with creatures
Cannot sing this song with me.

Naked Love Who spares nothing
In her wild overpassing,
Stripped of all accident
Finds again her simple nature.

In the abandonment of naked love
There must be detachment from all created aid,
For Love strips of all form
Those She receives in Her simplicity.

The poor in spirit are then free of all modes,
Strangers to all images;
This is the life they lead,
Here below.

It is not enough to exile themselves,
Nor to beg their bread or anything else;
The poor in spirit must be without thoughts
In the vast simplicity,

Which has neither beginning nor end,
Neither form nor mode, neither reason nor sense,
Neither opinion nor thought, nor attention nor knowledge,
Uncircumscribed in the vast immensity.

It is in this wild and vast simplicity
That the poor in spirit live in unity:
There they find nothing but the freedom of detachment
Which always opens up to Eternity.

This is said in a short poem,
But the road is long, as I well know,
For those who wish to reach the very end
Many a torment must suffer.

PART V

Marguerite Porete

(d. 1310)

Introduction

Marguerite and the Inquisition

We have no source of knowledge concerning Marguerite Porret, Poiret, or Porete (also known as Marguerite of Hainaut), apart from her famous *Mirror of Simple Annihilated Souls*, the records of her trials, and, in contrast to the condemnations contained therein, a few favorable yet wary judgments pronounced by theologians and spiritual men of those times. Moreover, the link between the *Mirror* and the Beguine Marguerite, victim of the Inquisition under Philip the Fair, was brought to light only in 1946, and this was thanks to the perspicacity of Romana Guarnieri. This text had been discovered in 1867 by Francesco Töldi, who did not hesitate to attribute it to Blessed Marguerite of Hungary, doubtless because some of the manuscripts were known to be in Vienna.[1] However, the little we know of Marguerite is the essential. She taught pure love and persevered in this teaching, such as it appears in her book, even if, already before 1306, it had been condemned by Guy II, Bishop of Cambrai, burned on the public square at Valenciennes and its use prohibited under pain of excommunication. Subsequently she was pursued by Philip of Marigny, Guy II's successor, and then accused by a higher authority, the Provincial Inquisitor of Haute Lorraine. Later on, during her eighteen months' imprisonment in Paris for having repeatedly refused to appear before an ecclesiastical court, to swear to tell the Inquisitor "the truth," and finally to retract when threatened with death, she was declared to be a relapsed heretic and on May 31, 1310, the Inquisition handed her over to the secular authorities.

The following day, June the first, she was burned at the stake on the Place de Grève—now Place de l'Hôtel de Ville— in the presence of the civil and ecclesiastical authorities and of an enormous crowd who were converted to her favor on witnessing her attitude to death.[2]

This final trial was instituted by the Inquisitor General of the Kingdom of France, the Dominican, Master William of Paris, who was King Philip's confessor and who, from 1307, in a notoriously sinister manner, had presided over the trial of the Templars. About this latter trial, it has been said that never in the Middle Ages did Inquisition and Crown collaborate so closely, and it seems that there were political reasons—apart from the strongly emphasized ecclesiastical or doctrinal ones—for Marguerite's condemnation. It has been suggested that this decision of the Inquisition was a compensation offered to the Pope and the Church after the ticklish question of the Templars. However that may be, those who love her are convinced that, if we seek a deeper explanation, it was "on account of her just love," as, according to Hadewijch, another Beguine, doubtlessly Aleydis, had been put to death a long time before by the first Inquisitor General of France, Robert le Bougre.[3]

In defense of the clergy who condemned Marguerite, it has been asserted that, on the basis of the documents presented to them, they could not have pronounced a different judgment. It was, in fact, common practice in the Middle Ages, as it still is in our own times, to allow polemics and persecutions to be nourished by quotations that have been either mutilated or severed from their context, and the duty to seek more complete information does not seem to have been the chief concern of the ecclesiastical courts. Perhaps this fact—which we cannot verify—helps to explain at least partially the obvious contradiction between the judgment pronounced by these theologians representing Paris University and the favorable opinions of the three equally competent exponents of the clergy who had "heard" her book, as Marguerite puts it. These three clerics were a Friar Minor named John (de Querayn according to the English version), a Cistercian called Frank of the Abbey of Villiers in Brabant, and lastly the famous theologian Godfrey of Fontaines who came from Flanders and was ex-regent of Paris University. "The selection could not have been more judicious or more complete: a representative of the most advanced and modern movements, a representative of the monastic tradition, and lastly an exponent of the scholastics and the secular clergy. The three attestations they wrote have an authentic and sincere tone and are important testimony in favor of Marguerite. At the same time, they throw light on the divisions existing in mysticism."[4] In fact, while the Cistercian's approval is without reserve, both Godfrey and the Franciscan, although expressing their deep admiration, consider that the book should be shown only to very few persons, for it might be a source of dangerous illusions to those who do not possess an adequate spiritual preparation.

These brief indications can help us to form a certain idea of the contacts and influence Marguerite had during her lifetime. We might also mention an episode—not bereft of a romantic touch—concerning a cleric who took her part in these vicissitudes. We refer to the Beghard Guiard de Cressonessart, arrested in Paris towards the end of 1308 by order of the Inquisitor William for having "aided and defended" Marguerite. When he gave witness before the Inquisition, Guiard admitted "that he had exposed himself on her behalf" in Paris. It seems that, by defending Marguerite, then strongly suspected of heresy, he had become as much distrusted as she was. Like her, for eighteen months (a lapse of time legally granted to the accused for reflection), he refused to appear before the Inquistion Court. At last, in March 1310, William convoked an assembly of theologians and canonists of Paris University to reach a decision on the two cases. On April 3 judgment was pronounced and it was declared that, unless they retracted, the two accused would be considered guilty of heresy and would be handed over to the secular authorities. This decision was meant to be a final threat. Guiard then retracted and was consequently condemned to life imprisonment instead of death. Marguerite, however, did not allow herself to be intimidated: she followed literally—a fact rare enough to be signaled—what she had written about the liberated soul: "This Soul replies to nobody, unless she wishes to, if he is not of her lineage; for a gentleman would not deign to answer a churl, if he called him, or challenged him. This is why whoever calls this Soul does not find her, and so her enemies have no reply from her."[5]

So all that was left for William to do was to gather in solemn assembly in the Church of Saint-Mathurin, the most renowned theologians of Paris University, twenty-one in number, among whom were John of Gent and Nicholas of Lyre, who unanimously condemned the *Mirror* and its author.

It is difficult to establish precisely the links which existed between Marguerite's doctrine and that of Guiard de Cressonessart, the latter having left nothing in written form, but it is known that he had Millenarian views, similar to those of Abbot Joachim of Fiore and St. Bonaventura. It results from his testimony before the Inquisitional Court that he believed he had been called to be the apostle of a new dispensation of the Faith. That is why he had his disciples call him the "Angel of Philadelphia," referring to a passage in Revelation (3:7) which attributes to the Angel of this church "the key of David." Guiard, in fact, was convinced that he had been given a prophetic power of the keys, higher than the merely ministerial power which he recognized in the Pope. Naturally this became the chief charge brought against him and led to his subsequent condemnation.

Although this perspective on the history of salvation does not at first glance strike the unprepared reader of the *Mirror*, it nevertheless seems to be reflected in the remarks concerning "Holy Church the Less," that is to say the official Church, distinguished from "Holy Church the Greater," composed of those souls who have been really freed, those who sustain and teach the whole of Holy Church. Marguerite says that "Holy Church the Less" is really less, for she will reach her end and she will rejoice at this.[6] This theme, which echoes the prophecies of Joachim of Fiore, frequently reappears in the *Mirror*.

Far from ceasing with Marguerite's death, the persecutions by the Inquisition continued and may be said to bear witness to the success of the *Mirror* in Europe in the fourteenth and fifteenth centuries. It overcame linguistic barriers as did no other contemporary mystical writing in the vernacular. Proof of this fact is furnished by the six versions which have been preserved, in Old French, Old Italian, Middle English and in Latin. (The German version, if it ever existed, has not been brought to light.) At present they are accessible in about fifteen manuscripts, while others have been reported to exist in various places but have then mysteriously disappeared.[7]

"But the history of the *Mirror* does not stop with its author's story. Its theological dossier is then transferred to Vienne, in Dauphiné, where, in 1311–1312, will be held the famous Council that will condemn northern mysticism in general, and more particularly Meister Eckhart's and that contained in the *Mirror*, confused, in its entirety, with the deviations of the Free Spirit sects. What remains of the documents of the various trials, as well as the articles of the Vienne Council, show how great the misinterpretation was. . . . With the condemnation of Vienne, the *Mirror* is henceforth labeled as a heretical work and was regularly confiscated by the Inquisitional authorities of the whole of Europe until the Renaissance, an eloquent proof of its success and diffusion. . . . The reputation for heresy and the limited number of manuscripts which survived the confiscations have certainly caused the importance of the *Mirror* to be underestimated in modern research.

"The fact that it met with great success during and after its author's life is amply testified by the impressive *mise en scène* of the various trials—all the authorities of the Sorbonne participating—by the efforts of the Inquisition to put a stop to its circulation, but above all by the traces it left in future spiritual literature, both orthodox and heretical. . . ."[8]

The first English version of the *Mirror*, dated fourteenth century, is in all probability the work of Michael of Northbrook, Bishop of London and co-founder of the London Charterhouse. As this text became an object of criticism, many years later he rewrote his translation, adding to it orthodox glosses. In the following century, the Carthusian, Richard Methley, produced a Latin version of this translation, insisting strongly in his preface that this book could be put into the hands of only a very restricted number of persons. (This Latin manuscript also contains a translation by Methley of the *Cloud of Unknowing*, the work of an anonymous English author on the mysticism of self-abandonment, of similar inspiration to that of the *Mirror*.) Recalling the extraordinary influence Marguerite's book had in England during the second half of the fifteenth and the first decades of the sixteenth century, Romana Guarnieri is led to the conclusion that its popularity had gone beyond the walls of the Charterhouses and, together with the doctrines of the Free Spirit, was having its effect on the mystical illuminism of the Quakers.

It was in the North of Italy, where it circulated in both Latin and Italian, (the earliest translations date from the end of the fourteenth century) particularly in the first half of the fifteenth century, that the *Mirror* seems to have provoked the most commotion. St. Bernadino of Siena, in the sermons he preached between 1417 and 1437, attacked it strongly and repeatedly; at Padua, in 1433, the Benedictines forbade it in their congregations; the Jesuates of Venice, accused of having made it their bedside book and of sympathizing with the Free Spirit heresy, were declared innocent by two inquirers named in 1437 by Pope Eugene IV, while the Inquisition continued to follow its course at Padua. The Venetian question came up again and finally the Pope himself was accused (after his deposition) of being favorable to the *Mirror*. This charge was made by a certain Mastro Giacomo, probably the Paduan Inquisitor who had written about this book "numerous execrations or reprobations." On the same occasion, in 1439, Mastro Giacomo reminded the Council of Bâle of the thirty articles of the *Mirror* judged as heretical by the Fathers of the Council and demanded that the thirty-six copies kept, according to him, by the Commission which had examined Marguerite's book, should be burned. We lose track of these vicissitudes after the Bâle Council. Nevertheless, in 1473, the error of the adherents of the simple soul (*lo errore di quelli de l'anima semplice*) is again denounced, this time by the Franciscan Pacificus of Novara who complains of the conduct of heretical groups. Finally, in a sixteenth century manuscript in the library of the Benedictine Monastery of Monte Cassino mention is found of a book entitled *De anima annihilata*, "in which are written the most secret of God's secrets, and all the secrets of the servants of love are contained in it." This certainly refers to a manuscript of the *Mirror* entitled *Speculum animarum simplicium alias Anima adnihilata*. This manuscript is now in the Vatican. It was finished being copied in 1521 at the Subiaco Benedictine Monastery where Rhenish mysticism was greatly appreciated. The Monte Cassino manuscript is impregnated with the spirit of the *Mirror*, and it seems that a group of mystics attached to St. Catherine of Genoa made use of it as a spiritual guide. Its publication had been planned, but a marginal note added later shows the disapproval of the censors and so the idea had to be abandoned.

In France, Jean Gerson, Chancellor of Paris University from 1395 to 1425, chanced to read a book on the love of God written by a certain Marie de Valenciennes. The mention of Valenciennes, Marguerite's town, where her book was burned for the first time, as well as Gerson's description of the book he had read, have induced the most serious critics to admit that it must have been the *Mirror of Simple Souls*— the first name, Marie, being simply due to an error on the part of the copyist. While recognizing that it was a work of "unbelievable subtlety," Gerson puts the reader on his guard against it.[9] But a century later the *Mirror* would find a supporter no less famous than this censor, in the person of

Marguerite of Navarre, Francis the First's beloved only sister. This Marguerite was on friendly terms with the nuns of the Madeleine Convent at Orleans from which comes the only accessible copy of the original version of the *Mirror*, in Old French, and now preserved at Chantilly. In the fifteenth century, when this copy was made, the Madeleine Convent played an important role in the reform of the famous Abbey of Fontevrault, where the queen poetess found one of the deepest inspirations of her mysticism. It is she who furnishes us with the most beautiful introduction to Marguerite Porete's book.[10]

The Mirror of Simple Annihilated Souls

In her *Prisons*, written in the last years of her life, Marguerite of Navarre mentions the *Mirror of Simple Souls* among the books "which follow unconditionally the intention of the Sacred Bible":

> But among all books I saw one by a woman,
> Written a hundred years ago, filled with the flame
> Of Charity, so very ardently
> That love and love alone was its concern,
> The beginning and end of all she said.
> ....
> Oh, how attentive this woman was
> To receive that love which burned
> Her own heart and those to which she spoke!
> Well she knew by her subtle spirit
> The true friend whom she named Noble.
>
> ....
> And her Far-Nigh, oh, how well-named He is
> He Who must be loved above all!
>
> ....
> He is noble and through His nobleness
> He makes her noble too;

He ennobles the soul with His bounty,
So she, from a churl, becomes a lady.[11]

We notice that it was the author's subtlety of mind that struck both Queen Marguerite and Chancellor Gerson. They did not dream of reproaching her, as worthy critics have later done, for not having obeyed a rational principle of composition when writing her book. Marguerite Porete's intention is to show, as in a mirror, the spiritual truth that she wishes to teach, a supra-rational truth which, if perceived, will, by itself, render the soul simple. By illuminating in turn the various facets of this truth, the author attempts to make the reader or listener progress in his or her understanding of the central theme: the liberation of the soul which one attains by annihilating oneself in God through love, thus being transformed into Him.

"The word (mirror) involves a very strong visual connotation and contains . . . an invitation to look at ourselves in order to draw closer to a reality we admire; here we have the Platonic, but more especially Christian, conception of knowledge. It is contemplation and not action that transforms us and makes us resemble what we contemplate: 'It is because we shall see God that we shall resemble Him,' St. John says, to explain the bliss of the elect. So the *Mirror of Simple Souls* is also a mirror which *renders the soul simple.*"[12]

The theme of liberation is expressed, as with our other Beguines, in the courtly language, in the literary and social schemas which allowed the author to be understood by the readers, or rather listeners, of those days: In fact, the text is presented in the form of a play, with allegorical characters, the chief ones being Soul and Lady Love. But there are also others, such as Courtesy, Understanding of Love, confronted with Reason, Understanding of Reason, and the Virtues. *Fine Amour*, the idealized love of the troubadours, leads us, when spiritually transposed, to Lady Love who represents an aspect of God, or rather, God Himself in His Essence.

"REASON: But who are you, Love? Are you not one of the virtues, just as we are, even if we admit you are above us?

LOVE: I am God, for Love is God and God is Love, and this Soul is God by condition of Love; I am God by divine nature and this Soul is so by the justice of Love, so that this precious friend of mine is taught and led by Me, without herself, for she is transformed into Me."[13]

The Soul no longer needs the outward rules of obedience which before she had observed scrupulously, for henceforth she is entirely passive to the motion of the Divine Will which operates in her "without herself"; that is to say, she takes no initiative. This is what Marguerite calls "to save oneself by faith without works" using a bold expression that was entirely misunderstood but which conveys the great theme of Rheno-Flemish mysticism—passivity to God:

And that is a work for God, for God works in me: I owe Him no work as He himself works in me, and if I did something myself, it would be undoing His work.[14]

Soul and Love try to explain these high truths to Reason. Bewildered and shocked by the paradoxes he hears, Reason ends up by dying, in the theatrical setting of the text. He thus leaves room for a higher comprehension of God while, at the same time, the Soul takes leave of the virtues, to rise above them in the sovereign freedom of Love.

As regards the way Marguerite expresses the spiritual combat of the Soul, until she finally reaches peace in abandonment, let us quote the words of Peter Dronke who has emphasized the "incomparable originality" of the *Mirror* as an imaginary construction and an expression of self-awareness:

"The lyrical and quasi-dramatic passages are integral to the construction. In her extended complex dialogues Marguerite never dispenses with narrative transitions—in this she is closer, for instance, to Ramon Lull than to Mechthild. Yet as in Mechthild's *Fliessendes Licht*, spontaneous dramatic tension can arise in the interchanges and conflicts between Marguerite's projections of inner and celestial forces, and among those forces (again as in Mechthild) Lady Love takes the lead. A further likeness lies in what we might call the lyrical continuum, which, in the *Mirror* as in the *Fliessendes Licht*, extends from rhythmic prose, filled with parallelism and homoioteleuta, to more sustained rhymed passages, to fully poetic forms."[15]

The theme of the Prologue to the *Mirror* seems to have been taken from the *Roman d'Alexandre*, written in the thirteenth century by Alexander of Bernay. The origin of this work, which greatly influenced the courtly literature of those times, goes back to Pseudo-Callisthenes, a Greek author of the second century. This legendary tale had already been sung by the troubadours ever since the beginning of the twelfth century. With Marguerite, the munificence of this Eastern monarch symbolizes the gratuitous nature of Divine Love. As is indicated in the full title of the Chantilly manuscript: *The Mirror of Simple Annihilated Souls who only Dwell in the Will and Desire of Love*, the knight—here the freed Soul—abandons everything to serve his Lady Love, without expecting any reward, except what She is ready to give of Herself, that is, Love, out of her great courtesy. (Courtesy, *curialitas* in the Latin versions, refers to the quality of the man, or woman, of court.)

"Although courtesy still remained an art of living based on politeness and chivalrous generosity (such as was attributed to Alexander the Great) now it began to express chiefly the will to pursue to its very end the plenitude of the experience of love, in literature as well as in life. *Fine Amour* is thus the real aim of the courtly quest and the *Mirror* often speaks of the simple annihilated soul as "demanding *Fine Amour*." In the early courtly literature, that of the langue d'oc troubadours, *Fine Amour* is the fruit of the intrepid fidelity of the lover in all the ordeals imposed on him by his lady. . . . and its essential feature is joy, a victorious enthusiasm and, at the same time, a sentiment linked to the complete possession of the beloved. In northern courtesy, from which the *Mirror* inherited, these notions become spiritual and inward, while losing nothing of their force. . . ."[16]

> LOVE: This Soul swims in the sea of Joy, that is to say, in the sea of delights which issues and flows from the Divinity; and so she feels no joy, for she herself *is* joy, and thus she swims and floats in joy without feeling any joy, for she dwells in Joy and Joy dwells in her; she is joy herself by the force of Joy that has transformed her into Itself.
> There is now a common will, the will of the lover and that of the beloved; they are like fire and flame, for Love has transformed this soul into Herself.
> SOUL: Ah, most sweet, pure, and divine Love, what a suave transformation it is to be transformed into what I love more than myself. And I am so transformed that I have lost my name in order to love, I who can love so little; it is into Love that I have been transformed; for I love nothing but Love.[17]

This transformation takes place when the Soul is entirely stripped of herself; then she finds her essential or original being, which is participation of God. Such is the theme of the return to God, expressed by Marguerite in striking terms, the equivalent of which we can find in the works of our other Rheno-Flemish Beguines, as also in Meister Eckhart:

> LOVE: He has peace who dwells in willing nothing, there where he was before he had willing.
> DISOBEYING WILL: I cannot be what I must be, until I am again there where I was; at that point where I was before coming from Him, as naked as He Who is; as naked as I was when I was [she] who was not. And I must have this, if I want to have back what is mine. Otherwise I shall not have it."[18]

She is adorned with this utter peace in which she lives, and continues, and is, and was and will be without [her own] being. For when iron is clothed in fire, it loses its appearance, because fire is the stronger and has transformed it into itself; so is this soul clothed in this "more," nourished by and transformed into this "more," for love of this "more," without taking into account the "less" [which she is]; and having been transformed into this "more" of utter eternal peace, she can no longer be found.[19]

Having abandoned her own being, the "less," she is transformed into the Being of God, the "more," and that is why she can no longer be found. With her name she has lost her individual identity, as a river that has emptied itself into the sea.

The condition of this annihilation is the abolition of the individual will or desire. This is, as has been already said, the central idea of the *Mirror*. The Soul no longer wills anything, in order to will exclusively the divine will. Such is "the King's straight highway through the land of wishing nothing" that Lady Knowledge, enlightened by divine grace, indicates to the "marred," or at least to those among them who seek this road. As Marilyn Doiron says in her edition of the Middle English version of the *Mirror*: "The marred life is a life hindered or arrested in the early stages by its adherence to a self-centered pursuit of the virtues. Though there is danger that it will never progress beyond this stage, it is possible for the 'marred' soul to rise to greater heights of perfection."[20] She can do so through self-knowledge, thanks to which the Soul finally understands that she is the "abyss of all poverty"[21] and "sees herself below all other creatures, in a sea of sin." "Reduced to nothing and less than nothing,"[22] she becomes aware that God alone is, while she herself is not. It is only then that the divine will can operate in her, "without her," that is to say, without her egocentric intervention. It is by no means a question of Quietism here, no more than it is with our other mystics. But henceforth the initiative belongs to Another. Moreover, on this point, Marguerite makes a statement which agrees perfectly with the Eastern doctrine of non-action: "Such people would govern a country, if it were necessary, but everything would be done without them."[23] (This is said of the souls who, having reached the fifth estate—the awareness that only God really is—have already "touches" of the sixth estate, a "flash" of the Far-Nigh, full glory belonging exclusively to the seventh estate, after death.) This non-acting and non-desiring, to Reason's great astonishment, do not prevent the Soul from making demands at a supra-conscious level: "It is the divine nature of the attraction of her [Soul's] love that formulates in her these demands without her knowing it, and her demands are beyond the frontiers of all countries where a creature can have access to knowledge."[24]

This non-willing is, as with Eckhart, the key of non-having and non-knowing, that of "non-thinking of the Far-Nigh."[25] For above rational knowledge and above egotistic desire, God is "neither known, nor loved, nor praised." He could not be (known, etc.) in the usual and human sense of these terms since His transcendency forbids it, and Marguerite's love is based on the "more" or the "surpassing."

It is a very long way from the land of the Virtues, where are the marred, to that of the forgotten, the naked, the annihilated or the glorified, who are in the highest estate, there where God is abandoned by Himself, in Himself. Then He is neither known, nor loved, nor praised by these creatures, except insofar as one can neither know, nor love, nor praise Him. This is the sum of all their love and the last estate of their way.[26]

To reach this estate, Marguerite had first to follow reason and the Virtues and feed the latter "to bursting point" before being able to say with St. Augustine: "Love and do what you like."[27] She had to overpass dogmatic knowledge of which she was far from ignorant: it is not without reason that in some manuscripts she is referred to as a *"béguine clergeresse"* or *"en clergerie moult suffisant."*

"In fact, we are astonished by the space that dogmatic formulae occupy in the *Mirror*. A whole chapter paraphrases the symbol of Nicée and Constantinople. . . . No less orthodox are the very dense formulae: 'He is Who is; therefore He is what He is by Himself: lover, beloved, love,' as well as the successful transposition of Trinitarian dogma to mystical form. . . . There are also numerous references to the mystery of the Incarnation and to that of the Redemption which is presented as the sole end of the Incarnation. . . . Marguerite even anticipates Pascal's *Mystère de Jésus*: 'If nobody had sinned except myself alone, You would nevertheless have redeemed my soul, turned from Your love, by being nailed naked to the Cross for me and by using Your well-ordained power to destroy sin. Thus, Lord, all You have suffered in Your sweet humanity You have suffered for me, as if nobody else had sinned, but myself alone.' "[28]

It has been more often Protestant authors who began to doubt Marguerite Porete's heterodoxy, but nevertheless one finds a good number of Catholic theologians supporting them. In this connection, we might mention Dom Porion and, more recently, Abbot Max Huot de Longchamp and Fr. Paul Verdeyen. The latter asserts that "the heretical character of her book is, to say the least, questionable."[29]

Moreover, Marguerite herself has furnished a wealth of explanations which should have enlightened the sincere reader endowed with sufficient humility. "For lack of this humility, which authorizes every reasonable person to read the *Mirror* without necessarily sharing in the experience, the Courts of the Inquisition sent our text and its author to the stake."[30]

Marguerite, like our other mystics, does not abolish dogma; for her it is an indispensable structure of thought to which her meditation and experience give a deeper significance. Properly speaking, we can say that this search for a more profound meaning has nothing original in it but is always confined within the tradition of the Greek Fathers and of

William of St. Thierry: this is the case, for example, in her ontological interpretation of union with God. What appeared suspect to the Inquisition, even more than this last point, was most certainly the indifference to outward practices—the freed Soul neither desires nor avoids masses and sermons—or to outward events, even of a religious nature: she does not care about Paradise or Hell since, participating in God, she is, by this very fact, in Paradise which "is nothing other than seeing God."[31]

In actual fact, the ecclesiastical institution felt threatened, particularly by the revendication, both thought and lived, (and, what is worse still, expressed in the vernacular) of the essential freedom of the soul. This doubtlessly explains why it was possible to confuse this revendication with those of the Free Spirit Sect. For, like the theme of poverty, from which it cannot be dissociated, the theme of freedom was at the heart of the real religious revolution which swept through the West from the thirteenth century onwards, a revolution which the official representatives of the Church tried too often to suffocate by the methods we already know.

". . . What penetrated religious practice and shook the ecclesial and moral order was the spirit of freedom and its consequences. The Church's condemnations of the Beghards and the Beguines, as well as the eight points . . . of the Council of Vienne were, almost without exception, directed against the idea of freedom, and we can say the same thing, in a slightly less exclusive manner, as regards Meister Eckhart's incriminated propositions. And so it is not surprising that Marguerite's Inquisitors rejected this conception of freedom. The cardinal point is cited in the first article: "That the annihilated soul takes leave of the Virtues, and is no longer in their service, for she no longer has any use for them, but the Virtues obey her will."[32]

It is true that, particularly in Chapters 6 and 8 of the *Mirror*, Marguerite joyfully dismisses the Virtues.[33] However, she insists, often in a most explicit manner, upon the fact that we must first pass through the virtues before we are able to overpass them. The virtuous life corresponds to the second of the seven estates of grace described by our author. The first estates, up to the third and fourth, which are those of the "marrred," no longer interest her at all, unless it is to call those who are capable of understanding and desiring *Fine Amour*, in order to rise to higher estates. But what she really prefers to speak of is the experience which constitutes the Soul in the estate of "blind annihilated life," consisting of detachment—"death of the spirit,"—and of a comprehension that can be reached neither by Reason, nor Philosophy, nor even by Theology.[34] One reaches this experience in an instant, or "a moment of time," thanks to that "flash" of the Noble Far-Nigh which characterizes the sixth estate, that of "illumined annihilated life."[35] Instead of speculating upon being, it is, in fact, rather a question of experiencing it in a "passivity" which is explained by the metaphysical structure of the two partners, since "He is . . . and I am not."[36] Then the "less" of the Soul, that is to say, what she is in her own created being, leaves room for the "more" of God, for the overpassing or the transcendency of the Uncreated Being.[37] "Thought has no longer sovereignty over her. . . . This is the accomplishment of her pilgrimage," at the end of which "her will is given back to her," since she no longer makes egotistic use of it.[38]

Having arrived so high, the soul is happy that she is never able to seize all the richness of her Lover, but can only partake of it in a negative kind of way. In this blessed ignorance, we recognize one of the great themes of Rheno-Flemish mysticism, inspired by Proclus' distinction—taken over by Denys—between the totally transcendent God and the participating God.

To those who love "without a why," Marguerite contrasts "those who expect large revenues from Love."[39] The contrast between the churl and the nobleman expresses in the *Mirror* the contrast between self-interested souls and those who "demand *Fine Amour*." We are reminded of Eckhart and his *German Sermons* in which he makes the same distinction between those who have understood pure detachment and those who save themselves in an outward and selfish manner.

As he does, and perhaps even more so, Marguerite uses many expressions of contempt when referring to the latter whom she calls asses or sheep: "seekers of earthly Paradises," "they save themselves in a far from courtly manner."[40] The spiritual hierarchy that she recognizes has no relationship with the constituted bodies. Among the "churls at heart," the "small minds," the "merchants," the "asses," and the "sheep," she includes the learned members of Paris University who condemned her, those of the Regular Orders who misunderstood her and the Beguines themselves whose incomprehension she had to face.

Beloved, what will Beguines say, and the pious throng,
When they hear the excellence of your divine song?
Beguines say that I am wrong, priest and clerk and preacher,
Austins and Carmelites and the Friars Minor,
Wrong in writing of the being of this noble Love.
I am not—no slight to their reason, that makes them tell me
    this:
Surely Desire, Will, and Fear rob them of cognizance, rob
    them of the flood
And union of the highest light of the ardor of divine Love.[41]
    (trans. Peter Dronke, Women Writers, p. 227)

From what is contained in these verses, we see why Marguerite so often repeats that she has written her book only for those who can understand the stripping involved in "willing nought," not for those to whom such comprehension is closed, or rather, those who close themselves to it. Some critics have spoken of esoterism concerning this point, without always seeing that it is exclusively the esoterism of spiritual detachment which doubtlessly involves a strictly closed number—*de facto* if not *de jure*. It is in this sense that Marguerite, following the most orthodox authors, speaks of the "glose" or hidden meaning of the Scriptures,[42] and with one of her usual witticisms she remarks that those who have nothing to hide have nothing to show either.[43]

We have drawn attention to the profound logic uniting

her life and her book in her refusal to appear before the Ecclesiastical Court and to retract for fear of being burned alive. This same sense of logic that governed her life led her to explain the contradiction, proper to mystical writers, between the impossibility of saying anything about God and the fact of writing about Him profusely. She specifies clearly that for her it was a necessity to write this book when she belonged to the number of the "marred," and before she became a freed soul.

"Certainly, it is necessary to do so before reaching completely the estate of freedom, of this I have no doubt. And yet, said the Soul who wrote the book, I was so foolish at the time I wrote it, or rather when Love wrote it for me, and at my request, when I put into words something precious which could neither be done, nor thought of, nor spoken of: as if you wanted to enclose the sea in your eye, carry the world on the point of a reed or illuminate the sun with a lantern or a torch. Yes, I was even more foolish than someone who tried to do such things.

When I expressed these precious unspeakable things,
I encumbered myself by writing these words.
But thus I took my élan
And by this I was helped
To reach the last stage
Of the estate of which we speak,
Which lies in perfection,
when the soul dwells in pure no-thingness and without thought, and not before.[44]

Together with the "Song of the Soul," which is the real conclusion to the book, we have here one of the rare autobiographical passages of the *Mirror*.[45] It is clear that what Marguerite reveals of her own life is there only to enlighten us on the situation of the human Soul, straying far from its Origin and struggling in vain to find it again until the moment when, thanks to self-knowledge, she finally abandons this "less" that she is in her own being by means of an annihilation which constitutes her in the only true being of God-Love. In spite of the "elitism" with which some have reproached her—and which goes no further than throwing light on the selfishness of human behavior even in spiritual research—the theme of *Everyman* is not far off, even if it is expressed in the ontological language of the Greek Fathers mingled with that of courtly love. It is not without reason that, in spite of so many persecutions, the *Mirror* so easily crossed all linguistic barriers in Europe during the Middle Ages and the Renaissance Period. This success is certainly to be attributed to the quality of an exceptional experience and to the simple yet learned manner of the maieutic approach to this experience. But, in our opinion, the success of Marguerite's work is also to be attributed to its universality, which opens up the King's straight highway to the land of wishing nothing for all those who really seek it. Let us hope that, in spite of its medieval form, there may be a revival in our own times of the success of this book, which has finally begun to be recognized as a major spiritual *oeuvre* of French literature.

Marguerite Porete's "Approbatio" and Excerpts from "The Mirror of Simple Souls"

Approbatio (The Approbation of the Three Clerics)

I, a creature made by God,[1] through whom the Creator made this book which comes from Him, for which persons I know not and neither do I wish to know (it suffices me that it is in the secret of divine knowledge and in hope). However, I greet them out of the love of the peace of charity of the Highest Trinity. May it deign to guide them by bearing testimony to their inner lives by the reports of the clerics who have heard this book.

The first of them was a friar minor, well known for the holy life he led, and he was called Brother John. What he said we are passing on to you in this letter of love: therefore receive this missive in your kind courtesy, for Love asks this of you, to the honor of God and His free servants and for the benefit of those who are not yet free but, God willing, will be so later on.

This friar said that this book was truly made by the Holy Spirit. And (he added) that if all the clergy in the world should hear it, presuming they understood it, they could not contradict anything at all contained in it. He asked, in God's name, that it should be wisely guarded and that few should see it. He also said it was so "high" that he himself could not understand it.

Afterwards, a Cistercian monk, called Dom Frank, of the

Abbey of Villiers, saw it and read it. He said it was in accordance with the Scriptures and that everything it said was the truth.

Then it was read by a master of theology who was called Master Godfrey of Fonteynes. And just like the others, he said nothing ill of the book. But he was right to say that he did not advise that many should have it because, so he said, they might lose their eternal life by aspiring to that higher life which perhaps they could never reach. So, on this account, they might be deluded. For, he said, this book has been made by a spirit so strong and fervent that few, or none, of this kind are to be found. Nevertheless he said that the Soul is not able to attain divine life or divine way of being until she has reached the way that this book describes, for all other ways of being—this master said—are inferior to it, as they are human. This alone is the divine way of being and no other but this.

This approbation was made for the peace of the listeners, and also for your own peace we relate these things to you, so that this seed may fructify a hundredfold in all those who will hear (this book) and will be worthy of it (Guarnieri, pp. 638–639; Doiron, pp. 249–250).

Prologue to "The Mirror of Simple Souls": In a Foreign Land.

LOVE: You, actives and contemplatives, perhaps even annihilated by true Love, you who are going to learn about certain powers of pure Love, noble Love, the high Love of the freed Soul, and how the Holy Spirit gave her a sail, as if she were His ship, I beseech you for Love's sake to listen very attentively, with the subtle understanding within you and with great diligence. For otherwise, all those who will hear these things will misunderstand them.

Now, in humility, listen to a little example of love here below and understand how it resembles divine Love.

Example: Once upon a time there was a lady, a king's daughter, whose heart was very worthy and noble and whose spirit was noble too, and she lived in a foreign land. Now it happened that this lady heard about the great courtliness and nobility of King Alexander; at once, in intent, she loved him for the great fame of his nobility. But this lady was so far from the great lord in whom she had placed her love that she could neither see nor possess him. That is why she was often disconsolate within, since no other love except this sufficed her. When she saw that this far-off love—though so close within her heart—was so far outside her, she thought she would seek comfort in her sorrow by somehow imagining the appearance of her beloved who so often brought suffering to her heart. Thus she had a portrait painted to the likeness of the king she loved, as close as possible to the way she pictured her beloved to be, according to the sentiment of love that pervaded her. And by means of this image, together with her other practices, she dreamed the king himself.

SOUL: Truly, it is just like that for me, said the Soul who had this book written: I heard of a very mighty king who was, by his great courtliness of nobility and bounty, a noble Alexander; but He was so far-off from me and I from him that I did not know how to find solace within me, and so that I should remember Him, He gave me this book which represents, in a certain manner, Love. But although I have His image, I still remain in a foreign land and far from the place where dwell the most noble friends of this lord, all of whom are pure, refined, and freed by the gifts of this king with whom they live (Guarnieri, pp. 521–522; Doiron, pp. 250–251).

The Noble Soul Desires Nothing

How Noble This Soul Is and How She Takes No Account of Anything Whatsoever—Chapter VII

LOVE: This Soul does not take account of shame or honor, poverty or wealth, comfort or discomfort, love or hatred, of Hell or Heaven.

REASON: Eh, in God's name, what's the meaning of your words?

LOVE: The meaning? Of course, he to whom God has given the understanding of these things knows what the meaning is, and nobody else does, for the Scriptures do not contain it, neither can human wit comprehend it, just as the efforts of a living creature cannot serve to understand it, or to comprehend it. This gift comes, rather, from the Most High Who has enraptured this Soul by plenitude of knowledge and she is brought to nought as to her understanding. And so such a Soul, having become nothing, possesses all and yet possesses nought, wishes all and wishes nothing, she knows everything and knows nought.

REASON: And how can it be, Lady Love, that such a Soul can desire what this book speaks of when it has already been said that she has no will?

LOVE: Reason, it is not at all her will that desires this, but rather the will of God that desires it in her. For it is not this Soul that dwells in Love (for then she would will this through some desire), but it is rather Love that dwells in her, Love Who has seized her will and does Her will through this Soul. And henceforth Love works in her, without her, so there can be no uneasiness within her.

This Soul can no longer speak of God for she is annihilated as regards all her outward desires, her inner feelings, and all strivings of the spirit, insofar as she does what she does out of good habits, or in obedience to a commandment of Holy Church, without any desire, for the will that gave her desire is now dead.

How These Souls Have No Will of Their Own—Chapter IX

LOVE: If anyone should ask them if they wished to be in Purgatory, these freed Souls, peaceful and confident, would reply no; if they wished, in this life, to be certain of their salvation, they would say no; as to whether they would like to be in Paradise, they would still say no. Besides, with what could they wish anything? They have no will, and if they wished something they would be severed from Love, for Love Who holds their will knows what is good for them, and that suffices them, without knowing it themselves and without further assurance. These souls live on knowledge, love and praise: such is their habitual practice, without acting of their own accord, for Knowledge, Love, and Praise dwell within them. Such souls cannot know whether they are good or evil; they have no knowledge of themselves and cannot judge whether they are turned towards God or from Him.[2]

Now, to speak more briefly, let us take one of these Souls as an example, one who neither desires nor rejects poverty and tribulations, Masses and sermons, fasting and prayers and who gives nature all that it requires, without prickings of conscience; but her nature is so well ordered, having been transformed by union with Love, to Whom this Soul's will is wedded, that it demands nothing that might be forbidden. This Soul is not solicitous about what she might need until the time comes when she needs it; but nobody can be free of this solicitude unless he is innocent.

REASON: Eh, in God's name, what does that mean?

LOVE: To your question, Reason, I shall give you an answer as I have done already, and I tell you once more: no master of natural wit [philosopher], no master of the Scriptures, none of those who go no further in love than obedience to virtues understand, or ever will understand, what there is to understand. Of this you may be certain, Reason, for nobody understands this except those who pursue *Fine Amour*. Certainly, if such Souls could be found, they would tell the truth, if they wished to speak; but do not think that anyone can understand them, except those who pursue *Fine Amour* and Charity.

This gift is sometimes given in one moment of time, and he who receives it must take great care of it for it is the most perfect gift that God can give to a creature. This Soul is now at the school of the Divinity; she sits in the valley of Humility and on the plain of Truth, and she rests on the mountain of Love. (Guarnieri, pp. 525–527; Doiron, p. 258).

Nine Points for Contemplatives

How, at the Request of Reason, Love Makes This Soul Known to Contemplatives, Explaining Nine Points Already Mentioned—Chapter XI

REASON: Now Love, in the name of contemplatives, of all those who desire to grow continuously in divine knowledge and who are and abide in desire for Love, I beg you, out of your courtesy, to explain the nine points of which you have already spoken. I mean those nine points possessed by the Soul pursuing *Fine Amour*, the Soul in whom Charity has fixed abode thanks to the annihilated life in which Pure Love allows the Soul to be abandoned.

LOVE: Name them then, Reason!

REASON: The first point of which you spoke, is that such a Soul cannot be found.

LOVE: That is true. I mean that this Soul knows only one thing within her: namely, the root of all her ills and the abundance of all her countless sins, without weight and without measure. But sin is nought and this Soul is quite crushed and terrified by her horrible faults that are less than nought; and by understanding this, she herself becomes less than nought as far as it depends on her. From this one may conclude that such a Soul cannot be found. For she is so annihilated by humility that, in her righteous judgment, if God should wish to take vengeance for the thousandth part of one single fault of hers, no creature who had sinned would ever deserve such great torments and such infinite confusion that she considers she merits. This humility, and none other, is true and perfect humility in the annihilated Soul.

LOVE: The second point is that this Soul is saved by faith without works.

REASON: Eh! In God's name, what do you mean by that?

LOVE: I mean that this annihilated Soul has within her such great knowledge, by virtue of faith, and that she is so occupied within herself sustaining what faith imparts to her of the power of the Father, the wisdom of the Son, and the goodness of the Holy Spirit, that nothing created can remain in her memory but passes swiftly away, because this other occupation has taken complete possession of her understanding. This Soul can no longer do works, and there is no doubt that she is amply excused and exonerated, without doing works, believing that God is good and incomprehensible. This Soul is saved by faith without works, for faith surpasses all works, as testified by Love Herself.

LOVE: The third point is that she is alone in Love.

REASON: In God's name, Lady Love, what does that mean?

LOVE: It means that this Soul finds neither comfort, nor affection, nor hope in any of the creatures God has made, neither in Heaven nor upon the earth, but only in God's goodness. Such a Soul neither begs nor asks anything of creatures. She is the phoenix, who is alone, for this Soul, feeding on herself, is alone in Love.

LOVE: The fourth point is that this Soul does nothing for God.

REASON: Hey! For God's sake, what are you saying?

LOVE: I mean that God has no use for what she does, and this Soul has no use for anything, except for what God does. She does not care about herself; let God care about her, He Who loves her more than she loves herself. This Soul has such great faith in God that she is not afraid of being poor, as her Beloved is so rich. In fact, faith teaches her that she will find God in the measure of her hopes and as, through her faith, she hopes that He is infinitely rich, she cannot be poor.

LOVE: The fifth point is that this Soul does not leave aside, for God, anything that she is able to do.

REASON: In god's name, Love, and what can this mean?

LOVE: It means she can do nothing other than the will of God, and so she cannot even wish anything else, and therefore she leaves aside no action, for God. In fact, she lets nothing enter her thoughts which would be against God and so she does not leave aside any of her actions, for God.

LOVE: The sixth point is that she can be taught nothing.

REASON: In God's name, that means?

LOVE: It means that this Soul is of such great constancy that if she had all the knowledge of all creatures who ever were, are, and shall be, this would seem nothing to her compared to the One she loves, Who was never known and never will be. This Soul loves better what is in God, which has never been given and never will be, than what she has and what she would have if she were to possess all the knowledge of all creatures who are and shall be.

SOUL: And this is nothing to what *is* really . . . but one can say nothing about it.

LOVE: The seventh point is that nothing can be taken away from her.

REASON: In God's name, Love, tell me the significance of that!

LOVE: The significance? But what could be taken away from her? There is no doubt nothing could be taken away from her, for if one should take from this Soul her honor, her riches, her friends, her heart, her body, and her very life, one would be taking nothing from her, if God still remains hers; and so it is clear that one can take nothing from her, no matter what effort he makes.

LOVE: The eighth point is that one can give her nothing.

REASON: For God's sake, Love, what is this, that one can give her nothing?

LOVE: What is this? But what could one give her? If she were given everything that ever was and ever shall be given, it would be nothing compared to what she loves and will love. . . . that is, God Himself.

SOUL: Lady Love loves and will love in me.

LOVE: . . . We shall say that God loves better the "more" of this Soul which is in Him than the "less" that she is by herself.

SOUL: There is no "less," there is only all; this I can tell you and this is the truth.

LOVE: I can say even more. If that Soul possessed all the knowledge, all the love and all the praise that ever were and ever will be given, of the Divine Trinity, this would still be nothing compared to what she loves, and will love; but she will never reach that love through knowledge.

SOUL: Oh, truly, Sweet Love, [by knowledge] I won't reach even the smallest point of my love, for there is no other God save He of Whom nothing can be known perfectly. In fact, He alone is my God, of Whom one can say not a single word and of Whom none of those in Paradise can reach one single point, no matter how much knowledge they have of Him. And in this "more" is contained the greatest mortification of love of my spirit, and in this lies all my soul's glory of love, an endless glory, like that of all those who ever understood this. This is a small point to listen to, compared to the greater of which nobody speaks! But I want to speak of it, even if I don't know what to say. And yet, Lady Love, my love is of such a quality that I prefer to hear you being spoken ill of, rather than not hear You being spoken of at all. And that, in fact, is what I do myself: I speak ill of You, for everything I say is nothing other than speaking ill of Your goodness. But what ill I say of You, You must forgive me for, God, he speaks well who speaks ill of You, as long as he always speaks of You, even if he never says anything of Your goodness. And I can tell you, the same applies to me: I never cease talking about You, whether in my questions or in my thoughts; nor would I cease listening, if anyone could tell me something about Your goodness. But the more I hear You spoken of, the more bewildered I am; indeed, it would be most uncouth on their part if men should think they have made me understand something about You when they talk about You. Those who believe this are deceived, for I am convinced that nothing at all can be said about You, but, please God, I myself shall never be deceived in this respect; and I never wish to listen to men telling lies about Your divine goodness. But I want to complete the task I have assumed: this book, of which Love is the mistress, Love who bids me bring to a conclusion all that I have undertaken.

For whenever, on my own, I question Love on something

concerning Her, then I am living a life of the spirit, in the shadow of the sun, where one can see the subtle images of the attractions of divine Love and of the divine generation.

But what am I saying? Even if I possessed all that has been said, it would certainly be nothing compared to what I love of Him and which He will give to nobody else but Himself and which He must withhold according to His divine righteousness. And so it is true when I say that men can give me nothing, whatever it may be. But this complaint which you hear me utter, Reason, is my all and my best, if one understands it well. Ah, how sweet it is to understand this! For the Love of God, understand it fully, for Paradise is nothing other than this very comprehension.

LOVE: The ninth point, Reason, is that this Soul has no will.

REASON: Eh, for God's sake, what are you saying? That this Soul has no will?

LOVE: Oh, most certainly she hasn't, for all this Soul wants and consents to is what God wants her to will, and she wants this in order to accomplish God's will and not at all her own will; and she cannot want this by herself but it is the will of God willing it in her; from which it results that this Soul has no will apart from God's will that makes her will all that she ought to will (Guarnieri, p.528; Doiron, pp.261–264).

The Soul Takes Leave of the Virtues

How the Soul Who Loves God, Living in the Peace of Charity, Takes Leave of the Virtues—Chapter VI

LOVE: The Soul who has this love can say that she has remained a long time and many a day in the service of the virtues.

SOUL: I confess to you, Lady Love, that was once so. But now things have changed: Your courtesy has delivered me from their bondage. That is why I am ready to tell them, to sing to them.

Virtues, I take leave of you for evermore,
I'll have a freer and happier heart;
Your service is too oppressive, this I well know,
Once I gave my heart to you, unconditionally.
You know that I had abandoned myself entirely to you;
I once was your slave, but now I am free of you.
I had given you my whole heart, of this there is no doubt,
And I lived a long time in great trouble,
Thus I suffered many a torment, bore many a pain.
It is a great wonder that I escaped alive;
But since it is so, all this no longer matters,
For I am severed from you.
For this I thank God on high: a good day it is for me.
I have left your dangers, the cause of many a woe.
Never was I free until separated from you;
I have left your dangers and now I dwell in peace.

(Guarnieri, p.525; Doiron, pp.254–255)

A Life Encumbered With Self

How Those Who Have Not Obeyed the Teachings of Perfection Remain Encumbered with Themselves until Death—Chapter LXXVII (end) and Chapter LXXVIII

LOVE: Now understand the secret meaning of this book, for a thing has value only insofar as we appreciate it and feel the need for it, and not otherwise. When I wished, when it was My good pleasure, and when I needed you (I say "needed" because I order you so), you have sent me away in the person of several of My messengers. Nobody knows this, except Myself alone. I sent you Thrones, to reprimand you and adorn you, Cherubim to enlighten you, and seraphim to enflame your hearts. By means of all these messengers I asked you to do My will, which they made known to you, as well as the estates in which I asked you to be, but you have never taken any notice. Seeing this, I left you to your own guidance to seek your salvation. But if you had obeyed, you would have been otherwise, as you yourself admit. Certainly, you will save yourself, by yourself, but it will be in a life encumbered with your own spirit, and never will it be entirely disencumbered. And this because you have not obeyed My messengers and the Virtues, when I so wished to enslave your body and free your spirit by means of these messengers. And it is also because you did not obey when I asked you to, through the subtle Virtues that I sent you, and through my angels by means of whom I followed you that I cannot give you by right the freedom that is Mine, for Justice cannot do that! But if you had obeyed, when I asked you to, the will of the Virtues that I sent you, and My messengers by means of whom I followed you, you would have had, by right, the freedom that is Mine.

Alas, Soul, how encumbered you are with yourself!

SOUL: Yes, my body is full of weakness and my soul full of fear. For often—whether I wish it or not—these two natures cause me a preoccupation that free [beings] have not, nor can have.

LOVE: Ah, weary Soul, how much trouble you have, and little profit. And all this is because you have not obeyed the teachings of perfection with which I have pursued you, to disencumber you in the flower of your youth. Nevertheless, you have never wished to change, never wished to do anything about it. On the contrary, you have always refused My requests that I made known to you through these noble messengers, as you have just heard. And people of this kind remain encumbered of themselves until the day of their death.

Ah, certainly, if they so wished, they could be delivered from this great servitude in which they remain and will continue to remain, with little gain. If they had so wished, they could have been delivered at very little cost. Yes, very little indeed, simply by surrendering themselves there, where I wanted them, when I showed them by the Virtues where their duty lay.

I say they would have been entirely free of both soul and body, if they had followed My advice by means of the

Virtues, obeying My will and doing what they had to do, so that I could dwell in them with My freedom. And because they have not done so, they have remained entirely in the state we have spoken of: that is, with themselves.[3] And those who are free and annihilated, adorned with delights, know this, for they are capable of seeing by themselves the servitude of these Souls. In fact, the true sun shines in their light and they see the motes within the sunbeam, thanks to the brightness of the sun and of the beam. And when this sun is within the soul, with these beams and this brightness, the body no longer feels weakness, the Soul no longer fears; for the true Sun of Justice never looked after or healed the soul without healing the body, when He performed His miracles on earth; and He still often does so, but to none of those who have not faith in these things.

Thus you can see and understand that whoever trusts in God is strong and great, entirely free and disencumbered of everything, for God sanctifies him.

I have said of those whom I pursued inwardly so that they should obey the perfection of the virtues and who have done nothing about it, that they shall remain encumbered of themselves until death. And I also say that if they worked every day [remaining] with themselves, to accomplish the perfection of the Apostles, by an effort of the will, they would in no way be disencumbered of themselves, either in the body or in the soul. Let no one expect this. No, and what is more, when this is not given either by interior force or pursuits, one cannot find it, and all that one does "with oneself" is to encumber everything with self. Let them know this, all those who undertake works "with themselves," without the ardor of inward ebullition (Guarnieri, pp.579–581; Doiron, pp.311–312).

Conclusion

To conclude this work we would like to call to mind the two essential themes that seem to be of particular interest for the modern reader. The first may be called "the lost story of feminine Christianity" and in actual fact the two Hadewijches, Beatrice of Nazareth and Marguerite Porete, were forgotten for centuries. The second of these themes, not unrelated to the first is, we might say, the alchemic operation by means of which our Beguines transmuted courtly love into a more precious essence, that of Eternal Love.

There is no doubt that there was a more or less conscious concealment of the works of our authors, as Hans Urs von Balthasar noted when speaking of Mechthild, ignored by theologians or, to put it mildly, underestimated by them for 700 years.

In our own times, the rediscovery of these mystics and the renewed interest manifested in their work seem to show that the moment has come for the reawakening of Sleeping Beauty. This long sleep is explained by reasons mentioned in our book, the chief ones being the widespread misogyny of the Middle Ages and the emphasis placed by the scholastics on intellect—symbolized by man—at the expense of imagination and the senses, considered as inferior powers—symbolized by woman.

It has been the happy lot of our times to rediscover what had been repressed or diminished: the creative and maternal art of our abbesses and Beguines whose writings are sometimes given the depreciative name of *Nonnenmystik*, i.e., nuns' mysticism. In their convents and Beguinages, they were able to preserve the most precious part of our mystical heritage, cast into oblivion by the scholastic theologians and logicians. With these women, we find the primacy of Love over intellect which marks the end of the Middle Ages and the beginning of modern times. But this primacy has often led to a certain voluntarism that is entirely alien to our Beguines, for whom will is impregnated with contemplation. In other words, with them, as with all other authentic contemplatives, what is essential is *to be passive* to God and not to be active in His regard. In this passivity lies the simplification of the soul who breaks free of the multiplicity of desires, no matter how holy or spiritual he or she may be, to be entirely united to God in the non-willing which is willing Him alone. This seems to us the most profound and perhaps least recognized characteristic of Western mysticism, such as it was transmitted from the time of the Greek Fathers to Teresa of Avila and John of the Cross. The latter, who sang of the encounter with God in the night of Love, put us on our guard against the illusion of "good" actions before the soul has been really transformed in God and receptive to Him. This tradition touches the human soul in her "essence," that is, in her most intimate bond with the Absolute. It was because he was able to express this that Eckhart has been recognized as a spiritual master by the Orientals. In fact, after asserting, in accordance with the Dominican tradition, that the name "man," which symbolizes intellect, is the noblest name for the soul, he does not hesitate to proclaim, most certainly under the influence of some of our mystics, that its noblest name is, in reality, that of "woman," because this name expresses receptivity towards God.

There is urgent necessity for our civilization to rediscover the importance and nobleness of non-willing which it has completely forgotten in its over-activism. Thus, together with the religious traditions which have preserved a deeper comprehension of Ultimate Reality, our world will be able to find once more an equilibrium, both spiritual and human. A return to the essential values symbolized by woman seems to be an indispensable condition for the survival of the world today, as had been prophesied by writers such as Berdiaev and Evdokimov.

We shall now give our attention to the second theme, that of courtly love and the manner in which it was transposed into the religious sphere by the Rheno-Flemish mystics. The texts translated in this book will have shown that their authors were, either in a broad or in a strict sense of the term, women troubadours, i.e., *trobairitz* of God. In fact, while the troubadours sang the praises of their ladies, women poets called *trobairitz* celebrated the virtues of their lovers. In our opinion, even Hildegard, who could have had no knowledge of courtly poetry, as it appeared only later in Germany with the *Minnesänger,* deserves this appellation in a broad sense, since she composed so many love poems to God. She deserves it in the original sense of the *langue d'oc* word "troubadour" or of "*trouvère*," the corresponding word in Northern French: he who *finds,* that is to say, invents. These two words denote poets and minstrels who, first in the courts of Provence, and later in those of Catalonia, of Northern France, Italy, and Germany, were not satisfied with merely reciting poems and songs and so actually created them. As for our Beguines they well deserve to be called troubadours or *trobairitz* of God, in the strict sense of the term. They have every right to be included in the tradition of courtly lyricism based on a new conception: the knight's "service of Love" to his lady.

Love has been called an invention of the twelfth century, for there is no doubt that courtly lyricism "invented" a more refined conception of love between the two sexes. A certain number of literary critics, in the wake of C. G. Jung, have held that the chivalrous ideal compensated for the contemptous and repressive attitude of the clerical world towards woman. Many authors have given their attention to this "invention of the twelfth century" in the hope of discovering its source: Arabian poetry, Christian idealism, or Cathar heresy? Diverse theories have been proposed, but none of them has explained in a satisfactory way the origin and development of this idealization of the lady.

"It is from you, Lady, that comes to me/ All the good that I say, or do," wrote the troubadour Arnaud de Mareuil. This quotation expresses the crystallization of a personal relationship which allows the lover to attain to a higher psychic and moral level and, in certain cases, even to Divine Love. It is not by mere chance that two out of three of the troubadours known to us ended their lives in monasteries.

It is in Dante's works that we find the most complete expression of this alchemy of Love. The poems of *Vita Nova*, written probably about 1292–1293, reflect in the most perfect manner the courtly ideal. They are already centered on Beatrice, the lady who raises Dante up and allows him to purify his sensuality at the cost of much suffering. After his philosophic study of Love contained in the *Convivio*, Dante, in his *Divine Comedy*, completed in 1319, reaches such a purification of his ideal that Beatrice has now the exclusive role of being the mediator of "that Love which moves the sun and the other stars."

Thus, first taking inspiration from courtly lyricism, Dante eventually succeeded in expressing the mysteries of Divine Love in a new manner which was destined to kindle the hearts and minds of the world at large. Similarly, our abbesses and Beguines, breaking free of scholastic and literary conventions, and using a vastly more comprehensible language, expressed these mysteries in a way that still stirs our spirits today.

Notes

Introduction

1. *Annales Palidenses, Monumenta Germaniae Historica, Scriptores*, t. 16, p. 90.
2. Lamprecht von Regensburg, *Tochter von Syon*, (Paderborn: 1880), V. 2838ff. The emphasis is ours.
3. *Ibid.* The term "old woman"—*vetula* in Latin—denoted complete ignorance: "I have never read any letter," are the words Villon puts into the mouth of his old mother. But we presume that the women of whom Lamprecht speaks were not necessarily all old.
4. *Ibid.*
5. *Daz ist Swester Katrei, Meister Ekehartes Tochter von Strasburg*, in F. Pfeiffer, *Deutsche Mystiker des 14ten Jahrhunderts*, t. 2, *Meister Eckhart* (Leipzig: 1984, reprint 1962), pp. 448–475.
6. In Hildegard, *Briefwechsel, Epistolae*, XVI, ed. Pitra, Analecta, t. 8, p.384; cf. p. 8.
7. U. Eco, *Il Nome della Rosa* (Milano: 1980), Eng. trans. *The Name of the Rose* (G. B: 1983).
8. J. Gerson, *De mystica theologia*, ed. A. Combes, (Padova: 1959).
9. H. Harph (Herp),*Theologia mystica*, collection of Herp's mystical works, (Cologne: 1538; reprint, Farnborough: 1966).
10. Cf. p. 209, note 34.
11. Hadewijch, *Lettres Spirituelles*; Beatrice, *Sept Degrés d'Amour*, French trans. from Mid. Dutch by J.-B. Porion, (Genève: 1972) *Introduction*, pp. 54–56.
12. Jacques de Vitry's most important testimony on the Beguine movement is to be found in his *Prologue* addressed to Foulques de Toulouse, AASS, Junii, t. 4, (Antwerpiae: 1707) 630–666. See also his Life of Marie d'Oignies: *Vita Mariae Oigniacensis*, ibid. 636–666.
13. Hildegard, *Ep. XLVII ad praelatos mogutinenses*, PL 197, 232–233.
14. See A. Schulze, *Predigten des H. Bernhard in altfranzösischer Übertragung*, einer Handschrift der königlichen Bibliothek zu Berlin herausgegeben, (Tübingen: 1894).

15. Hadewijch d'Anvers, *Poèmes des béguines traduits du moyen néerlandais par* J. B. Porion, (Paris: 1954, reprint 1985). *Introduction*, p. 26, note 27.

16. *Ibid.* p. 26.

17. *Ibid.* p. 11.

18. William was "the first to seek a Trinitarian foundation for the real and conscious unity of the spiritual man with his God." P. Verdeyen, "La théologie mystique de Guillaume de Saint-Thierry," *Ons Geestelijk Erf*, 51, 1977, chap. 2, p. 175. We acknowledge our debt to this remarkable study.

19. On this subject see W. R. Inge's excellent and still valid article: "The Doctrine of Deification," Appendix C, in *Christian Mysticism*, (London, 1899 etc.), pp. 356–372, which clearly shows the differences and even oppositions between the Greco-Oriental and Latin mentalities in this matter.

20. William of St. Thierry, *Epistola ad Fratres de Monte Dei*, PL 184, 307–354. "To be unable to will anything except what God wills—this is to be already what God is." *Epistola*, SC 223, pp. 348–350. Emphasis is ours.

21. Cf. Wm. of St. Thierry, *Adversus Abaelardum*, PL 180, 262D–263A.

22. Wm. of St. Thierry, *De natura et dignitate amoris*, PL 184, 379–408. See p. 127.

23. "You must cross over and overpass all the virtues; you must seize virtue only in that depth where it is one with the Divine Nature." Eckhart, *German Sermon* 16b. Cf. p. 110, 130, 196ff.

24. William of St. Thierry, *De contemplando Deo*, PL 184, 376D–377A.

25. Cf. p. 104. "And may He absorb you in Himself, in the depths of wisdom! There, in fact, He will teach you *what He is*, and how sweet it is when the loved one and the Beloved dwell in each other, and how they penetrate each other in such a way and neither can distinguish himself from the other. There is common and reciprocal fruition, mouth to mouth, heart to heart, body to body, and soul to soul; the same sweet *Divine Essence* flows through them both, flooding them, so that they are one single thing, one through the other and remain so *without difference*, forever." Hadewijch, *Letter IX*. Emphasis is ours.

26. Marguerite Porete, *Mirror*, chap. 113, ed. R. Guarnieri, p. 606.

27. Cf. Hadewijch, *Letter XVIII*, see p. 127. Cf. F. Brunner, "Le mysticisme de Maître Eckhart; Etude comparative," in the collection *Das "einig Ein." Studien zur Theorie und Sprache der deutschen Mystik*, ed. A. M. Haas and H. Stirnimann, (Freiburg, Scheiz: 1980), p. 68, and E. Zum Brunn, "Une source méconnue de l'ontologie eckhartienne," in the collection *Métaphysique, Histoire de la Philosophie*, (Neuchâtel: 1981), pp. 111–118.

28. Cf. p. 138.

29. F. Pfeiffer, *Deutsche Mystiker des 14ten Jahrhunderts*, t. 2, p. 520.
30. This seems a better translation than the term *lack* used by some scholars and translators, especially as it seems that Marguerite was conversant with the Flemish language and spirituality.
31. Cf. p. 212–213, note 26.
32. *Dreifaltigkeitslied*, ed. K. Bartsch, 1858. (Bartsch dates this anonymous *Trinitarian Hymn* as belonging to the second half of the thirteenth century, probably about the same time that Marguerite wrote her *Mirror*.)

> It is—but nobody knows what It is
> It is here, It is there
> It is far, It is nigh
> It is deep, It is high;
> It is such that
> It is neither this, nor that.
>
> It is light, It is brightness,
> It is very dark,
> It is nameless,
> It is unknown,
> Free of beginning and end,
> It is a calm place
> Flowing without essence.
> Who knows Its dwelling?
> Let him come out
> And describe Its form!
>
> Become like a child
> Become deaf, become blind!
> The something that you are
> Must become nothing;
> Every thing, every nothing
> Must be overpassed,
> Leave place, leave time,
> Leave also images.
> Go without a path
> Up the narrow hill;
> Thus you will reach the tracks of the desert.
>
> O my soul,
> Come out and enter God,
> Engulf all that is mine
> In the Nothingness of God,
> Sink into the fathomless waters!
> If I flee far from Thee,

Thou comest to me;
If I lose myself
I find Thee,
O super-essential Good!

Part I: Hildegard of Bingen

Introduction

1. The life of St. Hildegard was written by the monks Godfrey, prevost of the Rupertsberg, and by Dietrich of Echternach: *Vita sanctae Hildegardis*, PL 197, 91–130 Cit. *Vita*. This life contains several autobiographical passages which P. Dronke has inserted in his *Women Writers of the Middle Ages* (Cambridge: 1984), pp. 231–234, cit. *Women Writers*. Guibert of Gembloux began a *Life* of which a few fragments remain (ed. J. B. Pitra) *Analecta Sanctae Hildegardis opera spicilegio Solesmensi parata*, t. VIII (Monte Cassino: 1882), pp. 407–414, cit. *Analecta*. In German: A. Fuehrkoetter, *Das Leben der Heiligen Hildegard*, (Düsseldorf: 1968). In French: *Vie de sainte Hildegarde*, by the monks Théodore and Godefroid, (Paris: 1907).
2. *Vita*, I, II, 9–10, 97–98.
3. *Vita*, II, I, 20, 105. Cf. letter of Guibert of Gembloux to Bovon, a monk of Gembloux, *Analecta*, p. 406. Guibert relates that water was laid on in all the places where work was done.
4. M. Schrader, A. Fuehrkoetter, *Die Echtheit des Schrifttums der heiligen Hildegard* (Köln-Gratz: 1956), pp. 105–108.
5. *Vita*, I, I, 5, 94–95.
6. *Vita*, III, II, 47, 124, 48–51, 124–127. The rite contained in the Berlin fragment MS Lat. Qu. 674 has been translated and published by P. Dronke, "Problemata Hildegardiana," *Mittellateinisches Jahrbuch*, Bd 16, 1981, pp. 117–122, 127–129, cit. *Problemata*.
7. *Ep.* XLVIII, PL 197, 243–253.
8. *Ep.* X, *Analecta* pp. 348–351.
9. *Acta inquisitionis*, 6, PL 197, 135; *Ep.* XLVII, PL 197, 218C–221D; *Ep.* VIII, 159B–160D P. Dronke, *Women Writers*, pp. 196–199. Cf. *infra*, p. 23–27.
10. *Liber Divinorum Operum* (Cit.) LDO, vis. 10, 38, PL 197, 1037C.
11. *Vita*, III, II, 45, PL 197, 122.
12. *Vita*, I, I, 4, PL 197, 94; II, II, 21, 106.
13. *Vita*, I, II, 6, 8, 96–97.
14. Cf. n. 11; *infra*, p. 19–21.
15. Letters of warning to the Emperor Frederick, Barbarossa, after the schism: *Echtheit*, pp. 128, 129.
16. Letter to Richardis von Stade, *Echtheit*, p. 137. *Ep.* X (to Archbishop

Hartwig de Brême), PL 197, 161–163. Commentary in Dronke, *Women Writers*, pp. 154–159.

17. *Ep.* CXVI, PL 197, 336B–338C. P. Dronke, *Women Writers*, p. 165ff. We can notice the difference in tone of these two letters: Tengswich's is polite but critical, with references to the New Testament and the Fathers, while Hildegard's is like an apocalyptic flight above social contingencies. However, by a devious way of reasoning, she gets back to the Gospel, shifting the problem from the persons concerned to their works as an expression of the Divine Will.

18. *Vita* I, I, 2, PL 197, 93; *Ep.* II (to Guibert of Gembloux) *Analecta*, p. 333. Letter to St. Bernard of Clairvaux, *Echtheit*, pp. 104–105. Cf. *infra*, p. 22.

19. *Vita* II, I, 14, PL 197, 101.

20. On Guibert of Gembloux (1124/25–1213), M. Schrader, "Guibert de Gembloux," *Dictionnaire de spiritualité* t. 6 (1967), 1132–1135. Before becoming abbot in 1194, Guibert was a monk at the Benedictine monastery of Gembloux (in the Liège diocese) which was famous for its collection of books. He was an extremely cultured person. Hildegard's fame had reached both North and South Netherlands, as is proved by her correspondence with the Bishops of Utrecht and Liège. As he was anxious to know more about her, Guibert wrote to the abbess twice before he was able to meet her personally in the autumn of 1175. In 1177 he became her secretary as well as spiritual father to the Rupertsberg convent where he remained until 1180, after Hildegard's death. He was also abbot of Florennes from 1188 to 1194.

21. *Hildegardis Scivias*, ed. A. Fuehrkoetter, OSB; coll. A. Carlevaris, OSB, CC, Continuatio Mediaevalis, t. XLIII, (Turnhout: 1978), plate I. This edition presents the colored plates of MS 1 of the Hessische Landesbibliothek, Wiesbaden. Lost in 1945, this manuscript had previously been faithfully copied, together with the colored miniatures at the St. Hildegard Abbey at Eibingen between 1927 and 1933. It serves as a basis for all further reproductions. Cf. also *Wisse die Wege. Scivias*, trans. M. Boeckeler, (Salzburg: 1963). There exists, moreover, an illuminated manuscript of the *De operatione Dei* (Biblioteca Statale, Lucca, Cod. Lat. 1942), the images of which are reproduced in Hildegard von Bingen, *Welt und Mensch, Das Buch "De operatione Dei,"* trans. H. Schipperges, (Salzburg: 1965).

22. *Echtheit*, p. 184.

23. *Ep.* XVI, *Analecta*, p. 386, from Guibert to Hildegard: "The Apostle does not allow woman to teach in the Church but, when freed from this condition by the Holy Spirit and enlightened by His authority and wisdom, woman has understood in her heart and through her experience the words that are written: 'Happy are those whom you instruct and whom you teach by your law' (Ps. 93: 12)." On the

position of woman in the works of the philosophers and theologians: M. Th. d'Alverny, "Comment les théologiens et les philosophes voient la femme," *Cahiers de Civilisation médiévale*, t. 20, 1977, pp. 105–128; E. Goessmann, "Anthropologie und soziale Stellung der Frau nach Summen und Sentenzenkommentaren des Jahrhunderts," *Miscellanea Mediaevalia* 12 (Berlin: 1979), pp. 281–297.

24. P. Dronke, *Problemata*, pp. 107–117.

25. Cf. *Ep.* XIV, PL 197, 167–168; XLIII, 212–213; 1037–1054, CXXVIII, 353–355; 1037–1054.

26. H. Schipperges, "Einflüsse arabischer Medizin auf die Mikrocosmos-literatur des 12. Jahrhunderts," *Miscellanea Mediaevalia* 1, (Berlin: 1962).

27. P. Dinzelbacher, *Vision und Visionsliteratur im Mittelalter*, (Stuttgart: 1981), p. 29; A. Haas, "Traum und Traumvision in der deutschen Mystik." *Analecta cartusiana* 106, 1, (Salzburg: 1983), pp. 22–55, gives less emphasis to the differences between dream, ecstasy, and imaginary vision (pp. 31, 36; and, on Hildegard, p. 46, n. 122).

28. *Scivias*, Prologue (*Protestificatio*) CC 43, p. 4, l. 43ff.

29. *Vita* II, III, 35, 116. Hildegard expressed herself further on her visions in *Vita* II, I, 16, 102ff.; in *Liber vitae meritorum* (LVM), *Analecta*, pp. 7–8; *Liber divinorum operum* (LDO), PL 197, 741ff.

30. *De modo visionis suae, Analecta*, pp. 331–334; cf. *infra*, p. 22–23.

31. LVM, *Analecta*, p. 244.

32. This can be felt in the letters in which the visionary speaks as a seer: P. Dronke, *Problemata, Letter I*, pp. 129–130. On the function of symbols as a universal expression of faith, G. Dufour-Kowalska, *L'arbre de vie et la croix*, (Geneva: 1985), pp. 30–31.

33. For this work and the following ones, cf. *Bibliography*.

34. H. Schipperges, the German translator, opts for this interpretation rather than that of "Book of Life" with reference to the Apocalypse.

35. M. D. Chenu, *La théologie au douzième siècle*, Etudes de théologie médiévale XLV (Paris: 1957), ch. VIII, pp. 159–190.

36. Cf. n. 21. J. Schomer, *Die Illustrationen zu den Visionen der hl. Hildegard als künstlerische Neuschöpfung*, Diss. (Bonn: 1937).

37. LDO, Vis. 4, c. 105, PL 197, 888–889; Vis. 9, 7. For the explicit reference to Ex. 3:14: *Scivias*, I, Vis. 4, CC 43, p. 76, l. 524; P. Dronke, *Problemata*, p. 127 (Exorcism of Sigewize). In the letters, together with expressions such as the "living light," the "transparent source," and the "fire," which are a solemn introduction to Hildegard's words, the term *Who is* may also be used to emphasize a threat. (Cf. letter to the Emperor Frederick, *Analecta*, p. 561; to the abbot Ruthard, *Ep.* XXXI, PL 197, 195B; to the abbot of S. Anastase, *Ep.* XXXII, 196C; to the prior Friedrich, *Ep.* LXXXII, 304B.)

38. LDO, Vis. 10, 2, 998C.

39. LDO, Vis. 1, 7, 746AB.

40. LDO, Vis. 4, c. 105, 892A.
41. LDO, Vis. 4, c. 105, col. 896 D; *Scivias*, I, Vis, 6, 3, CM 43, p. 103.
42. LDO, Vis. 4, c. 104, 888C.
43. Vis. 8, c. 2, 979D.
44. LDO, Vis. 4, c. 57, 845–846.
45. LDO, Vis. 4, c. 98, 877ff.
46. *Vita* II, 35, 115.
47. LDO, Vis. 4, c. 100, 885B: "Man is the plenary work of God; it is through him that God is known and for him that God created all creatures."
48. LDO, Vis. 4, c. 100, 885C; Vis. 5, c. 43, 945C.
49. M. Th. d'Alverny, *Philosophes et théologiens*, pp. 107–115 and *passim*; E. Goessmann, "Das Menschenbild der Hildegard von Bingen und Elisabeth von Schönau vor dem Hintergrund der frühscholastischen Anthropologie," *Frauenmystik im Mittelalter*, hersg. von P. Dinzelbacher und D. R. Bauer (Stuttgart: 1985), 24–47.
50. *Carmina*, XI, *Analecta*, pp. 442–443. However, Eve is put on the same level as Mary: LDO, Vis. 7, c. 13, 974D: "Eve was not created from seed, but from the flesh of man, by the same force (*eadem vi*) by which God sent His Son into [the womb of] the Virgin, so that henceforth, there was no other woman similar to Eve, virgin and mother, or to Mary, mother and virgin."
51. *Causae et curae*, P. Dronke, *Women Writers*, pp. 245–46, 247–249.
52. *Causae et curae*, *Analecta*, pp. 447–478 (P. Dronke, *Women Writers*, p. 244).
53. LDO, Vis. 4, c. 100, 885; Vis. 1, c. 15, 749D.
54. LDO, Vis. 1, c. 17, 750D.
55. *Scivias* II, Vis. 3, c. 22, CM 43, p. 147, ll. 453–462.
56. *Scivias* III, Vis. 3, c. 8, pp. 380–381, l. 313.
57. *Scivias* III, Vis. 2, c. 20, p. 366, l. 586.
58. LVM, IV, XXIV, 32, *Analecta*, p. 158 (l. 7: Corr. *mendum* to *mundum*).
59. LVM XXVIII, 36, Analecta, pp. 160–161; LDO, Vis. 5, c. 43, 945C. Man has a greater strength (*Major fortitudo*), woman a softer energy (*mollior robur*).
60. LDO, Vis. 4, c. 51, 842D; Vis. 5, c. 23, 920D.
61. LDO, Vis. 4, 12, 812C.
62. LDO, Vis. 4, c. 13–14, 813; c. 29, 826D. Hildegard here employs the old topography according to which the North, a sunless world, was the sojourn of the dead and the dwelling of Hades. B. Maurmann, *Die Himmelsrichtungen im Weltbild des Mittelalters*, (München: 1976).
63. LDO, Vis. 5, c. 23, 920D.
64. LDO Vis. 5, c. 27, 925AB.
65. LVM, V, 5–7, *Analecta*, pp. 185–186.
66. LVM, III, 2, 3, *Analecta*, pp. 105–106, cf. *infra*, p. 33. M. Schmidt, " 'Discretio' bei Hildegard von Bingen als Bildungselement," *Spiritu-*

alität heute und gestern Analecta cartusiana, t. 35, 2, (Salzburg: 1984).

67. *Causae et curae,* ed. P. Kaiser (Leipzig: 1903), pp. 18, 19.

68. LVM, I, 7–8, *Analecta,* pp. 12–13.

69. Cf. n. 66.

70. *Scivias,* III, Vis. 12, c. 12, pp. 611–613.

71. LDO, III, Vis. 9, c. 14, 996–998.

72. LDO, Vis. 10, c. 37, 1036B.

Excerpts from Hildegard's Works

1. This letter, which makes reference to St. Bernard's preaching in favor of the Second Crusade (Vézelay, 1146), was written, therefore, after that date and before the Synod of Trier (Nov. 1147–Feb. 1148). Hildegard was at that time unknown and, still uncertain about her visionary charisma, she writes to a man who is famous throughout Christendom, a friend of Pope Eugene III. At that time Bernard had not yet read Hildegard's works; in his reply there is no doubt that he encourages her, but in rather vague and general terms. It is on the occasion of the Synod of Trier that he becomes acquainted with the Abbess' works and the report of the commission sent to the Disibodenberg Convent. He then asks the pope to confirm, by his authority, Hildegard's prophetic mission "so that the light shall not be smothered in silence" (Cf. *Vita* I, 5, 94–95).

   The text of Hildegard's letter and Bernard's reply is from the manuscript of Zwiefalten (Stuttgart, Landesbibliothek, Cod. theol. 4th, 141, fol. 31v–33r) which, with its awkward literary style, seems closer to the original than the transcription of the great Rupertsberg codex. Text of the letters: *Echtheit,* pp. 105–107. Commentary and discussion of their authenticity, pp. 104, 108–110.

2. The monk referred to is Volmar. Cf. *supra,* p. 7.

3. Sound is at the origin of creation. Cf. *supra,* p. 37.

4. *Echtheit,* p. 107.

5. On Guibert, cf. *supra,* n. 20, p. 185. The letter translated here is a reply to Guibert's urgent questions: Does Hildegard forget her visions after they have been written down? Does she dictate them in Latin or in German and then have them translated afterward? Is her knowledge of Holy Scripture the fruit of study or of the inspiration of the Holy Spirit? (*Analecta, Ep.* L, pp. 328–331).

   After general considerations on human life and on faith, Hildegard passes on to a description of her visions. She distinguishes the different degrees: "shadow of the living light" or "living light," the latter indicating a degree which is higher, but rarer. We can note the synthesis of audition and vision: the light speaks and words are like a shining flame.

In spite of her protests of weakness, in this letter Hildegard is much more self-confident about her vocation than she is in her letter to St. Bernard. Text of the letter: *Analecta, Ep.* II, pp. 331–334. On its date (1175), *Echtheit*, pp. 14–16. Commentary: Dronke, *Women Writers*, pp. 167–169.

6. This letter is addressed to the Chapter of Mainz Cathedral. At that time the Bishop, Christian von Buch, was in Rome, attending the Third Lateran Council (1179), and the canons, who were taking care of ordinary diocesan affairs, suddenly pronounced an interdict against the Rupertsberg Convent which had consented to bury a young nobleman who had once been excommunicated. However, before his death, he had been reconciled with the Church privately, but not publicly. Hildegard submitted to this interdict but refused to have the body exhumed. What is more, she had the grave mound flattened to prevent it being profaned, tracing a cross on the soil with her abbatial rod (*Acta inquisitionis*, ch. 6, PL 197, 135).

She was now writing to the Chapter to ask them to reconsider their decision. Having received a refusal, she was obliged to put her case before the Bishop himself; after receiving two letters, the latter was finally convinced of the justice of Hildegard's appeal.

This letter to the Chapter shows opposition between a juridical attitude (i.e., if it is not really certain that the young man did actually receive absolution, he cannot be allowed burial in consecrated ground—such was the position held by the canons), and the charismatic attitude of Hildegard. She accepts the sanction against her, thus submitting to the institutional Church but, out of respect for Christ's sacraments received by the deceased, she refuses to have his body exhumed. In her arguments she recalls the role of the sacraments, issuing from Christ for our sanctification, with a view of our union with God. These sacraments can be received with confidence if, *with a clear conscience* and *with pure intention*, one deems oneself to be free from grave sin.

The second theme is that of original *harmony*, which united the angelic choir and the voice of man. If the latter has lost the sweetness of his voice, prophets and musicians remind him of it by the variety of instruments and the sounds which they emit, as well as by the words of sacred songs. To forbid the nuns to sing the divine praise, the *opus Dei*, the principal office of the Benedictines, is to play into the hands of the Devil. Hence the reproach to the clergy.

The third theme is the *remembrance* of God underlying everywhere. Grave sin is forgetfulness of God the Creator. Faith and desire for God lie in a re-remembering (*recordatio*) which becomes a conscious re-insertion into God's plan. Hence the importance of the liturgical "memorial."

Text of letter: *Ep.* 47, PL 197, 218–221, with variants indicated by Dronke, *Women Writers*, pp. 314–315. Commentary *ibid.*, pp. 196–199. Cf. *Echtheit*, p. 158 and n. 13.

7. Cf. commentary on this psalm, *Scivias*, III, vis. 13, c. 16, 633ff.

8. Allusion to the "Guidonian hand" on which Guido d'Arezzo (c. 995– c. 1050) indicates the position of the notes.

9. *Scivias*, CM XLIII, pp. 124–132. This vision assembles the chief characteristics of Hildegard's art and thought. Its beauty is admirably reflected in the Rupertsberg illuminated manuscript: those luminous circles, at the center of which we behold the Son of God made man, contain all the symbolism of light created by the visionary: The bright silvery light represents God the Father, origin and source of all light; the rutilant fire, brilliant with its golden streaks, stands for the Holy Spirit, the fire of love, inflaming Father and Son; the blue of the central figure is less a color than a quality of divine light which is in some way concreted in human form through the Incarnation of the Son. These three lights form one single light, penetrating each other without merging, and this is Hildegard's way of expressing something about the mystery of the Trinity.

Time and time again, especially in her theological letters (Cf. *supra*, n. 25, p. 186), Hildegard returns to the mystery of one God in Three Persons. She thus echoes the controversy among the theologians of the day about the Trinitarian "names": fatherhood, filiation, procession, a controversy in which St. Bernard was opposed to Gilbert de le Porrée, the latter being condemned by the Council of Reims in 1148. (Cf. E. Gilson, *La théologie mystique de saint Bernard* (Paris: 1969), pp. 70–71). Like St. Bernard, Hildegard represents here the monastic theology rooted in the luminous obscurity of mystery, without attempting to clarify it, as opposed to the new scholastic theology which reasons about mystery, taking logical and grammatical categories as bases.

She approaches mystery by the method of analogies which describe "the greatest likeness in the greatest unlikeness," as it was defined in the thirteenth century. Hildegard insists more on the likeness: the structure of the elements is related in some way to the very Being of God, although there can be no identity with the Being of God, since God is incomprehensible. She takes three elements: mineral, fire, and air (specifically stone, flame, and speech). In stone which, according to her, (*Physica, III, De lapidibus*, PL 197, 1247–1250) resulted from the concretion of water when it contacted igneous mountains, there are, at the same time, fruitful humidity, fire, and mass solidity, qualities that are attributed to the Persons of the Trinity. As for flame, we find once more the three essential elements of the vision itself: light, viridity (*viriditas*) and ardor. The last analogy splits up speech into sound, the original power: word, which gives an intelligible form to the primordial sound, and breath, which propagates sound and word.

Finally the vision ends, as always, with an appeal to man to remember God and to seek to reach the plenitude of his humanity by means of the virtues.

A century later, Dante takes up this vision again in the last canto of his *Paradise* and it is through Hildegard's eyes that he contemplates the mystery of the Trinity in Unity (*Commedia*, III, *Paradiso*, cant. XXXIII, v. 115–137, Trans. H. F. Cary, Everyman's Library).

> In the deep and clear subsistence
> Of the lofty light,
> It seemed to me I saw
> Three orbs of triple hue
> And joined in one.
>
> ....
>
> And therein, I thought,
> In its own hue,
> I beheld our image painted
> And thereon I fixed my gaze.

10. *Causae et Curae*, 136–138, *Analecta*, pp. 477–478. Cf. P. Dronke, *Women Writers*, p. 244; comment. *ibid*, p. 176.

    In an archetypical manner, Hildegard here describes the union of man and woman. But even if carnal love, very frankly presented in the last image, changed its nature after the transgression, she still insists upon the beauty and fecundity of the man–woman encounter, woman being the earth that receives the germs of life coming from man's ardor.

11. CM 43, p. 32.

12. *LVM*, III, I, II, *Analecta*, 105–106.

13. *Scivias* III, vis. 12, c. 12, CM 43A, pp. 611–613.

14. *Scivias* III, vis. 13, c. 10, 11, 12, CM 43A, pp. 630–631.

15. The "bent" man is he who inclines himself towards the earth instead of straightening up towards Heaven. Cf. St. Bernard, *Sermones super Cantica Canticorum*. S. 24, 6–7.

16. *Scivias* III, vis. 13, c. 7, CM 43, p. 620. *Viriditas*, a notion proper to Hildegard, is a germinative, creative force, which is to be found at all levels of divine and terrestrial life. It is a radiating splendor of God and qualifies the work of the Word and of the Holy Spirit whose joint action sustains creatures in Being. While representing fecundity of the earth, viridity also expresses that of the soul which animates the body, nourishes the virtues, each of which is accompanied by its own particular viridity.

Part II: Mechthild of Magdeburg

Introduction

1. "It has always been asserted that Mechthild belonged to the nobility. In fact, in numerous passages of her book, there are allusions to the comfortable life she led in her youth and the riches of this world which would have been hers if she had not sacrificed all for God. She complains to Love for having taken from her the world and worldly honors and riches (I, 1). She speaks of noble women and their godlessness in such violent terms that one wonders whether this indignation did not perhaps correspond to facts that she herself had observed (V, 34. Cf. III, 21). On the other hand, from the information we have about Baldwin, Mechthild's brother, we learn that he, and presumably his sister too, had been brought up in all good customs and virtues. Most critics have understood this as a proof of their nobility. Moreover, Mechthild's comparisons and symbols, inspired by chivalry and courtly poetry, have been used as arguments in favor of her noble origin. However, we do not consider the question solved, and we remain only half convinced by all the pretexts brought forward. It is fairly obvious that Mechthild was of a well-to-do family, but we do not think it has been sufficiently proved that she belonged to the nobility, as is endlessly repeated in dictionaries and in prefaces introducing excerpts from her book. Against this widespread opinion, we have only one argument, but it seems to us of considerable weight: we refer to the silence of her first editors and of those who knew her. In fact, when a woman of religion has noble origins, her biographer never fails to tell us so. . . ." J. Ancelet-Hustache, *Mechthilde de Magdebourg: Etude de Psychologie*, (Paris: 1926), p. 52.

2. The texts we translate here are those of P. G. Morel's edition of Manuscript E of Einsiedeln: *Offenbarungen der Schwester Mechthild von Magdeburg oder Das Fliessende Licht der Gottheit, edited according to the only existing manuscript by P. Gall Morel*, (Regensburg: 1869), re-ed. (Darmstadt: 1980). As this edition contained errors, it is useful to refer to the Latin version, given in Tome II of *Revelationes Gertrudianae et Mechthildianae*, by the Benedictines of Solesmes, based on the two Latin manuscripts, A VIII 6 and B IX 11 of the University Library of Bâle, ed. L. Paquelin, (Poitiers-Paris: 1877). We have also used the complete translation in modern German by Margot Schmidt who, apart from the manuscripts already mentioned, has also utilized the 1929 edition by W. Schleussner of a fragment of Codex W I, 110 of Würzbourg. This fragment, containing more than a third of the work, does not come from E, but from a previous source of Alemanic form, like the shorter fragments of Stuttgart and Coblenz. Cf. M. Schmidt,

Mechthild von Magdeburg, Das fliessende Licht der Gottheit, introduced by M. Schmidt, with a study by H. U. von Balthasar, (Einsiedeln: 1955). The references to Mechthild's work given in the notes, or in parentheses in our text, indicate the parts, or books, in Roman numerals, the chapters in Arabic numbers.

3. "What is written in this book has sprung from the Living Deity into the heart of Sister Mechthild and is related here in an entirely faithful manner because it has been given to us by her very heart [and] by God and by her own hand. Deo gratias" (VI, 43). These lines were certainly written by Henry of Halle whose edition ends with this last text of Book VI.

4. Cf. study mentioned, note 2, by H. U. von Balthasar, "Mechthilds kirchlicher Auftrag," pp. 19–45, which we shall cite simply by the author's name.

5. Cf. p. 194.

6. Balthasar, pp. 19–21. She died about 1294.

7. P. Strauch, *Margaretha Ebner und Heinrich von Nördlingen: A Contribution to the History of German Mysticism*, (Freiburg in Brisgau und Tübingen: 1882). Letter 43, pp. 246–247. Cf. B. Gorceix, *Amis de Dieu en Allemagne au temps de Maître Eckhart* (Paris: 1984), p. 78ff.

8. Cf. W. Preger, *Geschichte der deutschen Mystik im Mittelalter nach den Quellen untersucht und dargestellt*. First part: *Geschichte der deutschen Mystik bis zum Tode Meister Eckharts*, (Leipzig: 1874) pp. 70–71, 91–112. J. Ancelet-Hustache, *Mechthilde* p. 3ff. gives the essentials of Preger's arguments.

9. A. Haas, "Mechthild von Magdeburg, Dichtung und Mystik" in *Sermo mysticus, Studien zur Theologie und Sprache der deutschen Mystik* (Freiburg, Switzerland: 1979), p. 71. Cf. also the fine study of Mechthild's language in H. Stierling, *Studien zu Mechthild von Magdeburg* (Nürnberg: 1907), pp. 27ff. The author shows that the courtly elements she employs are not merely superficial additions, but give force and realism to her mystical language. The images of chivalry, instead of being irritating allegories (as is often the case), give a clear intuition of the religious or moral reality—and this is a sign of consummate art.

10. Balthasar, pp. 22–23.

11. Balthasar, p. 24.

12. A. Haas, *Sermo mysticus*, p. 77.

13. Balthasar, pp. 32–33.

14. Balthasar, pp. 34–35.

15. Balthasar, p. 37.

16. Dante, *Purgatory*, XXVIII, 121–133; XXXI, 94–105.

17. J. Ancelet-Hustache, *Mechthilde*, p. 369. Cf. *Purgatory*, XXVIII, 37–47 (Trans. D.L. Sayers, *Comedy of Dante Alighieri the Florentine*. Penguin Books, 1955)

And there appeared to me

....

A lady all alone who wandered there
Singing and plucking
Flower on Flowerlet gay
With which her path was
Painted everywhere.
'Fair lady' that in love's warm ray
Dost sun theyself, if looks
That wont to be the index of the heart
Mean what they say,
Advance, said I. . . .

18. "It is not surprising that Dietrich, Mechthild's compatriot, since he was born near Iena and belonged to the Dominican convent of Erfurt, knew about her revelations; but the holiness of our mystic must have been very renowned for Dietrich to have spoken of her in a document of such importance." J. Ancelet-Hustache, *Mechthilde*, pp. 362–363. Cf. H. Stierling, *Studien zu Mechthild von Magdeburg*, pp. 5–15. (Let us recall the fact that it was due to Mechthild that her younger brother, Baldwin, entered the Dominican Order; he became sub-prior of the convent of Halle.)

19. "It is with deep emotion that we have noted that such a reliable critic as Alfonso Bertoldi . . . says that the source of the beautiful verses introducing the passage in which Dante celebrates St. Dominic is to be found in a few lines of Dietrich of Apolda; but Bertoldi is unaware that Dietrich borrowed these lines from the text of Mechthild of Magdeburg, omitting *only one word*!" J. Ancelet-Hustache, *Mechthilde*, p. 365. The three texts compared are: *Revelationes Gertrudianae et Mechtildianae*, t. 2, *Sororis Mechtildis . . . Lux Divinitatis*, p. 493; Dietrich of Apolda, *Life of St. Dominic*, AA.SS. August, t. 1, p. 627; and Dante, *Paradise*, XII, 37–45.

20. J. Ancelet-Hustache, *Mechthilde*, pp. 361–362. See her indications on Dante's critics for information about Matelda.

21. J. Ancelet-Hustache, *Mechthilde*, pp. 285–292. Cf. text of Mechthild, IV, 27: *Of the End of the Order of Preachers, of the AntiChrist, of Elias and Enoch.*

22. "Then God taught me how Christians should behave towards Jews. They must pay them no honor. They must not live with them, or pass the night with them. They must buy from them and sell to them without indulging in friendly company with them and without false cupidity" (IV,11). For the rest, as was customary in the Middle Ages, Mechthild sees both "pagans" and Jews in Hell, even if not as low

down as bad Christians who have had greater chances of reaching truth (III, 21). She foresees during the last days many conversions of "pagans" and Jews, a fact that will irritate the Antichrist considerably (IV, 27). We read in the Annals of Magdeburg, *Geschichte der Stadt Magdeburg*, I, pp. 102–104, that the Archbishop Ruprecht, on the day of the Feast of the Tabernacles, in 1261, had the richer Jews imprisoned, gave orders that their houses should be plundered and that they should be freed only on payment of a high ransom. The same thing happened at Halle, although here the inhabitants sided with the Jews, but in vain.

23. Cf. W. Schulz, *Der Gott der neuzeitlichen Metaphysik*, (Pfullingen: 1957.)
24. "There are passages in which Mechthild sings such high praises of her sex that they can be understood only in relation to the chivalrous cult of woman: the highest reward that human beings can ever obtain is attributed to the virgins who will be above the angels, the martyrs, and the Preachers." In fact, their place will be in the tenth choir, from which height Lucifer fell and in this degree of glory they will have only one masculine companion, John the Baptist (III, 1). This subversion of the traditional hierarchy of the sexes even in celestial beatitude seems rather to shock the above-quoted critic, H. Stierling, *Studien zu Mechthild von Magdeburg*, p. 28, as also does the description of the crowning of the virgins in Paradise: We see Christ standing up when they approach, like a knight, and "He crowns them standing up, as an imperial prince would do" (IV, 24).

Excerpts from Mechthild of Magdeburg's "The Flowing Light of the Godhead"

1. Cf. Song of Songs, 1:13: "My beloved is to me a bouquet of myrrh: he shall abide between my breasts."
2. We give here only an extract of the dialogue between God and the Soul, and between the Soul and the senses.
3. *nihtes niht*: absolutely nothing, that is, without any intermediary between God and the Soul.
4. Here we recognize the theme of the shedding or the overpassing of the [exterior] virtues to reach that which constitutes in a certain way the nature or the essence of the Soul: the love or desire for God.
5. Cf. n. 3; in other words, no intermediary between you and Me.
6. In their bodies, that is, still living on this earth and therefore still having a possibility of saving themselves.

Part III: Beatrice of Nazareth

Introduction

1. L. Reypens, ed., *Vita Beatricis, De autobiografie van de Z. Beatrijs van Tienen, Cist. Ord., 1200–1268*, (Antwerp: 1964). (Cit. *Vita*; the numerals in parentheses in the text refer to this work). On the manuscript tradition: *Vita*, pp. 17–25, 26–40; *Prologus*, pp. 13–14. The author (par. 1, p. 13) dedicates his work to the Prioress of Nazareth and her convent, considering himself as "brother and companion in God's service."

2. *Vita*, III, par. 274, p. 185. The author insists that his work is truthful, for could Beatrice have said about herself "things either false or invented?" (I, par. 5, p. 14).

3. In particular, the foundation documents connected with the activity of her father (*Vita, pp. 47–56*). On Cistercian convents in Brabant, E. Brouette, *Monasticon belge*, t. 4, *Brabant*, fasc. 2, (Liège: 1968). On Beatrice's father: *Vita*, pars. 8–15, pp. 17–21; *Bijlage* I, 3, pp. 193–196; *Bijlage* XI, pp. 260–262.

4. *Vita* I, par. 20, pp. 24–25. As was often the case, community life among these Beguines was previous to their establishment in a Beguinage (*curtis beghinarum*), which took place in 1242.

5. *Vita* I, pars. 30–40, pp. 30–35. The biographer draws attention to the fact that, in spite of her infected wounds, which barely allowed her to stand on her feet, she very rarely missed school. In fact, she managed to attend classes either by dragging herself along or else being led by other pupils "so as not to let any of her time pass without the viaticum of [sacred] knowledge."

6. On La Ramée, at Jauchelette, near Nivelles, cf. *Vita*, pp. 192–193. On Ida de Nivelles (circa 1199–1231), C. Henriquez, *Quinque prudentes virgines* (Antwerp: 1630), pp. 199–297. R. de Gank, "Chronological Data in the Lives of Ida de Nivelles and Beatrice de Nazareth," *Ons Geestelijk Erf*, 57, 1983, pp. 14–29.

7. Described as "indissoluble sentiment of love," indestructible bond, the feeling of spiritual friendship is a particular application of the unity of heart and spirit, a basis of the apostolic life (Acts, 4:32). The cult of such friendships forms a link between the ecstatic feminine movement of the thirteenth century and the Cistercian spirituality of the twelfth which fostered a veritable humanism. Cf. Aelred de Rievaulx, *De spirituali amicitia, Opera omnia*, ed. A. Hoste, C. H. Talbot (Turnhout: 1971), t. 1, pp. 285–350.

8. *Vita* I, par. 67, p. 54. So as not to seem holy, Beatrice had given up many of her habitual prayers and spiritual exercises. The result was an extreme "torpor" and Ida strongly advised her, in this trouble, to have recourse more frequently to the life-giving effects of the Eucha-

rist. On Ida's death, see *Vita* III, pars. 188–189, pp. 123–124. The life of Ida contains the account of a vision which she is said to have had at the same time as Beatrice. It is asserted that, on this occasion, they felt the love of the Virgin for the Trinity and were encompassed in this love. (*Vita, Bijlage* VI, pp. 218–220).

9. *Vita* III pars. 228–232, pp. 147–150. Before establishing themselves in the new convent, Beatrice and her sisters spent six months copying the liturgical books necessary for the community's divine office.

10. *Vita* III, par. 185, p. 122; pars. 219–221, pp. 141–143. This desire goes as far as frenzy, rendered by a whole series of expressions: delirium, paralyzing passion, etc. There is mention of inundation, ebullition, tornado. But, paradoxically, instead of being crushed by this host of emotions, her spirit rises out of it all "purer and stronger."

11. Richard of Saint Victor, *Quattuor gradibus violentae caritatis* ed. G. Dumeige (Paris: 1955), pp. 88–200. G. Dumeige, *Richard de Saint-Victor et l'idée chrétienne de l'amour* (Paris: 1952), pp. 117–122. Richard considers this mad desire, this insatiable love for God, to be "sane and saintly folly," in line with God's wisdom in accordance with 1 Cor. 1:25.

12. In certain convents, sisters who were unable to control themselves after Holy Communion were forbidden henceforth to partake of the Divine Repast.

13. *Vita* II, par. 120, p. 86. In the spiritual convent (II, par. 112) the abbess represents reason and is the source of discernment; the prioress is wisdom. Discernment is obtained by means of research (*inquisitio*), by exploration, and by a critical, purifying examination (*circumspectio, perlustratio*). Cf. St. Bernard, *De gradibus humilitatis*, III, 6 (*Opera*, t. 3, p. 20); William of St. Thierry, *Lettre aux Frères du Mont-Dieu*, ed. J. M. Dechanet, SC 223 (Paris: 1975), pars. 228–229, pp. 326–328.

14. "The two cells of her heart," "The five mirrors of her heart," "The spiritual monastery" (where each office is represented by a virtue), *Vita* II, pars. 101–117, pp. 76–84.

15. *Vita* II, par. 123, p. 88; III, par. 197, p. 129; par. 236, p. 152. This doctrine of the image and likeness was developed by the Cistercian School: St. Bernard, *De gratia et libero arbitrio* (*Of Grace and Free Will*), IX, 28, *Opera*, t. 3, p. 185; *Super Cantica Canticorum* (*On the Song of Songs*), S. 81, *Opera* t. 2, pp. 287–291; S. 82, pp. 292–298; William of St. Thierry, *De la nature et de la dignité de l'amour*, ed. M. M. Davy, (Paris: 1953), par. 5, p. 75; *Exposé sur le Cantique des Cantiques*, ed. J. M. Dechanet, SC 82 (Paris: 1962), par. 1, p. 71; pars. 88–89, pp. 208–210; E. Gilson, *La théologie mystique de saint Bernard* (Paris: 1969), p. 67ff. R. Javelet, *Image et ressemblance au 12ème siècle*, 2 vols. (Paris: 1967), t. 1, ch. VI–VII, pp. 169–297.

16. *Vita* II, par. 166. pp. 110–111. The impression of the divine seal on

the wax of the soul, now become soft, (Cf. Ps. 21:5) renders it conformable to the divine image and likeness.

17. Cf. William of St. Thierry, *De la nature et de la dignité de l'amour*, par. 5, pp. 131–132.

18. The sweetness of these abundant consolations leads to a spiritual inebriety well known to mystics (ref. Eph. 5:18).

19. Editions: *Beatrijs van Nazareth, Seven manieren van minne*, critisch uitgegeven door L. Reypens en J. Van Mierlo (Leuvense Studieën en Tekstuitgaven), (Leuven: 1926) (cit. *Seven manieren*). *Beatrijs van Nazareth, Van seven manieren van heiliger minnen*, uitgegeven naar het Brusselse handschrift . . . door H. W. J. Vekeman en J. Th. M. Tersteeg (Zutphen: 1971). French translations: Dom J. Kerssemakers, *Une mystique des Pays-Bas au 13ème siècle, Béatrix de Nazareth* (1205–1268), *Vie spirituelle*, Supplément, March 1929, pp. 316–332; Béatrice de Nazareth, *Sept degrés d'amour*, translated from Middle Dutch by J. B. Porion (Geneva: 1972).

20. J. H. Kern, *De Limburgsche Sermoenen* (Leiden: 1895), pp. 570–582. The Limbourg Sermons (about 1331) are a collection of sermons and spiritual texts. They contain Hadewijch's 10th *Letter*.

21. L. Reypens, *Vita*, Bijlage IX, "De 'Seven manieren van minne' geinterpoleerd" pp. 237–256. P. Wackers, "Het interpolatie probleem in de 'Seven manieren van minne' van Beatrijs van Nazareth" ("The Problem of Interpolation in the 'Seven Manners of Love' of B. of N."), *Ons Geestelijk Erf*, 45, 1971, pp. 215–230.

22. H. Vekeman, "Vita Beatricis en 'Seven manieren van minnen': Een vergelijkende studie" ("a comparative study"), *Ons Geestelijk Erf*, 46, 1972, pp. 3–54. Although the biographer confines the life and works of Beatrice within the frame of the Cistercian theology of love, we can perceive something else—the outlines of a more speculative trend which would develop later on with Hadewijch.

23. *Seven manieren*, I, p. 3, ll. 3–5: "On the return of human nature and, thanks to it, the return of all creatures, within the eternal ideas from which it proceeded, on its return and its restitution to its original dignity . . . " Cf. J. Scotus Erigena, *De divisione naturae* (*The Division of Nature*), PL 122,862A, cited by J. B. Porion. *Hadewijch/Beatrice*, Annex B, p. 290. For William of St. Thierry and St. Bernard, the return is linked to the theory of the image (Cf. n. 15) and of love. St. Bernard, *On the Song of Songs*, S. 83, 4 (*Opera*, t. 2, p. 299): "What a great thing love is, provided it comes back to its principle, returns to its origin and, flowing back towards its source, receives from it all that is necessary to proceed uninterruptedly."

24. *Seven manieren*, II, p. 7, ll. 4–6: "sonder enich waeromme." The Latin source of this expression is thought by J. B. Porion to be the beginning of St. Bernard's treatise *De diligendo Deo*: "The reason why one must

love God is God Himself" (*Opera*, t. 3, *De diligendo Deo*, I, 1, p. 119).
J. B. Porion, *Hadewijch d'Anvers* (Paris: 1954), p. 147, n. 6.

25. St. Bernard, *De diligendo Deo* I; 1: "The measure of this love, it is to love without measure" (*Opera*, t. 3, p. 119).

26. *Seven manieren*, III, p. 11, ll. 24–25. With the adjective *onwesenlec* ("which does not belong to one's essential being"), Beatrice emphasizes the difference between her ideal being in God and the human condition. This notion of "lack" is to be found throughout Rheno-Flemish mysticism. Cf. J. B. Porion, *Hadewijch d'Anvers*, pp. 135–136. It appears on several occasions in St. Bernard's work, *On the Song of Songs*, S. 9,2 (*Opera*, t. 1, p. 43): "I have received more than I deserved, but much less than I desired." This theme is linked to that of languor—found, for example, in William of St. Thierry. *Exposé sur le Cantique des Cantiques*, ed. J. M. Dechanet, M. Dumontier (Paris: 1962), par. 120, pp. 258–260. This lack is the very motive force of spiritual progress; it ceaselessly urges the creature beyond himself. Cf. *La contemplation de Dieu*, ed. J. Hourlier, SC 61 bis (Paris: 1968), par. 6, p. 76.

27. *Seven manieren*, IV, p. 15, l. 25. It has been thought that this expression was created by Beatrice; however, it is to be found in St. Bernard's *On the Song of Songs*, S. 83, 5 (*Opera*, t. 2, p. 301): "Pure love, it is that of the Bride, because the Bride is all love."

28. *Seven manieren*, V, p. 23, ll. 77–80.

29. *Seven manieren*, VI, p. 24, ll. 20–24. Equality (*effenheit*) in the sense of a resemblance.

30. *Seven manieren*, p. 25, ll. 35–42. To describe the same state, the biographer uses also traditional images, such as the drop of water lost in the ocean, the liquefying fire of love. (*Vita*, par. 206, p. 133). This sovereign liberty is the fruit of the unity of the Divine Spirit and of human will, in accordance with 1 Cor. 6:17. E. Gilson, *Théologie mystique*, pp. 148–152. William of St. Thierry, *Lettre aux frères du Mont-Dieu*, ed. J. Dechanet, SC 223 (Paris: 1975), par. 275, pp. 364–367: "The perfection and true wisdom of man is when he embraces all the virtues, when he clasps them to himself, not as elements borrowed from an outward source, but as if sown within him by nature, according to that resemblance to God Who is Himself all that He is. Then just as God is That which is, so, as regards the good of virtue, the disposition of the good will in the good spirit is so much consolidated that, thanks to its ardent adhesion to unchangeable good, it seems that this will can in no way turn away from Him Who is."

31. *Seven manieren*, VII, p. 31, l. 36; p. 36, ll. 140–141. Here we can notice the use of the superlative. In the Sixth Manner, Beatrice employed comparatives: "a nearer being" (*naerren wesene*); "a higher knowledge" (*in hogeren bekinne*).

32. "Common" love refers to those who can love beings and things only in the love of God. St. Bernard, *De diligendo Deo*, IX, 26 (*Opera*, t. 3, p. 141). William of St. Thierry, *Letter aux frères du Mont-Dieu*, par. 263, p. 354, explicitly compares this love with intra-Trinitarian relationships. This notion will be developed with great theological accuracy by Ruysbroeck. B. Fraling, *Mystik und Geschichte. Das "ghemeyne leven" in der Lehre des Jan van Ruysbroeck* (Regensburg: 1974).

Excerpts from Beatrice of Nazareth's "Vita" and "The Seven Manners"

1. This Trinitarian vision goes back to a traditional Scriptural theme, that of the source of life and the rivers which flow from it (Cf. Gen. 2:10–14; Ps. 35:9–10; John 4:14; Rev. 22:1). Eccles. 24:32–47 is particularly interesting in this regard, since it compares Wisdom to the river which irrigates the land as far as the sea, but also leads up to Paradise. (v. 41), associating the two movements of exit and return. Cf. G. de Champeaux, Dom S. Sterckx, *Introduction au monde des symboles*, (La Pierre-qui-Vive: 1980), pp. 213–214. The Fathers of the Church have applied these texts to Christ. A. Thomas, "Brunnen," *Lexikon der christlichen Ikonographie*, I (1968), 330–336.
2. *Vita*, III, pars. 213–218, pp. 137–140.
3. The *acies oculi* is the point where the whole visual force of the eye is concentrated. In the same way, in the soul, the *acies mentis* is the point towards which all powers of the soul converge, the organ through which the soul is capable of uniting with God. It is given various names by different authors: the summit of the soul, the fine point, the spark, or, in a more scholastic way, synderesis.
4. Cf. Mt. 13:47. For the image of the net of charity, cf. St. Augustine, *In Ps.* 49:9 (CC 38, pp. 583–584). St. Bernard, *De diligendo Deo*, XV, 40, (*Opera*, t. 3, p. 153).
5. *Vita*, III, pars. 234–237, pp. 151–152.
6. This vision is the experiential outcome of Beatrice's reflection on an important text of St. Bernard concerning "the love of self for the love of Christ." Since she is perfectly detached, she now dominates the world, represented by a wheel, and she at last succeeds in seeing the world, and also herself in the perspective of divine Love. We have not found this precise text in St. Bernard's works. However, the thought it contains is certainly his: When man has found once more the divine likeness, love of self is not destroyed but is simply assimilated in his love for God. We love ourselves as God loves us and for His sake. *De diligendo Deo*, XII, 39 (*Opera*, t. 3, pp. 152–153). E. Gilson, *Théologie mystique*, pp. 139–140.
7. Trans. from edition of L. Reypens and J. Van Mierlo.

8. *Seven manieren*, pp. 28–29. Cf. *supra*, p. 79.
9. St. Augustine, *Confessions* II, X, 18, on Mt. 25:21.

Part IV: Hadewijch of Antwerp

Introduction

1. Jan van Leeuwen, *VII tekene der sonne* (*The Seven Signs of the Zodiac*) cited by J. Van Mierlo, *De Visioenen van Hadewijch*, II (Leuven: 1925), p. 137: "Thus also speaks a saintly and glorious woman of the name of Hadewijch, a true 'mistress' [of spirituality]. For the books of Hadewijch are certainly good and just, born of God and revealed by Him. . . . But Hadewijch's teachings are not equally profitable to all, for there are many who cannot understand them: those whose inner eyes are too dimmed, not yet opened by the love that adheres to God in the nakedness and silence of fruition."
2. In the *Revue Encyclopédique* of Paris, July 1897, Maeterlinck wrote an article on Flemish mysticism, ten years after publishing his translation of Ruysbroeck's *Spiritual Espousals*. Referring to Hadewijch, he wrote: "Among the mystical spirits of that age, she is one of the most curious and the most powerful." Cited by R. Pouillart, "Maurice Maeterlinck and Flemish Mysticism. Complementary Notes," Dr. L. Reypens-Album, *Studien en Tekstuitgaven van Ons Geestelijk Erf*, 16 (Antwerp: 1964) pp. 281–302.
3. There are three manuscripts in Middle Dutch of the 14th century: Brussels, Bibl. roy. cod. 2879–80; cod. 2877–78; Ghent, Bibl. univ. cod. 941 (the earliest one). These three manuscripts contain Hadewijch's four works. An early 16th century manuscript (Ruysbroeck-Genootschap, Antwerp, cod. 385) contains almost all the poems, but not the letters. Critical editions: J. Van Mierlo (ed.), *Visioenen* I (text); II (Introduction), (Leuven: 1924–25), (cited *Visioenen*); *Strofische Gedichten* I (text); II (Introduction), (Leuven: 1924) (cited SG); *Brieven* I (text); II (Introduction) 1947, (cited L.); *Mengeldichten*, (Leuven: 1952), (cited MD).
4. Complete bibliography: F. Willaert, in G. Jaron Lewis *Bibliographie zur deutschen mittelalterlichen Frauenmystik* (Bibl. zur deutschen Literatur des Mittelalters 9, Berlin: 1984).
5. *The List of the Perfect*, edited after *Vision XIV*. It contains the names of 85 persons, some dead, some still living "clothed as love," among whom "a Beguine whom Maître Robert killed, on account of her just love, the 29th" (*Visioenen*, p. 125). On this woman, cf. H. Grundmann, *Religiöse Bewegungen im Mittelalter*. . . . Historische Studien 267, (Berlin: 1935) p. 189. Hadewijch also cites: "Hildegard who saw all her visions, the 28th" (p. 189), "A recluse called Marie, the 22nd, who before was

a nun . . . and Madame de Nazareth knew her well" (p. 188). Perhaps this is a reference to Beatrice of Nazareth.

The *List of the Perfect* is interesting not so much for the historical information that can be gleaned from it as for the fact that it traces a network of the "friends of God" in the 13th century, a network which is not confined to the Netherlands, but spreads to Cologne, Thuringen, Bohemia, Paris, Jerusalem, and England.

As to the difficulty in giving precise dates for Hadewijch, cf. J. Reynaert, "Over Hadewijch naar anleiding van 3 recente publikaties," *Ons Geestelijk Erf* 54, pp. 280–292.

6. In *Letter I*, she expresses herself with authority: "I exhort you, I command you, I order you" (19–21). Cf. L.XV,l.52ff.; L.XXIX,l.8ff. On the separation from her friends: "Others would willingly attract you to them in order to separate us: it is our fidelity that they cannot bear" (L.XXIII,ll.23–25). Cf. L.XXV, L.XXIX. At times it would seem that these trials were imposed not by some authority, but by a "competitive" group: "Above all, I order you, beware of the eccentricities which are very numerous there" (L.XXIII,ll.12–16). This is obviously a warning.

7. On assistance to one's neighbor, to the sick: L.II, L.XVI, L.XXIV. On her own ascesis: "I have had little to do with men's customs, as regards eating, drinking or sleep; I have not concerned myself with clothes, colors or outward splendor." (L.XXIX,ll.28–33). Let us note that, if Hadewijch speaks much of the suffering of being separated from Love, the "suffering body" is hardly ever mentioned. Hadewijch seems to differ from Beatrice and the contemporary Beguines by the moderation of her ascesis, which is shown as wholly inward.

8. Cf. Bibliography, *Hadewijch, the Complete Works*, Translation and Introduction by C. Hart, OSB. Preface by P. Mommaers. (New York: 1980; London: 1981).

9. P. Zumthor, *Essai de poétique médiévale*, Paris: 1972. R. Dragonetti, *La technique poétique des trouvères dans la chanson courtoise. Contribution à l'étude de la rhétorique médiévale.* (Bruges: 1960).

10. "Although the winter is still cold/ the days short and the nights long, proud summer is hastening on, to free us of our sadness,/ behold the new season/ the hazelnut trees are in bloom,/ no sign is more faithful. . . ." (SGI)

11. On the poetic art of Hadewijch and its links with contemporary courtly poetry: N. De Paepe, *Hadewijch. Strofische Gedichten, Een studie van de minne inhet kader der 12e en 13e-eeuwse mystiek en profane minnelyriek,* (Ghent: 1967); F. Willaert, *De pöetica van Hadewijch in de "Strofische Gedichten."* (Utrecht: 1984.)

12. "My shield has received so many blows/ that there is no room for another stab." (SG III, st. 3)

13. "The cruel aliens/ afflict me without limit/ in this weary exile/ by their

false counsels; they are pitiless towards me/ and have often frightened
me:/ they condemn me in their blindness, and never will be able/ to
understand the love/ the desire of which holds me captive" (SG XXIV,
st. 8).

14. Cf. SG XXIX. Cf. William of St. Thierry: ". . . You her guest, O God,
Who are Yourself her love in her, let her love You through You, O
You her love, love Yourself through her and do all through and in
her." *Exposé sur le cantique*, ed. J. Dechanet, SC 82, par. 131, pp. 278–
279. This corresponds with the last verse of MD XV:

> "Ah, sweet Love, were I but love, and could love you, Love,
> with love itself!
> Ah! Sweet Love, grant me for Love's sake
> That love may fully know love!"

15. Cf. MD XVI, verse 3 (*live ember*); verse 4 (*fire*).
16. Cf. SG I, last stanza; SG VII, *supra*, p. 115. L. XXX: In the intra-
Trinitarian relationships, the flux in the Persons and the reflux in
Unity are a constant renewal: "This demand which is eternally new,
eternally one in possession and in being" (ll.54–56).

This insistence on *novelty* caused Hadewijch to be accused of
belonging to the sect of the New Spirit (*De novo* spiritu). B. Spaaken
refutes this accusation: "Hebben onze 13de-eeuwse mystieken iets
gemeen met de broeders en zusters van de vrije geest?" *Ons Geestelijk
Erf* 40, 1966, pp. 369–391; "The Movement of the 'Brethren of the
Free Spirit' and the Flemish Mystics," *Revue d'ascétique et de mystique*,
t. 42, 1966, pp. 423–437. On the patristic and medieval sources of
the *novitas*, cf. J. Reynaert, *Beeldspraak*, pp. 392–401.

17. P. Zumthor, *Poétique médiévale*, p. 206.
18. H. I. Marrou, *Les Troubadours*, (Paris: 1971), pp. 161–163.
19. R. Guiette, *D'une poésie formelle en France au Moyen-Age* (Paris: 1972),
p. 69: "The aim of formal poetry is not to express something (a
subject), but to reveal a form in its development."
20. For a study of these symbols and their sources, cf. J. Reynaert,
Beeldspraak, ch. I to ch. VIII, particularly pp. 175–186.
21. F. Willaert, *Poëtica*, pp. 388–391.
22. MD XIII. These were the lines that aroused Maeterlinck's enthusiasm.
23. On the interpretation of the visions: B. Spaapen, "Hadewijch en Het
vijfde Visioen" ("Hadewijch and the Fifth Vision"), *Ons Geestelijk Erf*
44, 1970, pp. 1–44, 113–141, 353–404; 45, 1971, pp. 129–178; 46,
1972, pp. 113–199. These important articles are a study of the whole
of Hadewijch's spirituality. H. Vekeman, " 'Angelus sane nuntius,'
een interpretatie van het visionnenboek van Hadewijch" ("An Interpretation of the Book of Hadewijch's Visions"), *Ons Geestelijk Erf* 50,

1976, pp. 225–259. P. Dinzelbacher, "Hadewijchs mystische Erfahrungen in neuer Interpretation," *Ons Geestelijk Erf* 54, 1980, pp. 267–279. F. Willaert, "Hadewijch und ihr Kreis in den 'Visionen,'" *Abendländische Mystik im Mittelalter*, ed. K. Ruh (Stuttgart: 1986), pp. 368–387, insists on the didactic and exemplary character of the visions, teaching for those whom Hadewijch directed.

24. F. Willaert, *Hadewijch und ihr Kreis*, stresses the fact that Hadewijch's exaltation is closely connected to her apostolic mission.

25. Translations of the *Letters*, cf. Bibliography. Special mention of C. Hart, *Hadewijch, the Complete Works*, pp. 43–121.

26. In the *Letters*, particularly, Hadewijch adds to this theme that of a debt (*scout*) which cannot be paid to God (doubtlessly a ref. to Rom. 8:12). L.IV, l.55: "Hope leads them to rely on the things they will never attain, for they are too lazy and do not pay their debt to God, nor towards love to whom we owe our pains till death." This debt is a debt to the Divine Unity and the Son has been acquitted of it (L.VI,ll.109–114; L.XXXl.64ff.).

27. A. M. Haas, "Trage Leiden geduldiglich, Die Einstellung der deutschen Mystik zum Leiden," in *Lerne leiden, Leidensbewaltigung in der Mystik*, (Karlsruhe: 1985).

28. The community "helps to love Love": "As you are one of those [in the community] who at present can favor or retard this progress towards the common good, I advise you to be attentive and to devote yourself in all things to the kingdom of just love." (L.XII,ll.145–150). We give to the expression *int ghemeyne vorderen* the sense Beatrice gave it (Cf. supra, n. 32), the same sense it will have with Ruysbroeck.

29. Cf. MD XVI,ll.181–182:

> Light teaches us the customs of love,
> And reveals her will in all its forms.

30. J. Reynaert, *Beeldspraak*, pp. 82–88.

31. William of St. Thierry, *De la nature et de la dignité de l'amour*, ed. M. M. Davy, paras. 25–26, pp. 100–102. J. van Mierlo; "Hadewijch en Willem van St-Thierry," *Ons Geestelijk Erf* 3, 1929, pp. 45–59; P. Verdeyen, "De invloed van Willem van St-Thierry op Hadewijch en Ruusbroec," *Ons Geestelijk Erf* 51, 1977, pp. 3–19. L.XX,ll.81–85.

32. J. Reynaert, *Beeldspraak*, pp. 191–198, on the various meanings of the word *anschijn* and their sources.

33. This expression is often used by Hadewijch who, however, shows that it is impossible to reach this state unless we first suffer with Christ. "We all wish to be God with God, but there are few of us who wish to be men with His Humanity (L. VI,l.230ff.). On the success of this expression in Rhenish mysticism, E. Zum Brunn and A. de Libera,

Maître Eckhart. Métaphysique du Verbe et Théologie négative, Bibliothèque des Archives de philosophie, 42 (Paris: 1984), pp. 31–70.

34. William of St. Thierry, *Letter to the Brethren of Mont-Dieu*, ed. J. Dechanet (SC 223) par. 258, pp. 348–350: "To wish what God wishes is already to resemble God; to be incapable of wishing other than what God wishes is already to be what He is: for Him, in fact, to be and to wish are the same thing."

35. In Hadewijch, among others, MD XVI,ll.90–91: "Who never received the intimate touch of this fire finds nothing too wide or too narrow."

36. This hymn is the "Alpha et O, magne Deus," PL 171, 1411, of which Abélard's authorship has been refuted. For this source and others, cf. F. Willaert, "Hadewijch en Maria-Magdalena" (in press).

37. The definition of the Father as Origin goes back to the Councils of Tolède (638 and 675). It was taken up again by William of St. Thierry; P. Verdeyen, "The Mystic Theology of William of St. Thierry," *Ons Geestelijk Erf* 52, 1978, pp. 160–161.

38. The authenticity of this letter has been questioned. F. Willaert, "Is Hadewijch de auteur van de XXVIIIe brief?" *Ons Geestelijk Erf* 54, 1980, pp. 26–36, concludes in favor of its authenticity. For its interpretation, cf. H. W. J. Vekeman, "Hadewijch, een interpretatie van de Br.I,II,XXVIII,XXIX als documenten over de strijd rond de wezenmystiek," *Tijdschrift voor Ndl. Taal- en Letterkunde* 90, 1974, pp. 336–366.

39. "The soul is a free way for the passage of God from His profound depths; again, God is a way for the passage of the soul into her freedom, that is to say, into the abyss (*grond*) of the Divine Being which can be touched only by the abyss (*diepheit*) of the soul" (L.XVIII).

Excerpts from the Works of Hadewijch I and Hadewijch II

1. *Strophische Gedichten*, V, p. 30–34. This poem is on the "whims" of Love and the vicissitudes to which the soul who loves totally is exposed. There is, as it were, a game of approach and withdrawal between the soul and Love, a game of courtly love to which Hadewijch gives a spiritual sense, since it is a question of meeting Love in her most intimate bower, in her very essence (st. 6). The succession of contrasts allows us to appreciate—even in a different language—the rhythmic art of our poetess. On these contrasts see also, besides the *Poems in Stanzas*, the *Mengeldichten* XIII and XVI.

2. Traditional allusion to nature, here to contrast winter to the constancy which much be possessed by the loving soul.

3. The more the soul progresses, the more she feels her insufficiency.

4. The "touch" of Love is a mystical term that will have a more exact

meaning later on with Ruysbroeck. Here, it refers to the awakening of the soul by Love. Cf. St. Augustine, *Confessions* X, xxvii, 38: "You have touched me and I am inflamed for your peace."

5. "Nameless," as above, "strange" (unheard of), refers to the secret character of divine life and to the darkness in which the spiritual seeker must advance: he proceeds by intuition rather than knowledge. This expression is developed in *Letter XX* on the "Twelve Nameless Hours." The first of these hours describes the "sudden touch of Love, all the nobleness of which one does not yet imagine."

6. Here, the "debt" refers to the demands of Love who wants the whole person. For a more theological explanation, cf. L. XVIII, p. 126 and n. 6, p. 209.

7. This expression will have great success, with the Far-Nigh of Marguerite Porete (cf. *supra*; p. 150 and 156). We find it again in the *New Poems*, MD.XVII, among others, cf. *supra* p. 133.

8. "*Avontuere*" in the text—a term often used by Hadewijch with obvious reference to the *chansons de geste*.

9. *Strofische Gedichten*, VII, pp. 40–48. This poem is an arabesque on the theme of "novelty" or "newness." Cf. *supra*, p. 203, n. 16. St. 1: Rebirth of nature and promise of love; st. 2: Joyful discovery of love in the communion of those who serve her; st. 3: The creative power of love: st. 3 and st. 5: Dialectic of the old and new; st. 4 and st. 6: Love steals away, creating a desire that always deepens; st. 7: Appeal to taste newness in its plenitude, by participation in the divine life.

10. Cf. 2 Cor. 4:16.

11. Cf. Eph. 4:24, John 3:5.

12. There is an old age that is a refusal of love; there is another—wisdom—which is like being rooted in love (st. 5). On the opposition between youth and old age, cf. E. Koehler, "Sense and Function of the Term 'Youth' in the Poetry of the Troubadours," *Mélanges René Crozet*, t.I (Poitiers: 1966), pp. 569–583.

13. Cf. William of St. Thierry, *De natura et dignitate amoris*, PL 184,391D. SG XXVIII:

> At the school of lofty Love
> One learns the sublime madness
> For a man of former sense
> Becomes a wandering vagabond.

14. Cf. Song of Songs. 2: 16.

15. *Visioenen* I, pp. 106–122. The vision includes two tableaux: (1) That of the divine abyss in which she sees concrete images (the Lamb, David with his harp, religious feasts) and has spiritual intuitions: the birth of God in souls, the knowledge of their profound being and (2), the scene of the two eagles swallowed up by the phoenix.

The account continues with a series of reflections in the state of wakefulness: she regrets having been united to God with St. Augustine, when it is her wish to be detached from all affective human ties. Then she places herself in the spiritual universe: her relation to God which is marked by suffering and awaiting; to the already glorified saints; to men and women close to God or far from Him. The latter are her greatest concern and she goes as far as the "impossible supposition," that is, to be hated by God to buy His love for them. This meditation gives us a good idea of the spiritual universe of Hadewijch who, far from thinking only of herself and her fulfilling relation to God through being engulfed in the Divine Essence, remains open to the needs of mankind, in the communion of saints.

16. The phoenix, which is reborn from the flames is, according to Christian authors, the symbol of the Resurrection. Hadewijch here applies it to the Uni-Trinity which swallows up souls (to make them re-live within It). A similar metaphor can be found in *Mengeldichten XVI* where the phoenix burns and is transformed in the fire of the salamander. Cf. J. Reynaert, *Beeldspraak*, pp. 110–113.

17. The image of the eagle often appears in Hadewijch's works (Vis. 5, 7, 10, 11, 12; L.22), with reference both to St. John and, as here, to the life of souls. P. Dinzelbacher, "Die Mittelalterliche Adlerssymbolik und Hadewijch," *Ons Geestelijk Erf* 54, 1980, pp. 5–25.

18. We can thus summarize the relations between the *old* and *new* as they appear in these very dense lines: the *oldness* is at the same time the *perfection* which is in one's eternal nature in God (the young eagle has gray feathers), and the *plenitude of love* personified by St. Augustine; the *new*, or *youth* is at the same time a certain *imperfection* of human nature (Hadewijch) and the *eternal youth* of love which never ceases to grow (the old eagle has young feathers). Moreover, the power of renewal possessed by love has an effect on others (Hadewijch's love for Augustine has rejuvenated the old eagle's feathers). Old age and youth converge in union within the Trinity.

19. This purity seems to us to refer to her being in God, a purity that is not yet entirely hers. (Cf. last paragraph). This intermediate state leaves her a certain margin of choice in which she can prove her love for God.

20. *Brieven*, pp. 137–145. For commentary on this letter cf. *supra*, p. 110.

21. Cf. *supra*, "Excerpts from the Works of Hadewijch I & II," n. 37.

22. Cf. Mt. 25:12. This compassion for straying souls is a particular feature of Hadewijch's spirituality (cf. *supra*, Vis. 11). At the same time she does not wish to go against the judgments of God.

23. The justice of God is the integrity of the Divine Nature.

24. *Brieven*, pp. 146–160. Although she is addressing one particular person, as in the previous letter, Hadewijch alternates between *thou* and *you*, a proof she is writing also for the community.

25. In the *Sixth Manner of Love*, Beatrice described the free soul as "mistress of the house" (*huusvrouw*). The image is prosaic but conveys the idea of the sovereignty of Love over free souls. Ruysbroeck expressed this sovereignty (using the image of a king) in his *Kingdom of Lovers* (Werken, t. 1, pp. 99–100) and in *Spiritual Espousals* (Werken, t. 1, pp. 136, 137).

26. This admirable phrase seems an answer to William of St. Thierry's question: "Who could love what he does not see? How could he appear lovable, whose glance cannot be perceived?" (*De contemplando Deo*, PL 184, 368D–369A).

27. Cf. *supra*, "Hadewijch of Antwerp," p. 104 and n. 31.

28. To William's text, Hadewijch adds this phrase which takes up that of p. 127 about the depths (*gront*) of the soul and the abyss (*afgrond*) into which souls are projected. Cf. *Letter XX* (4th and 12th "nameless hours"). This notion will be developed in the *New Poems* and in the 14th century by Meister Eckhart, Ruysbroeck, and their disciples.

29. Prov. 14:10.

30. It is interesting to note that Hadewijch adds this adverb to William's text.

31. John 13:23–25.

32. Job, 4:12.

33. *Mengeldichten*, pp. XXVII–XXXIII. J. B. Porion, *Hadewijch d'Anvers*, pp. 45–55.

34. Cf. *supra*, "Hadewijch of Antwerp," n. 35.

35. *Hadewijch d'Anvers*, pp. 133–185. Dom Porion's French translation is enriched by numerous doctrinal notes. Cf. *supra*, *Introduction*, p. 000.

36. J. Reynaert, "Ruusbroec en Hadewijch," *Ons Geestelijk Erf*, 55, Louvain: 1984, pp. 193–232. G. Epiney-Burgard, "L'influence des Béguines sur Ruusbroec."

37. *The Sources, Content and Sequels of His Mysticism*, ed. Ruusbroec, Werken, t. 4, p. 5. P. Mommaers, N. De Paepe (Leuven: 1984), pp. 68–85.

38. *Mengeldichten* XVII, pp. 86–91. The two themes of this poem are *naked knowledge* of the Deity, beyond intelligence, images, forms and *lack*, that gap between what has been received and what is still to be received. Paradoxically, it is in this gap that is to be found union with the Divine Principle.

39. *Uncreated*. This word, for which Eckhart was later reproached, refers to the being we possess from all eternity in the divine thought.

40. *Mengeldichten* XIX, pp. 111–115. To the theme of nakedness and non-knowing, there is added that of transformation, analogous to death, by a return to inwardness in one's simple depths, with the image of the *desert*.

41. *Mengeldichten* XXVI, pp. 135–137. Poem on "poverty in spirit," total detachment which leads to the simple One, unqualifiable, unlimited. On the success of this theme, cf. Porion's *Hadewijch d'Anvers*, pp. 54–56.

Part V: Marguerite Porete

Introduction

1. Romana Guarnieri, "Lo 'Specchio delle anime semplici' e Margherita Poirrette," in the *Osservatore Romano*, June 16, 1946, p. 3. All research on the *Mirror* and its author must take into account the considerable work of Romana Guarnieri, *Il Movimento del Libero Spirito. Testi e Documenti*, Edizioni di Storia e Letteratura (Rome: 1965). *Archivio Italiano per la Storia della Pietà*, IV, 23, pp. 363–708. Text of the *Mirror* from the Chantilly MS, pp. 513–635. The abovementioned article in the *Osservatore Romano* is in Appendix 6, pp. 661–663. We give references to the *Mirror* from the Guarnieri edition and, when possible, to the Middle English translation edited by Marilyn Doiron (Rome: Edizioni di Storia e Letteratura, 1968). *Archivio Italiano per la Storia della Pietà*, V, 17. Editions henceforth will be cited Guarnieri and Doiron.

2. It is significant that the documents of Marguerite's trial were preserved by the ministers of Philip the Fair: William of Nogaret and William of Plaisians. These documents are now in the *Layettes du Trésor des Chartes*, (Paris: 1863–1909), t. 2. Part of them have been published by Henry Charles Lea, *A History of the Inquisition of the Middle Ages* (New York: 1888; repr. New York: 1955) t. 2, pp. 575–578 and reproduced without corrections in Paul Fredericq, *Corpus documentorum inquisitionis haereticae pravitatis Neerlandicae*, t. 1 (Ghent: 1889), pp. 155–160 and t. 2 (Ghent: 1896), pp. 63–65. Curiously enough, part of these documents were neglected by Charles-Victor Langlois, who wrote a short article on Marguerite Porete in 1894; moreover, in the criticism made by H. S. Denifle and his assistant E. Chatelain in their *Chartularium universitatis Parisiensis* (Paris: 1889–97) t. 3, pp. 660–661, there is no mention of the documents ignored by Langlois. A complete list can be found in Robert E. Lerner's study, "An *Angel of Philadelphia* in the Reign of Philip the Fair: the Case of Guiard of Cressonessart," in *Order and Innovation in the Middle Ages: Essays in Honor of Joseph Strayer*, ed. by William C. Jordan *et alii* (Princeton: 1976), pp. 343–364, 529–540. On all this, cf. the excellent article by P. Verdeyen, "Le Procès d'Inquisition contre Marguerite Porete et Guiard de Cressonessart (1309–1310)," *Revue d'Histoire ecclésiastique* (Louvain:

1986), vol. LXXXI, pp. 47–94. It is to be hoped that the author will soon publish the complete dossier of the charges brought against Marguerite, as he seems to promise.

3. "Om hare gerechte minne," in the *List of the Perfect*, edited at the end of *Vision 14, De visioenen van Hadewijch*, ed. J. van Mierlo (Leuven: 1924), p. 189, cited re Marguerite by K. Ruh, "Beginnenmystik. Hadewijch, Mechthild von Magdeburg, Marguerite Porete," in *Zeitschrift für deutsches Altertum und deutsche Literatur*, t. 106, 1977, p. 268.

4. Guarnieri, *Il Movimento del Libero Spirito*, p. 638. Cf. text p. 163–164.

5. *Mirror*, chap. 85; Guarnieri, p. 586. It is worthwhile citing here a remark of Longchamp on the real sense of Marguerite's refusal to appear before the Inquisition. Max Huot de Longchamp, *Le Miroir des Ames simples et anéanties*, A modern French translation of the *Mirror* (Paris: Albin Michel, 1984), Introduction, pp. 25–26: ". . . The result will be new denunciations and a new diocesan trial, now that the Bishop of Cambrai is Philip of Marigny, the demon-angel of Philip the Fair and one of his accomplices in the persecutions of the Templars; this higher judicial summons led Marguerite Porete before the Inquisition of Haute Lorraine, and from there before the Paris Inquisition, where she fell into the hands of William of Paris, he too entirely compromised in the struggle against the Templars. It is when she is face to face with these executioners that we must judge the prisoner's attitude: her refusal to take an oath of loyalty which would have made her become a collaborator of an unjust system; then her refusal to receive absolution for faults she considered she had not committed. It is clear that one cannot just simply identify this double refusal with a refusal of the ecclesiastical institution as such, and of its sacraments."

6. *Mirror* chaps. 43 and 66, Guarnieri, pp. 555, 571; Doiron pp. 288–289. It is not necessarily a question of a gnostic thesis, as Edmund Colledge and Romana Guarnieri had initially thought in "The Glosses by 'M. N.' and Richard Methley to the 'Mirror of Simple Souls,' " *Archivio Italiano per la Storia della Pietà*, in Doiron, pp. 357–382. This thesis consists of opposing in a radical manner the human and legalist institution of Holy Church the Less, to Holy Church the Great, composed exclusively of those who are saved by gnosis. But it cannot be assumed, as the inquisitors did, that, after the manner of the Valentinian Gnostics, Marguerite taught that this Lesser Church was bad in the very principle of its creation, in virtue of the malignity inherent in matter. In fact, we cannot forget that in the first centuries of Christianity, this distinction is made between the two Churches by orthodox authors who do not attribute to it the same meaning. We find it in Denys the Areopagite who explains it in his *Celestial Hierarchy*: he distinguishes between the message Christ teaches to His disciples,

who are the initiated, and that received by the crowds compared (according to Matt. 7:6) to the swine before whom one must not throw pearls. "In Marguerite's views on the two 'Churches' there may be no more than this ancient and reputable tradition." E. Colledge and J. C. Marler, " 'Poverty of the Will': Ruysbroeck, Eckhart, and *The Mirror of Simple Souls*," in *Jan van Ruusbroec: The Sources, Content and Sequels of his Mysticism, Mediaevalia lovaniensia*. Series I/ Studia XV, (Leuven: 1984) p. 35. Cf. Denys, *Celestial Hierarchy*, PG3,II,2-II,5. (Paris: 1958), pp. 76–77.

7. The six versions include: 1. The text in Old French is MS Condé F XIV 26 at Chantilly. 2. A Latin translation of the original version, made in the 14th century. 3 & 4. Two Italian translations of this Latin version, made in the 14th century. 5. A version in Middle English dating from middle to end of the 14th century. 6. This last mentioned version was translated into Latin by Richard Methley. For a description of the manuscripts, see Guarnieri, pp. 501–509. We draw attention to the very important discovery of a fifth Latin manuscript by Fr. Verdeyen at the Vatican Library, the Chigiano B IV 41, which contains the text of the first Latin version, written before 1310. Encouraged by this fortunate discovery, he began the comparison of the various manuscripts which give the same Latin translation, promising us a bilingual edition in *Corpus Christianorum* in the near future. Cf. P. Verdeyen, "The First Latin Translation of the Mirror of Marguerite Porete," in *Ons Geestelijk Erf* (1984), 58, pp. 388–389.

8. Longchamp, *Introduction*, pp. 26–28.

9. *De distinctione verarum revelationum a falsis* in J. Gerson, *Oeuvres complètes*, ed. Glorieux, t. 3, *L'oeuvre magistrale* (Tournai: 1962), pp. 51–52.

10. On all this, cf. Guarnieri, *Il Movimento del Libero Spirito*, pp. 353–499.

11. Marguerite de Navarre, *Les Prisons*, ed. and comm. by Simone Glasson, (Geneva: 1978) pp. 179–180. We have modernized the text somewhat. " 'Loingprès,' 'Far-Near,' is a personification of the *ludus amoris*, the *Minne spêl*, the *va et vient* between the Soul and her Divine Lover which all the expositors, following Hugh of St. Victor, insist is a necessary and lamentable consequence of the human condition. That Hugh's *De arrha animae* is the inspiration of the personification Margaret shows without all doubt when, in Chapter 61, the 'spouse of the Soul' says: 'Je vous ay par mon Loingprès les erres envoiees,' 'I have sent you my bridal gifts by my Far-Near'. . . . 'Loingprès' is one certain example—others are possible—of Margaret devising a French equivalent for notions or terms already current in the Netherlands and Rhineland literature of Christianized *Minne*, courtly love. 'Loingprès' is her translation of 'Verre bi,' 'far off—close at hand'. . . . This raises the whole question, not yet adequately explored, of transmission." E. Colledge and J. C. Marler, " 'Poverty of the Will':

Ruysbroeck, Eckhart, and *The Mirror of Simple Souls* in *Jan van Ruus-broec: The Sources, Content and Sequels of his Mysticism, Mediaevalia lov-aniensa.* Series I/Studia XV (Leuven:1984), pp. 39–40.

12. Longchamp, *Introduction*, p. 16. "A mirror reflects the image of the person who looks in it. . . . A mirror thus evokes knowledge of self, with the idea of a purification, an assimilation to a moral ideal. . . . Moreover, the Latin word *speculum* in its derived sense indicates paintings or representations; thus it signifies *picture, portrait,* even description. A "mirror" thus becomes a means of knowledge and brings instruction which is either purely informative or normative. During the Middle Ages and later on, this derived sense gave rise to an abundance of *Specula*." Margot Schmidt, article on *"Mirror"* in the *Dictionnaire de Spiritualité,* t. 10, (1979), pp. 1290–1291.

13. *Mirror*, chap. 21, Guarnieri, p. 541; Doiron, 275.

14. *Mirror*, chap. 84, Guarnieri, p. 586; Doiron, p. 317.

15. P. Dronke, *Women Writers of the Middle Ages, a Critical Study of Texts from Perpetua (203) to Marguerite Porete (1310),* (Cambridge: Cambridge University Press, 1984), p. 218.

16. Longchamp, *Introduction*, p. 24. "Her tongue is French, but an attentive reader of the *Mirror* can notice numerous Flandricisms, a sign of a nearby linguistic frontier. Her excellent knowledge of contemporary Flemish mysticism leads us to believe that she knew the language." *Ibid.* p. 22.

17. *Mirror*, chap. 28, Guarnieri, p. 545; Doiron, p. 278.

18. *Mirror*, chap. 111, Guarnieri, p. 605; Doiron, p. 334.

19. *Mirror*, chap. 52, Guarnieri, p. 561; Doiron, p. 294.

20. *Mirror*, chap. 57, Guarnieri, p. 565; Doiron, p. 297, note to ll. 10–11. The Old French word *marri* corresponds to the *tristitia* of St. Bernard who, in the same sense, also employs the term *amarus,* derived from the verb *amarare* from which the word *marri* certainly comes: "Whoever, amongst us, has found once again the free respiration of hope after the sadness and tears of the beginnings of conversion, (*post illa amara et lacrimosa conversationis suae primordia*) has known the joy of rising on the wings of grace towards a sky of infinite consola-tions." *Sermones super Cantica Canticorum,* 37, 4, in *Sancti Bernardi Opera,* ed. J. Leclercq, C. H. Talbot, H. M. Rochais, (Rome: 1957–1958) t. 2, p. 11. This text, together with others, has been brought to our attention by Brigitte Saouma.

21. *Mirror*, chap. 38, Guarnieri, p. 552; Doiron, p. 286.

22. *Mirror*, chap. 40, Guarnieri, p. 554; Doiron, p. 287.

23. *Mirror*, chap. 58, Guarnieri, p. 566; Doiron, p. 299.

24. *Mirror*, chap. 106, Guarnieri, p. 601; Doiron, p. 330.

25. *Mirror*, chap. 84, Guarnieri, p. 586; Doiron, p. 317.

26. *Mirror*, chap. 95, Guarnieri, p. 594; Doiron, p. 324. "If we read her

book with due attention, we see that 'wanting nothing, knowing nothing, having nothing' are among its most frequently recurring themes." E. Colledge and J. C. Marler, " 'Poverty of the Will,' " p. 36. See comparison with *German Sermon* 52, *Beati Pauperes Spiritu*, by Meister Eckhart, p. 16ff, one of a series of comparisons made between the *Mirror* and Eckhart's German work.

27. *Mirror*, chap. 13; Guarnieri, p. 534; Doiron, p. 267. Cf. Augustine, *In Epistola Iohannis ad Partos*, VII, 8. "But I can very well tell you, says this freed Soul, that, before reaching [this point], one must do the very opposite of one's will, feeding the virtues to the full. . . ." *Mirror*, chap. 90; Guarnieri, p. 591; Doiron p. 321.

28. J. Orcibal, "The 'Mirror of Simple Souls' and the 'sect' of the Free Spirit," *Revue de l'histoire des religions* 88 (1969), t. 176, pp. 44–45. Cf. Blaise Pascal, *Pensées et Opuscules*, ed. L. Brunschwig (Paris: Hachette, 1909), No. 553, pp. 574–578.

29 P. Verdeyen, "Le procès d'Inquisition contre Marguerite Porete et Guiard de Cressonessart," p. 47.

30. Longchamp, *Introduction*, p. 19 " . . . Where Marguerite Porete speaks of the overpassing of virtues and morals, her judges read an opposition to virtue; where she speaks of union with God, they read an identification with God; where she speaks of inward peace, they read perverse nihilism; where she speaks of adoring God in spirit and in truth, they understood the sacrilegious denial of Christian institutions. This could not have been avoided by any of Marguerite Porete's warnings, by any of her professions of Catholic Faith in the *Mirror* (in chapters 14 and 15, for example) and not even by her clearly expressed affirmations of the *necessity for man to do, on his part, everything that comes from reason, as the part of love is that of God and Him alone.* 'I tell all those who will hear this book, that we must reproduce in ourselves as much as we can—by devout thoughts, by works of perfection, by the exigencies of Reason—all the life that Jesus Christ led and that He preached to us. . . . This we must do to have victory over ourselves. And if we did this as much as we could, we would succeed in possessing it, at the same time putting outside of us all thoughts, all works of perfection and all exigencies of reason, for we would not know what to do with them: the Divinity would then operate its divine works within us, for us and without us' (chap. 113). In each condemnation, it is clear that what we have already called the 'contemplative point of view' is at stake, and that, as regards liberation from the Law, Marguerite's judges envisaged only the immoral Libertinism of that age, with all its black masses, unclean sacrifices and fornication." *Ibid.* pp. 26–27.

31. *Mirror*, chap. 97; Guarnieri, p. 595; Doiron, p. 325.

32. Cf. *Mirror*, chap. 8; Guarnieri, p. 526. K. Ruh, " 'Le miroir des Simples

Ames' der Marguerite Porete," *Verbum et Signum*, t. 2: *Beiträge zur mediävisten Bedeutungsforschung. Studien zu Semantik und Sinntradition im Mittelalter. Festschrift F. Ohly* (München: Wilhelm Fünk Verlag, 1975), p. 378. (There remain only three of the fifteen propositions extracted from the *Mirror* and condemned by the doctors of the Sorbonne. See text compared with similar propositions attributed to the Beghards and condemned by the Council of Vienne in Guarnieri, p. 416.) However right Professor Kurt Ruh's analysis concerning the concept of freedom may seem to us, in the lines immediately preceding those we have cited, we must point out an error which on its own would justify the accusation of heresy to which Marguerite was victim. We quote the passage in question: "It is with the life of the *Freed Soul* that one touches the most virulent aspect of the *Mirror*, from the dogmatic point of view. Doubtlessly, the ontological equality with God of the "annihilated" soul—*I am God by divine nature* (541, l. 13) was already unorthodox. . . ." Ruh bases what he calls ontological equality of the annihilated soul with God upon a quotation which is, in fact, contained in the *Mirror*: "*I am God by nature*" (Guarnieri, p. 541, l. 13). But these words are pronounced by Love, that is to say, by God Himself, while the soul says she is God only *by condition of love*, or *by justice of love*! See these lines of chapter 51 of the *Mirror* which we have cited in full above, p. 152.

33. See p. 172–173.
34. See p. 171.
35. "In the beginning, this Soul lived the life of grace, grace that is born in the death of sin. After, says Love, she lived the life of the spirit, the life that is born in the death of nature; and now she lives the divine life, that divine life which is born in the death of the spirit. This soul, who lives the divine life, is always without herself. . . .when she is nowhere of her own initiative, neither in God, nor in herself, nor in her neighbor, but in the annihilation which this 'flash' operates in her." *Mirror*, chap. 59; Guarnieri, pp. 566–567; Doiron, p. 299.
36. *Mirror*, chap. 101; Guarnieri, p. 598; Doiron, p. 328.
37. On the neo-Platonic theme of "being more" and "being less" and the way Augustine has utilized it, see E. Zum Brunn, St. Augustine, *Being and Nothingness in the 'Dialogs and Confessions'*, esp. ch. 3, trans. from the French by Ruth Namad. (New York: Paragon House, 1987). On Eckhart's use of this same theme, see E. Zum Brunn and A. de Libera, *Maître Eckhart: Métaphysique du Verbe et Théologie négative* (Paris: Beauchesne, 1984), p. 31ff., 127ff.
38. *Mirror*, chap. 110; Guarnieri, p. 604; Doiron, p. 333.
39. *Mirror*, chap. 49; Guarnieri, p. 560; Doiron, p. 292. The expression "without a why" is often repeated by Marguerite, for example: "she has given everything freely, with no why," chap. 81; Guarnieri, p. 583; Doiron, p. 315.

40. *Mirror*, chap. 62; Guarnieri p. 569; Doiron, p. 301. " . . . As regards this estate, there are people who have feet and no road, hands and no work, a mouth and no speech, eyes and no light, ears and no hearing, a reason without reason, a body without life and a heart without understanding." *Mirror*, chap. 86; Guarnieri p. 587; Doiron, p. 318. "These people, whom I call asses, in order to adore God, seek Him in creatures, in monasteries, in created paradises, in human words and in the Scriptures. . . . It seems to novices that these people, who thus search Him through hills and vales, consider that God is submitted to His sacraments and His works. Alas, what a pity for all the troubles they have, and will continue to have, as long as they go on in this way. On the other hand are those who make good use of time, adore God not only in temples and monasteries, but in all places, in union with the divine will." *Mirror*, chap. 69; Guarnieri, p. 573; Doiron, p. 306.

41. *Mirror*, chap. 122; Guarnieri, pp. 618–619.

42. "We mean to say, said Holy Church, that these Souls live above us, for Love dwells in them and Reason dwells in us; but that is not against us, said Holy Church the Less: on the contrary, we are happy about this and render praise for it, in the secret sense of our Scriptures." *Mirror*, chap. 43; Guarnieri, p. 555; Doiron, p. 288–289. See note 6, p. 210.

43. "Ah, sheep that you are! said this Soul, how bestial your understanding is! You leave the grain and take the chaff! And I tell you that when Jesus Christ was transfigured before three of His disciples, He did so that you should know that few people would see the glory of His transfiguration and he shows this only to His intimate friends; that is why there were [only] three of them. And this still happens in this world when God gives Himself by the ardor of His light to a creature's heart. Now you know why there are only three of them, and I am going to tell you why it was on the mountain. It was to show that nobody can see divine things as long as he or she is concerned with, and involved in, temporal matters, that is to say, in things that are less than God." *Mirror*, chap. 75; Guarnieri, p. 547; Doiron, p. 309.

44 *Mirror*, chap. 97; Guarnieri, pp. 595–596; Doiron, p. 325.

45. Cf. *Mirror*, chap. 122; Guarnieri, pp. 616–619, Doiron, pp. 343–345. The chapters which follow, without doubt written before the *Mirror*, or else rewritten, are "considerations for those who are in the estate of the 'marred' and who ask the way to the land of freedom." *Mirror*, chap. 123; Guarnieri, p. 620; Doiron, p. 345. These chapters contain points of meditation which Marguerite herself used when, as she tells us, she was still one of the 'marred,' when she lived on milk and broth and was still foolish. (*Ibid.*).

Marguerite Porete's
"Approbatio" and Excerpts from
"The Mirror of Simple Souls"

1. This text is not in the Chantilly MS. It is to be found as an epilogue to the *Mirror* in the Latin translations and is included in the prologue to the English translation. As this was based on the original French MS, it follows that the text must have been contained in it, and not only in the Latin version.

2. Cf. the famous question put to Joan of Arc when she was interrogated in 1431: "Do you know whether you are in God's grace?" and her answer: "If I am not, may God bring me there, and if I am, may God keep me there. . . ." R. Pernoud and M.-V. Clin, *Jeanne d'Arc* (Paris: 1986), p. 176.

3. This is a fundemental theme of the *Mirror*: every action we undertake "with ourselves" (that is, being attached to ourselves), however holy it may seem, merely carries along with it this encumberment of ourselves. On the contrary, Marguerite uses the expression "without herself," referring to the Soul, cf. *supra*, p. 166, that is, disencumbered of herself: "And henceforth Love works in her without her."

Suggested Reading

The following is a brief list of highly recommended works for the reader who wishes to further pursue this area of study. A complete bibliography follows this list of suggested reading.

General

Bogin, M. *The Women Troubadours*. New York & London: Paddington Press, 1986. The author draws attention to the existence of women troubadours and brings their poems back to light.

Dronke, P. *Women Writers of the Middle Ages: A Critical Study of Texts from Perpetua (203) to Marguerite Porete (1310)*. Cambridge: Cambridge University Press, 1984. Stresses the importance of a series of great Christian women writers from the 2nd to the 13th centuries, including penetrating studies on Hildegard and M. Porete.

Eco, U. *The Name of the Rose*, trans. W. Weaver. G.B.: Martin Secker and Warburg, 1983. This novel gives an excellent picture of the orthodox and heretical movements which developed in 13th century Italy, based on the new ideal of poverty opposed to the attachment to wealth and power of the higher ranks of the clergy.

Marrou, H.-I. *Les Troubadours*. Paris: Seuil, 1971. An extremely well-documented treatment of courtly lyricism and its sources by a great French historian. Accent is placed on the religious nature of the knight's devotion to his lady.

McDonnell, E. W. *The Beguines and Beghards in Medieval Culture*. New York: Octagon Books, 1969. An exhaustive scholarly study of the origins and development of the Beguine movement. The author analyzes in great detail the diverse aspects of this movement: social, literary, and spiritual, and gives particular attention to the problems of orthodoxy and heresy.

Petroff, E. *Medieval Women's Visionary Literature*. New York: C. Bynum, 1986.
Wilson, K. M., ed., *Medieval Women Writers*. Manchester: Manchester University Press; Athens, Georgia: University of Georgia Press, 1984. Includes discussions of and excerpts from Hildegard, Mechthild of Magdeburg, and M. Porete, among others.

Hildegard of Bingen

Dronke, P. *Women Writers of the Middle Ages* contains an excellent Introduction to Hildegard's life and works, with an English translation of important passages and corresponding Latin texts.
Neuman, B. *Sister of Wisdom. St. Hildegard's Theology of the Feminine*. Scholars Press, 1987. Gives an interesting commentary on the maternal aspect of God, as well as on Hildegard's treatment of woman from the physiological and psychological perspectives.

The German translations of Hildegard's works indicated in the *Bibliography, Primary Sources*, are all also preceded by excellent introductions.
Gorceix, B. *Hildegarde de Bingen: Le Livre des Oeuvres Divines*.
A French translation of the *Book of Divine Works* with a detailed historical introduction and reflections on the interpretation of Hildegard's visions.
Several of her liturgical hymns have been recorded, e.g., *Sequences and Hymns*, Gothic Voices with Emma Kirby, directed by Christopher Page. London: Hyperion Records, 1982. Hildegard von Bingen *Ordo virtutum sequentia*. Ensemble für Musik des Miltelalters, Köln, Germany: Harmonia Mundi, 1982.
In the fields of Medicine and Dietetics, a series of books based on Hildegard's teachings has been published recently, in Germany, e.g.:
Breindl, E. *Gesund kochen mit der heiligen Hildegard von Bingen* (*Healthy Cooking with Holy H. of B.*), Aschaffenburg: Pattloch Verlag, 1984.
Herztka, G. *Das Wunder der Hildegard-Medizin* (*The Marvels of Hildegard's Medicine*). Stein am Rhein: Christianer Verlag, 1986.

Mechthild of Magdeburg

Mechthild of Magdeburg, The Flowing Light of the Godhead, trans. Lucy Menzies. London: 1953.
Mechthild von Magdeburg. Das fliessende Licht der Gottheit, modern German trans. with introduction and notes by M. Schmidt. Einsiedeln: Benziger Verlag, 1955. Very faithful translation and exhaustive documentation. This book also contains the inspired essay by H. U. von Balthasar,

"The Ecclesial Mission of Mechthild," of which the reader will find large excerpts in our book. See also M. Schmidt's penetrating study: "*minne du gewaltige kellerin*: On the nature of *minne* in Mechthild of Magdeburg's *fliessende licht der gottheit*," in *Vox benedictina: Women and Monastic Spirituality* 4, 1987, 100–125.

J. Ancelet-Hustache. *Mechthilde de Magdebourg: Essai de psychologie religieuse.* Paris: Champion, 1926. This is still one of the most complete and most readable books on Mechthild. It treats on the one hand her mysticism and realistic psychology, and on the other shows what interest she took in the events of her times, especially in the feud between Pope and Emperor, and how she participated in the growing hopes for a coming age.

Beatrice of Nazareth

Hadewijch, Lettres Spirituelles—Béatrice de Nazareth, Sept Degrés d'Amour, French translation J.-B. Porion. The Introduction contains, pp. 39ff., a good analysis of Beatrice's *Seven Degrees of Love* and of the relationship between her mysticism and that of Eckhart and of Ruysbroeck.

McDonnell, E. W. *The Beguines and Beghards in Medieval Culture.* Contains interesting information concerning Beatrice. Cf. his index.

Hadewijch of Antwerp and Hadewijch II

Hart, C. *Hadewijch, The Complete Works.* New York: Paulist Press, 1980. This book contains a translation of Hadewijch's *Letters*, *Poems*, and *Visions*, preceded by an excellent preface by P. Mommaers, as well as by an exhaustive introduction by the translator, C. Hart.

Porion, J.-B. *Hadewijch, Lettres Spirituelles—Béatrice, Sept degrés d'Amour.* Genève: Claude Martingay, 1972. French translation with profound theological comment and comparisons of Hadewijch with other representatives of Rheno-Flemish mysticism, as well as with contemporary Jewish mysticism.

Porion, J.-B. *Poèmes des béguines.* Paris: Seuil, 1954; reprint, 1985. French translation of Hadewijch's *Stanzaic Poems*, as well as of the poems by Hadewijch II, with an important historical introduction.

Marguerite Porete

Margaret Porete. "The Mirror of Simple Souls": A Middle English Translation ed. by M. Doiron. Roma: Edizioni di Storia e Letteratura (*Archivio Italiano per la Storia della Pietà*, t. 5), 1968, with a brief and interesting introduction on various Middle English manuscripts of the *Mirror*. There is an important and lengthy appendix by E. Colledge and R. Guarnieri on "The Glosses by M. N. and Richard Methley to *The Mirror of Simple Souls*," glosses which were to defend this work against certain accusations of heresy.

Marguerite Porete. Le Miroir des Ames simples et anéanties, Introd. trad. et notes par M. Huot de Longchamp, Paris: Albin Michel, 1984. Modern French translation with a good introduction.

Lerner, R. E. "An Angel of Philadelphia in the Reign of Philip the Fair: The Case of Guiart of Cressonessart," in *Order and Innovation in the Middle Ages: Essays in Honor of Joseph R. Strayer*, ed. by W. C. Jordan et al., (Princeton: Princeton University Press, 1976), pp. 343–364, 529–540. An absorbing and well-documented history of the trials of Marguerite Porete and her defender, Guiart.

Bibliography

Primary Sources

Aelred de Rielvaux, *Opera omnia*, ed. A. Hoste and C. H. Talbot, CCCM, 1971.

Albrizzi, *AASS*, die quarta Augusti. I, 558–628. Venice: 1750.

"Annales Palidenses," in *Monumenta Germaniae Historica, Scriptores*, t. 16 (Hannover: 1859). pp. 48–98. Reprint: Anton Hiersemann–Kraus Reprint Comp., Stuttgart–New York: 1963.

Anonymous. *Dreifaltigkeitslied*. Ed. K. Bartsch, 1858.

Apolda, Dietrich of. *Life of St. Dominic*, Ed. J.-B.

Beatrijs van Nazareth, *Des degrés du saint amour*, trad, J Kersseinakers, "Une mystique des Pays-Bas au 13c siècle. Béatrix de Nazareth (1205–1268)," in *Vie Spirituelle*, Supplément 1929, 316 332.

———, *Sept degrés d'amour*. Trad. J. B. Porion, in *Hadewijch: Lettres Spirituelles*. Genève: Claude Martingay, 1972.

———, *Seven manieren van minne*, ed. L. Reypens and J. Van Mierlo. Leuven: De Vlaamsche Boekenhalle, 1926.

———, *Van seven manieren vanheileger minnen*, ed. H. W. J. Vekeman and J. J. Th. M. Tersteeg. Zutphen: N. V. W. J. Thieme & Cie., 1971.

———, *Vita Beatricis: De autobiografie van de Z. Beatrijs van Tienen O. Cist*, 1200–1268, ed. L. Reypens. Antwerpen: Ruusbroec-Genootschap, 1964.

Bernard de Clairvaux, *Oeuvres mystiques*, trans. A. Béguin. Paris: Seuil, 1953.

———, *Sancti Bernardi Opera*, ed. J. Leclercq, C. II. Talbot, H. M. Rochais, t. 1–7. Romae: Editiones Cistercienses, 1957–1974.

Dante, *Comedy of Dante Alighieri the Florentine*, Trans. D. L. Sayers. Penguin Books, 1955.

———, *The Divine Comedy*, Trans. H. F. Cary. Everyman's Library, 1955.

Denifle, H. (et Châtelain), *Chartularium Universitatis Parisiensis*. Paris: Delalain, 1889–1897.

Denys the Areopagite, *The Celestial Hierarchy*, PG 3, 120A–340B.

Eckhart (Meister), in F. Pfeiffer. *Deutsche Mystiker des 14ten Jahrhunderts*, t. 2. Aalen: Scientia Verlag, 1962 (reprint of Leipzig, 1857).

———, *Die deutschen Werke*, ed. Deutsche Forschungsgemeinschaft, t. 1–5. Stuttgart: Kohlhammer, 1936 ff.

———, *Meister Eckhart, Teacher and Preacher*, trans. and introd. B. McGinn with the collab. of F. Tobin and E. Borgstädt. New York: Paulist Press, 1986.

———, *Meister Eckhart: The Essential Sermons, Commentaries, Treatises and Defense*, trans. E. Colledge and B. McGinn. New York: Paulist Press, 1981.

Pseudo-Eckhart, *Daz ist swester katrei: Meister Ekehartes Tohter von Strasburg*, ed. Pfeiffer, t. 2, 448–475.

———, *The "Sister Catherine Treatise [Daz ist swester katrei . . .]* trans. E. Borgstädt, in *Meister Eckhart, Teacher and Preacher*, ed. B. McGinn. New York: Paulist Press, 1986, 347–386.

———, *Telle était Soeur Katrei*, trans. A. Mayrisch Saint-Hubert, in *Maître Eckhart, Traités et Sermons*. Paris: Cahiers du Sud, 1954, 23–73.

Fredericq, P., *Corpus documentorum inquisitionis hereticae pravitatis Neerlandicae*, t. 1–5, Ghent: J. Vuylsteke, 1889–1906.

Gerardo de Borgho San Donnino. *31 propositions de l' Evangile Eternel de Gérard de Borgho San Donnino*, in *Chartul. Univ. Paris* I, no 243, p 272 ff. Text improved in E. Benz, "Joachim-Studien II—Die Exzerpsätze der Pariser Professoren aux dem Evangelium aeternum," *Zeitschrift für Kirchengeschichte* (51), 1932, 415–455.

Gerson, J. *De distinctione verarum revelationum a falsis*, in *Oeuvres Complètes*, ed. P. Glorieux, t. 3. Paris: Desclée, 1962.

———, *De mystica theologia*, ed. A. Combes. Padova: Antenore, 1959.

Gertrude of Helfta. *Revelationes Gertrudianae*, in *Revelationes Gertrudianae et Mechtildianae*, ed. L. Paquelin. Paris-Poitiers: H. Oudin Frères, 1877. *Geschichte der Stadt Magdeburg*, I, in *Encyclopaedia Judaica*, Jerusalem, t. 11.

Hadewijch, *The Complete Works*, trans. and intr. C. Hart. New York: Paulist Press, 1980.

———, *Die Werke der Hadewych*, trans. and comm. J. Plassmann. Hannover: Orient-Buchhandlung Heinz Lafaire, 1923.

———, *Strophische Gedichten*, Introd., text and comm. J. van Mierlo. Antwerpen: Staandard, 1942.

———, *Mengeldichten*, ed. J. van Mierlo. Antwerpen: Staandard, 1952.

———, *Hadewijch d'Anvers: Poèmes des Béguines traduits du moyen néerlandais*, ed. J. B. Porion. Paris: Seuil, 1954; reprint, 1985.

———, *Hadewijch: Lettres Spirituelles*, Introd. and trans. J. B. Porion. Genève: Claude Martingay, 1972

———, *Hadewijch: Visions*, trans. J. B. Porion. Paris: O. E. I. L., 1987.

Harph (Herp). *Theologia mystica*. Cologne: Melchior Novesanus, 1538; reprint, Farnborough: Gregg Press, 1966.

Hildegard von Bingen, *Opera Omnia*, PL 197, 1882.
————, *Der heiligen Hildegard von Bingen Wisse die Wege, Scivias*, German trans. M. Boeckeler. Salzburg: Otto Müller Verlag, 1976.
————, *Der Mensch in der Verantwortung: Das Buch der Lebensverdienste (Liber vitae meritorum)*, trans. and comm. H. Schipperges. Salzburg: Otto Müller Verlag, 1976.
————, *Heilkunde: Das Buch von dem Grund und Wesen und der Heilung der Krankheiten. (Causae et curae)*, trans. and. comm. H. Schipperges. Salzburg: Otto Müller Verlag, 1976.
————, *Hildegardis Scivias*, ed. Führkötter and A. Carlevaris. *CCCM* XLIII, 2 vol., 1978.
Lieder (Carmina), ed. P. Barth, M. I. Ritscher and J. Schmidt-Goerg. Salzburg: Otto Müller Verlag, 1969.
Naturkunde, (*Liber subtilitatum diversarum naturarum creatarum*), trans. and comm. P. Riethe. Salzburg: Otto Müller Verlag, 1959.
Welt und Mensch. Das Buch "De operatione Dei," trans. and comm. H. Schipperges, Salzburg: Otto Müller Verlag, 1965.
Ordo virtutum, trans. A. E. Davidson. Kalamazoo, Mich.: Medieval Institute Publications, 1984.
The Life and Visions of St Hildegard, trans. F. M. Steele. London: Heath, Cranton and Ousely, 1914.
Le Livre des Oeuvres divines, trans. B. Gorceix. Paris: Albin Michel, 1982.
Hugh of Saint-Victor, *Soliloquium de arrha animae*, PL 176, 951–970.
Jacques de Vitry, *Prologue à Foulques de Toulouse*, ed. W. Papebroch, *AASS*, June, t. 4, Antwerpiae, 630–636
————, *Vita Mariae Oigniacensis*, ibid. 636–666.
Lamprecht von Regensburg, *Tochter von Syon*, ed. Karl Weinhold. Paderborn, 1880.
Marguerite de Navarre, *Les Prisons*, ed. S. Glasson. Genève: Droz, 1978.
Marguerite Porete, *Le "Miroir des simples âmes,"* ed. R. Guarnieri, in *Il Movimento del Libero Spirito* (*Archivio italiano per la Storia della Pietà*, t. 4), Introd., text and appendices Roma: Ed. di Storia e Letteratura, 1965, 501–636, 637–708.
————, *"The Mirror of Simple Souls": A Middle English Translation*, ed. M. Doiron (*Archivio Italiano per la Storia della Pietà*, t. 5). Roma: Ed. di Storia e Letteratura, 1968.
————, *Margaretae Porete: Speculum simplicium animarum*, cura et studio P. Verdeyen. *Le mirouer des simples âmes*, ed. R. Guarnieri (juxtaposed) *CCCM* 69, 1986.
Mirror of Simple Souls, trans. C. Kirchberger. London: Orchard Books, 1927.
Le Miroir des âmes simples et anéanties, Introd., trans., notes M. Huot de Longchamp. Paris: Albin Michel, 1984.
Mechthild of Hackeborn, *Revelationes Mechthildianae*, in *Revelationes Gertru-*

dianae et Mechthildianae, ed. L. Paquelin. Paris-Poitiers: H. Oudin
Frères, 1877.
Mechthild of Magedeburg, *Offenbarungen der Schwester Mechthild von Magde-
burg oder das Fliessende Licht der Gottheit*, ed. Gall Morel. Regensburg:
G.-J. Manz, 1869; reprint, Darmstadt, 1980.
———, *Lux divinitatis*. Paris-Poitiers: H. Oudin Frères, 1877. *Mechthild von
Magdeburg: Das fliessende Licht der Gottheit*, Introd., trans. M. Schmidt.
Einsiedeln-Zürich-Köln: Benziger Verlag, 1955.
———, *The Flowing Light of the Godhead*, trans. Lucy Menzies. London:
1953.
———, R. A. Dick. *Mechthild of Magdeburg's "Flowing Light of the Godhead":
An Autobiographical Realization of Spiritual Poverty*. Stanford University,
1980 (Xerografie, Ann Arbor, Mich.: Univ. Microfilms. Intern., 1986).
Richard of St-Victor, *Les quatre degrés de la violente charité*, ed. G. Dumeige.
Paris: Vrin, 1955.
Ruybroeck or Ruusbroec, Jan van, *Werken*. Tielt: Lannoo, 1944–1948. 4
vol./CCCM CIII-CIII A. Turnhout: Brepols, 1988.
Theodoricus and Godefridus, *Das Leben der Heiligen Hildegard von Bingen*,
ed. and trans. A. Führkötter. Düsseldorf: Patmos Verlag, 1968.
———, *Vie de sainte Hildegarde écrite par les moines Théodoric et Godefroid*,
Traduite du latin en français. Paris: R. Chamonal, 1907.
William of St-Thierry, *De contemplando Deo*, PL 184, 367–380.
———, *De natura et dignitate amoris*, PL 184, 379–408.
———, *Disputatio adversus Petrum Abaelardum*, PL 180, 249–282.
———, *Expositio in Cantica Canticorum*, PL 180, 473–545.
———, *Lettre aux Frères du Mont-Dieu*, ed., intr. and trans. J. M. Déchanet,
SC 223. Paris: Cerf. 1975.
———, *The Golden Epistle of Abbot William of St-Thierry*, trans. W. Shewring.
London: 1973.

Secondary Sources

Ancelet-Hustache, J. *Mechthilde de Magdebourg: Etude de psychologie religieuse.*
Paris: Champion, 1926.
Balthasar, von, H.-U. "Mechthilds kirchlicher Auftrag," in *Mechthild von
Magdeburg: Das fliessende Licht der Gottheit*, ed. M. Schmidt. Einsiedeln-
Zürich-Köln: Benziger Verlag, 1955, 7–45.
Colledge, E. and R. Guarnieri. "The Glosses by 'M.N' and Richard Methley
to the *Mirror of Simple Souls*," An Appendix to *Margaret Porete, "The
Mirror of Simple Souls": A Middle English Translation* ed. by M. Doiron
(*Archivio Italiano per la Storia della Pietà*, t. 5) Roma: Edizioni di Storia
e Letteratura, 1968, 357–382.
Colledge, E. and Marler, J. C., "Poverty of the Will: Ruusbroec, Eckhart
and the *Mirror of Simple Souls*, in Jan van Ruusbroec, *The Sources*,

Content and Sequels of His Mysticism, ed. P. Mommaers, N. de Paepe Leuven: University Press, 1984, 14–47.

De Paepe, N. Hadewijch. *Strofische Gedichten: Een studie van de minne in het kader der 12e en 13e-eeuwse mystiek en profane minnelyriek.* Gent: 1967.

Dinzelbacher, P. *Vision und Visionsliteratur im Mittelalter.* Stuttgart: Hiersemann, 1981.

Dronke, P., *Women Writers in the Middle Ages: A Critical Study of Texts from Perpetua (203) to Marguerite Porete (1310).* Cambridge: University Press, 1984.

Eco, U. *Il Nome della Rosa.* Milano: Fabbri-Bompiani, 1980.

———, *The Name of the Rose,* trans. W. Weaver. G. B.: Martin Secker and Warburg, 1983.

Epiney-Burgard, G., "L'influence des Béguines sur Ruusbroec," In *Jan van Ruusbroec: The Sources, Content and Sequels of His Mysticism* (Leuven: University Press, 1984), 68–85.

Gössmann, E., "Anthropologie und soziale Stellung der Frau nach Summen und Sentenzkommentaren des 13ten Jahrhunderts," in *Soziale Ordnungen im Selbstverständnis des Mittelalters* (Berlin: W. de Gruyter, 1979), 281–297.

Grundmann, H. *Religiöse Bewegungen in Mittelalter.* Darmstadt: Wissenschaftliche Buchgesellschaft, 1961.

Guarnieri, R. *Il Movimento del Libero Spirito: Testi e Documenti (Archivio Italiano per la Storia della Pietà).* Roma: Edizioni di Storia e Lettteratura, 1965.

Haas, A. M. "Mechthild von Magdeburg, Dichtung und Mystik," in *Sermo mysticus: Studien zur Theologie und Sprache der deutschen Mystik.* Freiburg, Schweiz: Universitätsverlag, 1979.

Huot de Longchamp, M. *Marguerite Porete: Le Miroir des âmes simples et anéanties,* Introduction, traduction et notes. Paris: Albin Michel, 1984.

Javelet, R. "L'amour spirituel face à l'amour courtois," in *Entretiens sur la Renaissance du XIIe siècle,* cd. M. de Gandillac, E. Jeauneau. Paris–La Haye: Mouton, 309–336.

Langlois, C.-V. "Marguerite Porete," *Revue historique* (54), 1894.

Lea, H.-C. *A History of the Inquisition of the Middle Ages,* t. 1.3. London: Sampson Low and Co., 1888; reprint 1955.

Lerner, R. E. "An Angel of Philadelphia in the Reign of Philip the Fair: The Case of Guiart of Cressonessart," in *Order and Innovation in the Middle Ages: Essays in Honor of Joseph R. Strayer,* ed. by W. C. Jordan et al. (Princeton: Princeton University Press, 1976), 343–364, 529–540.

Marrou, H.-I. *Les Troubadours.* Paris: Seuil, 1971.

McDonnell, E. W. *The Beguines and Beghards in Medieval Culture.* (New York, Octagon Books: 1969).

Neumann, B. *Sister of Wisdom: St Hildegard's Theology of the Feminine.* Scholars Press, 1987.

Orcibal, J. "Le *Miroir des simples âmes* et la secte du Libre Esprit," *Revue d'histoire des religions* 88, t. 176, 1969, 35–60.

Petroff, E. *Medieval Women's Visionary Literature.* New York: C. Bynum, 1986.

Preger, W. *Geschichte der deutschen Mystik im Mittelalter nach den Quellen untersucht und dargestellt,* t. 1. Leipzig: Dorfling und Franke, 1874.

Reeves, H. *The Influence of Prophecy in the Later Middle Ages: A Study of Joachimism.* Oxford: Clarendon Press, 1969.

Reynaert, J. *De Beeldspraak van Hadewijch.* Tiel/Bussum: Lannoo, 1981.

Ruh, Kurt. "Le *Miroir des Simples Ames* de Marguerite Porete," in *Verbum et Signum,* t. 2, Festschrift F. Ohly, München: Wilhelm Funk Verlag, 1975, 365–387.

———, "Beginnenmystik: Hadewijch, Mechthild von Magdeburg, Marguerite Porete," *Zeitschrift für deutsches Altertum und deutsche Literatur* 106, 1977, 265–277.

Sargent, M. S. "Le *mirouer des simples âmes* and the English Mystical Tradition," in *Abendländische Mystik im Mittelalter,* ed. K. Ruh (Stuttgart: 1986), 443–465.

Schmidt, M. *"minne du gewaltige kellerin*: On the Nature of *minne* in Mechthild of Magdeburg's "fliessendes licht der gottheit," *Vox benedictina: Women and Monastic Spirituality* 4, 1987, 100–125.

Schrader, M. und Führkötter, A. *Die Echtheit des Schrifttums der heiligen Hildegard, Archiv für Kulturgeschichte,* fasc. suppl. 6. Köln: Böhlau, 1957.

Schulz, W., *Der Gott der neuzeitlichen Metaphysik.* Pfullingen: Neske, 1957.

Schulze, N. A. *Predigten des H. Bernard in altfranzösischer Ubertragung.* Tübingen: Bibliothek des literarischen Vereins in Stuttgart, 1894.

Spaapen, B. "Le mouvement des Frères du Libre Esprit et les mystiques flamandes," *Revue d'ascétique et de mystique* 42, 1966, 423–437.

Stierling, H. *Studien zu Mechthild von Magdeburg.* Nürnberg: J. L. Stich, 1907.

Strauch, P. *Margareta Ebner und Heinrich von Nördlingen.* Freiburg in Brisgau und Tübingen: Mohr, 1882.

Van Mierlo, J., "Hadewijch en Willem van St-Thierry," *Ons Geestelijk Erf* 3, 1929, 45–49.

Verdeyen, P. "De invloed van Willelm van St-Thierry op Hadewijch en Ruusbroec," *Ons Geestelijk Erf* 51, 1977, 3–19.

———, "La première traduction latine du Miroir de Marguerite Porete," *Ons Geestelijk Erf* 58, 1984, 388–389.

———, *La théolgie mystique de Guillaume de Saint-Thierry: Ons Geestelijk Erf* 51, 1977, 327–366; 52, 1978, 152–178, 257–295; 53, 1979, 129–220, 321–404.

———, "Le procès d'Inquisiton contre Marguerite Porete et Guiard de Cressonessart (1309–1310)," *Revue d'histoire ecclésiastique* 81, 1986, 47–94.

Walker, Bynum, C. *Studies in the Spirituality of the High Middle Ages.* Berkeley, Los Angeles, London: University of California Press, 1982.

Willaert, F. *De poetica van Hadewijch in de "Strophische Gedichten."* Utrecht: H. and S., 1984.

Wilson, K. M., ed. *Medieval Woman Writers.* Manchester: Manchester University Press; Athens, Georgia: University of Georgia Press, 1984.

Zum Brunn, E. "Une source méconnue de l'ontologie eckhartienne," in the collective work *Métaphysique, Histoire de la Philosophie,* Hommage à Fernand Brunner. Neuchâtel: 1981, 111–118.

Zum Brunn, E. and A. de Libera, *Maître Eckhart: Métaphysique du Verbe et Théologie négative.* Paris: Beauchesne, 1984.

Index